Emile Durkheim

ON MORALITY AND SOCIETY

THE HERITAGE OF SOCIOLOGY

A Series Edited by Morris Janowitz

Emile Durkheim

ON MORALITY

AND SOCIETY

Selected Writings

Edited and with an Introduction by

ROBERT N. BELLAH

THE UNIVERSITY OF CHICAGO PRESS
CHICAGO AND LONDON

Robert N. Bellah is Ford Professor of Sociology and Comparative
Studies at the University of California at Berkeley. He specializes
in the sociology of religion and the study of Japanese society and
is the author of numerous publications.

1973

THE UNIVERSITY OF CHICAGO PRESS, CHICAGO 60637
THE UNIVERSITY OF CHICAGO PRESS, LTD., LONDON
© 1973 by The University of Chicago
All rights reserved. Published 1973
Printed in the United States of America
International Standard Book Number: 0–226–17335–6 (clothbound)
Library of Congress Catalog Card Number: 73–76594

Contents

PREFACE   vii

INTRODUCTION *by Robert N. Bellah*   ix

I. THE FRENCH TRADITION
   OF SOCIAL THOUGHT

1. Sociology in France in the Nineteenth Century   3

II. SOCIOLOGY AND
    SOCIAL ACTION

2. Address to the *Lycéens* of Sens   25
3. The Principles of 1789 and Sociology   34
4. Individualism and the Intellectuals   43
5. The Intellectual Elite and Democracy   58

III. THE EVOLUTION
     OF MORALITY

6. Progressive Preponderance of Organic Solidarity   63
7. Organic Solidarity and Contractual Solidarity   86
8. Division of Labor in Society: Consequences   114
9. Division of Labor in Society: Conclusion   134

v

IV. THE LEARNING
OF MORALITY

10.   The Dualism of Human Nature and Its Social
      Conditions   149

V. SOCIAL CREATIVITY

11.   Origin of the Idea of the Totemic Principle or Mana   167
12.   Elementary Forms of Religious Life   187

NOTES   225

BIBLIOGRAPHY   243

Preface

THERE IS AN ANECDOTE from Georges Davy about an occasion when Davy and Marcel Mauss, Durkheim's nephew and disciple, had, on a warm summer day, left off work for a few minutes to have a beer in a sidewalk café. Catching a glimpse of his uncle coming out of the Sorbonne courtyard, Mauss said to Davy, "Quick hide me! Here comes my uncle!" and escaped behind one of the orange trees decorating the café. After working on this book off and on for five years and exposing myself for long stretches at a time to Durkheim's unrelieved tone of high moral seriousness, I have had moments of sharing the feelings of Marcel Mauss on that occasion. But I have also come to admire, more than ever before, not only the complexity of Durkheim's mind, but the definiteness with which he knew who he was and what he believed. We are, most of us in American social science, more in his debt than we imagine.

This volume includes five articles newly translated and published here for the first time (chapters 1–5). I wish to record my gratitude to Mark Traugott for making these translations and for assistance at every stage with the work for this book. His suggestions and corrections have immeasurably improved it. Albert Craig, Clifford Geertz, Morris Janowitz, Talcott Parsons, David Riesman, Irwin Scheiner, and Edward Shils were also kind enough to read the Introduction and give me the benefit of their reactions to it.

Introduction

THERE IS NO WORD in Durkheim's writings more difficult, and none commoner, than "society." To grasp the many meanings of that word and its many levels of meaning would be almost equivalent to understanding the whole of Durkheim's thought. At times the word is simple and obvious—it refers to some specific social group. At other times its meaning is darker and more mysterious.[1] It is not identical with "the group of individuals that compose it and their dwelling place." Rather, "it is above all a composition of ideas, beliefs and sentiments of all sorts which realize themselves through individuals. Foremost of these ideas is the moral ideal which is its principal *raison d'être*. To love one's society is to love this ideal, and one loves it so that one would rather see society disappear as a material entity than renounce the ideal which it embodies."[2] Not only is society not identical with an external "material entity," it is something deeply inner, since for Durkheim it is the source of morality, personality, and life itself at the human level. It is something on which we all depend whether we know it or not. He refers to those "not without nobility" who find the idea of dependence on society "intolerable. But that is because they do not perceive the source from which their own morality flows, since these sources are very deep. Consciousness is a bad judge of what goes on in the depths of a person, because it does not penetrate to them."[3] When we read in *The Elementary Forms of the Religious Life* that society is the "real" object to which the word "God" points, it is well to remember that Durkheim uses the word "society" in ways closer to classical theology than to empirical science. It is not that Durkheim makes an empirical society into an idol. It is that he so elevates, purifies, and deepens the word "society" that it can, not unworthily, take the place of the great word it supersedes.

If morality, then (and even divinity), is not a concept external to society but rather part of its essence, that implies a notion of sociology not identical with what currently goes by that name in the United States. Durkheim is known as one of the founders of scientific sociology, and not without reason. His contributions to the theory and methodology of empirical sociology have probably not been equaled by any other man. But he was not only a sociologist in the strict sense. He was a philosopher and a moralist in the great French tradition of moral thought. He was even more than that. He was a high priest and theologian of the civil religion[4] of the Third Republic and a prophet calling not only modern France but modern Western society generally to mend its ways in the face of a great social and moral crisis. In this selection from Durkheim's writings and in this introduction I have chosen to concentrate on this broader aspect of Durkheim's self-conception, partly because this is what determined the nature of his life work and partly because this broader aspect is perhaps more relevant to the present crisis in our society and our discipline than the somewhat more specific influence Durkheim has had on American sociology.

The first two groups of selections set the context for the development of Durkheim's sociology of morality, his central preoccupation. Section I gives Durkheim's picture of how his sociology is to be situated relative to the French tradition of social thought. Section II, "Sociology and Social Action," shows Durkheim grappling with moral and political issues in his society and indicates the immediate social context of his thinking. The remaining sections indicate some of the major substantive areas of Durkheim's sociology of morality. Section III, taken from *The Division of Labor in Society*, indicates his basically evolutionary approach to the development of moral norms in society. Section IV gives examples of Durkheim's work on socialization, the learning of morality. Finally, section V deals with the important question of how new moral norms arise in society. It is here that Durkheim's conceptions of the sources of social creativity can be found. In the introduction I hope to shed some light on the broad issues raised in these selections and to provide some commentary on most of the specific selections as well.

It seems unlikely that we will ever have a very intimate picture of Durkheim as a person. The sort of material that Arthur Mitzman utilized in his recent biography of Max Weber[5] does not seem to exist for Durkheim. The picture we get from those few writings which attempt to describe him is of a man extraordinarily serious, extraordinarily dedicated, extraordinarily sincere. He seems to have carried a characteristic atmosphere of gravity even from his school days. Trivial diversions were of no interest to him, though he was by no means averse to the society of others. Passionate in discussion, he was apparently an inspiring lecturer. According to Davy, "he gave to those who heard him the impression that they had before them the prophet of some newly born religion."[6] Language was his medium and he used it effectively, whether written or spoken, but there was nothing "literary" about him, and indeed he abhorred the *"litterateurs"* so characteristic of the French academy of his day.

Emile Durkheim was born on 15 April 1858, in Epinal, a French-speaking town in the Vosges near the Alsace border. His father was Moise Durkheim, a rabbi who became Grand Rabbi of the Vosges.[7] It was intended that Emile become a rabbi in accordance with family tradition, and he studied Hebrew in his youth. But, according to a tantalizingly obscure reference by Georges Davy,[8] Durkheim underwent a religious crisis under the influence of a Catholic governess or teacher (*institutrice*). He did not convert, but he did settle on a secular career as a professor, through which he could express in another form the religious aspirations of his youth, a career which he always viewed as, in Davy's words, "a veritable calling."

The social context in which Durkheim came to define his life work was decisively affected when he was twelve years old by the crushing defeat of France by Germany in the War of 1870, and by the subsequent fall of the Second Empire and establishment of the Third French Republic. This great social change became the objective reference point for his developing sense of calling. Even when preparing for the Ecole normale supérieure "he felt himself called to something other than mere teaching: he must teach a doctrine, have disciples and not just students, play a role in the social reconstitution of a France wounded in defeat."[9] Durkheim's growing concern for and love of French culture and society was not rejected by the established powers. Unlike so many young Jewish intellectuals in Wilhelminian Germany, who found all official doors closed to their advancement in the university,[10] Durkheim's career was one of continuous ascent to the highest academic post in France, a professorship at the Sorbonne. Anti-Semitism was certainly not absent in France, as became clear during the Dreyfus case into which Durkheim threw himself so passionately in the 1890s. But even then he spoke without self-consciousness, as a Frenchman and not as a Jew. His references to Judaism, as to Christianity, are always respectful, but it is clear that in his opinion both were outmoded in the modern world. His own highest commitments were to rationality, science, and humanity and to French society insofar as it embodied these ideals.

It was a strangely sober boy from the provinces, a boy who seemed older than his years, who arrived at the Ecole normale in 1879, a year behind Bergson and Jaurès, and he was soon dubbed "metaphysician" by his classmates.[11] Somewhat out of sympathy with the prevailing classical, literary, and aesthetic interests of many of his teachers, Durkheim early turned toward social and political philosophy. During his first year at the Ecole normale he began to read Renouvier, a French neo-Kantian who had been deeply influenced by Saint-Simon and Comte, and probably in his second year he began to read Comte himself. Although he accepted neither uncritically, Kant and Comte were perhaps the two formative influences on Durkheim's thought. In Kant he found a compelling description of moral obligation which resonated deeply in his own personality. In Comte he found a conception of society as a field of creative forces from which religion, morality, and science emerge. By his third year at the Ecole normale Durkheim had decided to become a sociologist, not only because sociology held an intellectual fascination for him but also because he saw in it a source of the moral reconstitution of his society.[12]

Durkheim did not spend all his time at school reading. He engaged in many animated conversations and debates with his fellow students, particularly the future socialist leader Jean Jaurès. He participated in the public life of Paris, for example when he spent the day in the streets sharing the popular enthusiasm during the first celebration of the fourteenth of July in 1880.[13] Efforts to create a new republican France were in the air he breathed and continually affected him.

After graduating from the Ecole normale in 1882, Durkheim spent five years teaching in various *lycées*. We are fortunate that Edward Tiryakian has recently discovered the graduation address which Durkheim gave at the end of his first year of teaching, at the Lycée of Sens, in August 1883.[14] It indicates Durkheim's preoccupation with the problem of the individual and society as well as his dislike for the literary elitism of a figure like Renan. During these years the plan of his doctoral dissertation, later published as *The Division of Labor in Society*, was beginning to take shape, and the first draft was completed in 1886. Lifelong preoccupations were already taking form well before he was thirty. It is not true that Durkheim's thought underwent no change during his lifetime, though there was less change on some issues than many commentators have thought. But Durkheim was one of those men who write essentially only one book, though in a number of versions. The development is merely the unfolding of what is clearly evident in germ from the beginning.

As an example of the striking consistency in Durkheim's work we might consider his inaugural lecture in 1887 at Bordeaux, where he had been appointed to give the first course of lectures on social science in the history of French universities. In this very first lecture he gave a remarkably accurate conspectus of his remaining life work.

The first part of the lecture is a brief history of sociology.[15] He traces the gradual emergence of a subject matter, society or social facts, and of a method, "observation and indirect experimentation, in other words the comparative method."[16] In particular Durkheim notes the emergence of subfields and specific problems which always arise when a science reaches a certain stage of maturity. In the early stage there are only a few grand theories developed by men of outstanding genius. Later, particular problems arise which can be worked on by men of various talents, often in collaboration. Since a science itself is a natural growth, its subdivisions cannot be predicted on logical grounds alone but emerge of themselves. Durkheim discerned several such emerging subfields. First is what he called social psychology, which turns out to be a study of common ideas and sentiments such as popular legends, religious traditions, political beliefs, language, and so forth. A second field is concerned with those ideas and sentiments which have an additional quality, namely that they are concerned with practice and are obligatory. This is the field of morality, and Durkheim proposed to develop a "science of morality which would treat moral beliefs and maxims as natural phenomena of which one could seek the causes and the laws."[17] A third field is concerned with those moral maxims which are felt to be so obligatory that the society takes precise measures to enforce them. Specially authorized representatives are in charge of maintaining respect for them, and they are not left to the sanction of public opinion alone. Such moral judgments become juridical formulas, and there is a science analogous to the science of morality which concerns itself with them—the science of law—though there are close and continuous relations between the two fields. Finally, there is a fourth field of sociology concerned with economic phenomena. It differs from economics in that it is not studied in isolation but deals with economic phenomena in their full social context. In studying all of these phenomena Durkheim says one should be concerned with the role they play and the constitution of whatever group they are a part of—in other words function and structure.[18] But he stresses the study of function over structure: "Structure is function consolidated, action which has become habitual and is crystalized. If then we don't wish to see things in their most superficial aspect, if we desire to reach to their roots, it is to the study of functions that we will above all apply ourselves."[19]

Finally Durkheim closes his magisterial opening lecture with some comments on the usefulness of sociology for students of various other subjects such as philosophy, history, and law, and more generally the role of sociology in society. During the course of these remarks he indicates that it is to the study of morality that he has committed himself. What he hoped to accomplish becomes clear from the following passage:

For a century there have been disputes about whether morality should take precedence over science or science should take precedence over morality: the only way to put an end to this antagonism is to make of morality itself a science, alongside the others and in relation to them. It is said that there is today a crisis of morality, and indeed there is such a break in continuity between the moral ideal conceived by certain minds and the reality of the facts that, following circumstances and personalities, morality swings between the two poles without knowing where definitively to rest. The only way to put a stop to this instability and inquietude is to see in morality itself a fact the nature of which one must investigate attentively, I would even say respectfully, before daring to modify.[20]

In his last paragraph Durkheim summarizes the practical benefits which may flow from the study of sociology:

We live in a country which recognizes no master but opinion. In order that this master not become a mindless despot it is necessary to enlighten it, and how if not by science?[21]

Further, French society has for a long time been enfeebled by an excessive spirit of individualism. Sociology will teach how much the individual owes to society and how much he depends on it. It will thus help to revivify the solidarity of French society.

Durkheim, it is clear from this inaugural lecture, was not what we would today call an alienated intellectual. On this point he never changed. If we are not to make false assumptions about

Durkheim's lack of alienation, assumptions based on other times and other places, we must consider more closely the social milieu in which his thought took shape.

The establishment of the Third Republic was the most recent effort to deal with the legacy of the French Revolution. It is perhaps difficult for Americans to realize how disturbed French political life had been in the century before Durkheim began to write. The Third Republic was the eighth regime since 1789. There had been three monarchies, two empires, and two republics in the period between 1789 and 1870. These eight regimes had produced fourteen constitutions. The period of twenty years just preceding 1870 was particularly distasteful in the memory of Durkheim's contemporaries, as it was dominated by the petty and narrow despotism of Napoleon III. We must remember that Durkheim was born under Napoleon III and was already old enough at the time of his overthrow to have some personal memories of that regime.

If Durkheim early developed a fundamentally positive attitude toward the Third Republic and maintained it throughout his life, this cannot, under the circumstances, be equated with a generalized conservatism. Indeed, to be a conservative in the 1880s in France meant specifically *not* to be committed to the Third Republic. To the extent that the Third Republic stood for an appropriation of the ideals of the French Revolution and their stable institutionalization in a social order, to be in favor of the Third Republic meant that one was necessarily a democrat, a political liberal, and probably if not a socialist at least concerned with major reforms of the social and economic order, all of which Durkheim was. Although he was all his life concerned with social policy, Durkheim seldom involved himself in direct political action. The great exception, his active defense of Dreyfus in the great legal case which convulsed France in the late 1890s, indicates unmistakably where he must be placed politically—in the opposite camp from the conservatives who so vigorously sought to uphold Dreyfus's conviction.[22]

Durkheim's high evaluation of society and of social integration has sometimes been incorrectly interpreted as an indication of his conservatism by those who overlook his lifelong preoccupation with orderly, continuous social change in the direction of greater social justice. But in this respect too it is well to keep in mind the specific social context. After nearly a century of grave social conflict and turmoil when the very existence of French society was frequently threatened by total civil war, it is not surprising that a French intellectual might be concerned with social integration, especially under a regime which he saw as embodying the ideals of the revolutionary tradition and the potential for a greater realization of them.

Durkheim can be seen with some justice as a semiofficial ideologist of the Third French Republic or even, as I have suggested, as a theologian of the French civil religion. There is no doubt that his intellectual and educational ideals did fit well with those of the regime. It was Louis Liard, French director of higher education, who instigated Durkheim's appointment in 1887 to give the course on social science at the University of Bordeaux, the beginning of Durkheim's distinguished university career culminating with a professorship at Paris in 1906.[23] Liard was motivated by a belief that science could provide a basis for moral reconstruction in the Third Republic, and in this belief Durkheim certainly concurred.[24] Durkheim's rise from the elite Ecole normale through the university hierarchy to the highest pinnacle of French academic and intellectual life took place in an atmosphere of basically cordial feeling between him and established political authority. Durkheim's wholehearted support of the French war effort during the First World War is only the last example of his positive attitude toward his society.

But if Durkheim had been only a narrow nationalist or a hack defender of a political regime we would have no reason to be interested in him today. Durkheim had a strong love of France and of the French tradition, especially its rationalist, democratic, and humanist strands, but he was no narrow nationalist. He believed that schoolchildren should be taught to love their nation, but he specifically opposed any teaching which would suggest that France was superior to other nations.[25] He argued that any particular nation has value only insofar as it embodies universal values such as the ideal of humanity, and not for itself alone.[26] However important the Third Republic and France itself were to Durkheim, his own intellectual sphere was far broader. The breadth of his comparative interests was rivaled only by Max Weber himself. None of Durkheim's major writings is confined to facts drawn from his own contemporary society. Most of his work involves several societies over extended time periods. The work of Durkheim's that most resembles much contemporary sociology, *Suicide*, drew its statistics from all of Europe and used examples from many other societies as well. His greatest book dealt with the Australian aborigines. This vast sweep of Durkheim's work was necessitated by his most fundamental intellectual concern, namely the crisis of modern society. In depicting this great crisis such a date as 1870 or even 1789 sinks to secondary importance. It is not the crisis of one society alone or even of a group of societies. It is the crisis of all traditional societies in the face of rationalism, industrialism, and individualism. What is to be the basis of the new social order, the new moral order in the face of forces which undercut all the bases of the old order? That is Durkheim's question.

It is as a philosopher of order that Durkheim stands in the tradition of Plato, Montesquieu, Rousseau, Saint-Simon, and Comte. All of them lived under conditions of disorder and sought to determine the foundations of order. Durkheim's work reflects the great preoccupations of his predecessors: religion, law, morality, and education—in short, the various ways in which social and individual action are ordered and controlled. And many of his central problems are classical as well: how to reconcile freedom and authority, rational choice and the weight of tradition, individual autonomy and social cohesion. But his answers, though indebted to many influences, were new.

If it is inappropriate to try to force Durkheim into the conservative side of some conservative/liberal or conservative/radical dichotomy, it is equally inappropriate to force him into the category of idealist as against materialist, collectivist as against individualist, or even, in any ultimate sense, sociologist as against psychologist. As with other great innovative thinkers, Durkheim's thought transcends the categories of his predecessors, even though, as has also been the case with others, critics have long failed to understand him and have continued to think of him in terms of categories he had left behind.

Marxists have sometimes argued that Durkheim's thought as a whole is "idealistic." Others have felt that idealist tendencies emerged in his late writings. In fact, Durkheim is quite clear almost from the beginning that neither the traditional materialist nor the traditional idealist positions were adequate as a foundation for social science.[27] The essential position is established in his 1887 article "La science positive de la morale en Allemagne." There he asserts that moral facts (in other writings he clearly extends this to social facts generally) are sui generis and, as the idealists have held, not reducible to any other kind of reality but, as the materialists have held, are natural facts capable of explanation through objective empirical scientific investigation.[28] In other words, the idealists have guarded the specificity of moral life and have often been admirable in their subtle descriptions of it, but have resisted any attempt at scientific explanation. Kant's perception, for example, that obligation is a decisive component of morality was always accepted by Durkheim as an accurate observation which any scientific theory of morality would have to account for. On the other hand, the materialists, who did accept a scientific approach to the understanding of morality, ended by explaining it away in reducing it to economic or other nonmoral causes. Durkheim's solution to the idealist/materialist impasse, which came very early and was never abandoned, was to accept the specificity of the idealists' description of the moral life but to develop a new, autonomous, but naturalistic science to account for it.

Durkheim saw mind not as some ultimate ontological reality or some transphysical influence, but as an emergent property of biological organisms, having its own autonomous existence which could not be reduced to physiology, but at the same time dependent on the organized matter which forms its substratum. Similarly, collective consciousness and representations are entirely natural phenomena to be studied objectively. They result from the interaction of individual consciousnesses and cannot exist without them, but cannot be reduced to them either. This position cannot be identified with that of collectivism or "social realism" if by that term is meant a belief in a group mind, oversoul, or any Hegelian notion of "objective spirit," all terms which have been used to describe Durkheim's position. In one of his earliest publications, in 1885, Durkheim stated the position which he many times later reiterated:

Undoubtedly a society is a being, a person. But this being has nothing metaphysical to it. It is not a substance more or less transcendent; it is a whole composed of parts. But isn't it the first problem for the sociologist to decompose this whole, to enumerate its parts, to describe and class them, to seek how they are grouped and divided? [29]

In *The Division of Labor* he says that society "has, after all, no other bases than individual consciences."[30] In the 1898 essay "Individual and Collective Representations" Durkheim makes a particularly clear statement of his position:

In fact individualistic sociology is only applying the old principles of materialist metaphysics to social life. It claims, that is, to explain the complex by the simple, the superior by the inferior, and the whole by the part, which is a contradiction in terms. The contrary principle does not seem to us any less questionable. One cannot, following idealist and theological metaphysics, derive the part from the whole, since the whole is nothing without the parts which form it and cannot draw its vital necessities from the void.[31]

It is clear, then, that for Durkheim collective life is an emergent process of human action with its own systematic properties but has neither greater nor lesser ultimate reality than individual life.

It has often been asserted that Durkheim was "antipsychological" or that he wanted to create a sociology entirely independent of psychology. In a sense, however, Durkheim was radically psychological. Two of his most fundamental terms, *"conscience"* and *"representation,"* refer to mental or psychic realities. In fact Durkheim frequently referred to social facts as "mental," "moral," "spiritual," or "ideal." He was constantly preoccupied with mind, with consciousness and with conscience. He even went so far as to say that "collective psychology is sociology, quite simply."[32] Nor did Durkheim have any antipathy to what he called "individual psychology." In the late 1880s he gives evidence of being widely familiar with French and German academic psychology. Later he showed familiarity with William James and other American and English psychologists as well. From the work of Ribot and Janet, he adopted the notion of the unconscious, extending it to the collective psyche as well as the individual. What Durkheim objected to was certainly not psychology in general, since he considered sociology a kind of psychology, nor even to individual psychology as such, but only to the attempt to explain social facts in terms of individual psychology instead of collective psychology (or social psychology or sociology). This was the main ground for his rejection of Tarde. He felt that an effort to reduce social reality to a mere epiphenomenon of individual psychology was strictly comparable to the effort to reduce individual psychology to physiology. It is certainly true that Durkheim never adequately dealt with the interrelations between sociology and psychology, though the article "The Dualism of Human Nature and Its Social Conditions"[33] is a valuable attempt in that direction. But any sensitive reader of Durkheim's monographs will be struck by their frequent psychological insights. One can mention his treatment of the various types of suicide, of the functions of ritual in *The Elementary Forms of the Religious Life*, and of the attitudes and motives of students and professors in medieval French universities in *L'évolution pédagogique en France*, as outstanding examples.

In all of these respects, then, both intellectually and ideologically, Durkheim tried to avoid making a narrow doctrinaire choice between allegedly incompatible opposites. Rather, he strove to attain a new synthesis, a unity of opposites, a *coincidentia oppositorum*, which would provide a new level of analytic insight.

One more dichotomy that Durkheim attempted to transcend, that between reason and tradition, was particularly salient in his conception of sociology and of the "science of morals" which was so central a part of it. Durkheim was very skeptical of the power of the unaided reason to penetrate the complexities of social and moral reality:

Social facts are almost always much too complex to be able to be embraced in their integrity by a human intelligence, however vast it might be. Rather, most moral and social institutions are due, not to reasoning or calculation, but to obscure causes, to subconscious sentiments, to motives without relation to the effects which they produce and which they cannot consequently explain.[34]

Consequently Durkheim tends to treat all "social facts" with respect. They are the result of obscure causes that we only partly understand. They fulfill functions which have been vital in the past, and we abandon them at our peril. He is far from believing that the progress of society will be furthered by abandoning all "inherited prejudices" and following the dictates of "reason." Abstract reason without the painfully accumulated results of science is helpless before the complexity of social existence. Even though we may expect the role of science to increase continuously, it will never be able to replace religion, which from his earliest essays Durkheim felt was an essential component of social existence. He wrote in 1886:

A society without prejudices would resemble an organism without reflexes: it would be a monster incapable of living. Sooner or later custom and habit will recover their rights and it is just that which allows us to presume that religion will survive the attacks of which it is the object. As long as there are men who live together there will be some common faith between them. The only thing we cannot foresee and that the future alone will decide is the particular form in which that faith will be symbolized.[35]

Durkheim begins, then, with what is, toward which he is never inclined to act lightly. But this does not mean that he is satisfied with what is or that he is not concerned with changing it. On the contrary, a major function of sociology is to provide the basis for effecting social change. Of course sociology itself does not provide directives for social action. The "science of morality," in Durkheim's view, can never tell us what is right, but only why people believe that certain things are right. But sociology and the sociological study of morality can tell us what the nature of a certain kind of society is, what its needs are, and what tendencies in it are amenable to intervention. It can thus direct us toward lines of action which are sensible and have a chance of success. Thus Durkheim had, both in his understanding of social facts and in his understanding of the process of social change, what might be called a strong "piety toward the real." His conception of sociology was a central expression of that piety.

Durkheim's *The Division of Labor in Society* is one of the inexhaustible classics of the sociological tradition. Published in 1893, it was his doctoral dissertation and had been in preparation for about ten years. Among his writings it is the trunk of which all the other writings, even his masterpiece, *The Elementary Forms of the Religious Life*, are the branches. *The Division of Labor* lays out Durkheim's conception of the historical evolution of the moral or normative order of society and locates the great moral crisis of modern society. Although the central idea of the book, the shifting predominance from mechanical solidarity based on likeness to organic solidarity based on the division of labor, owes much to previous writers such as Comte and Spencer and has certain similarities to the *Gemeinschaft/Gesellschaft* dichotomy of Tönnies, it is also profoundly original. As an imaginative construction its depths have been by no means entirely plumbed by later writers.

According to Durkheim, early and relatively simple societies are characterized by a common conscience enforced by coercive or repressive sanctions. But gradually, over time, "all social links which result from likeness progressively slacken."[36] Instead there emerges a system of cooperative relations based on the division of labor and characterized by restitutive sanctions. Above all Durkheim is concerned with the social and moral nature of the emergent form of social solidarity. Although he sees the role of the individual as much more important in the second type of social solidarity, he by no means repeats the common nineteenth-century idea in which the fundamental dynamics of history are seen to lie in the opposition of individual and society. For Durkheim, on the contrary, the shift is between two kinds of social organization which give very different places to the individual. In a later essay he states succinctly the argument of the *Division of Labor* when he points out that in societies where the division of labor is advanced,

Society has consecrated the individual and made him pre-eminently worthy of respect. His progressive emancipation does not imply a weakening but a transformation of the social bonds. The individual does not tear himself from society but is joined to it in a new manner, and this is because society sees him in a new manner and wishes this change to take place.[37]

Durkheim's analysis of mechanical solidarity is relatively easy to understand. Mechanical solidarity requires a generalized conformity from everyone in the society, and deviance from group norms is viewed as a kind of criminal action calling for more or less severe punishment. He gives as critical examples of mechanical solidarity criminal law and religion, both of which recede steadily though never completely before the rise of organic solidarity.

Durkheim's analysis of organic solidarity is much more complex and difficult to understand. He considers it on several different levels and his treatment is not wholly consistent, though the unresolved problems of *The Division of Labor* provided him with fruitful starting points for later reflection. Durkheim treats the classical analysis of economic interdependence only as a starting point for understanding the division of labor and not as its essence. The mere maximization of self-interest based on exchange of goods could not, in Durkheim's eyes, explain the moral basis of advanced societies. For Durkheim, under the division of labor there is "an occupational morality for each profession"[38] which has an imperative quality, even though it includes only a part and not all of society and even though the sanctions for violating it are restitutive rather than repressive. A work ethic requiring commitment to a definite specialized occupation seems also to be a part of organic solidarity in Durkheim's eyes. More and more, "public sentiment reproves" the tendency of "dilettantes" when they "refuse to take any part in occupational morality."[39]

Many writers—Maine, Spencer, Tönnies, and others—had emphasized the importance of contract as characteristic of modern society. Here, as for economic interdependence, Durkheim recognizes the salience of the characteristic but denies that it is fundamental. For Durkheim what is essential in organic solidarity is not contract but the moral basis of contract or the "noncontractual elements" in the contract.[40] If contract were simply a temporary truce between conflicting self-interests and subject to every pressure a stronger party could enforce, it would provide far too capricious a foundation for a society based on the division of labor. A stable form of organic solidarity requires an institutionalized system of enforcing good faith and the avoidance of force and fraud in contract. It requires, in a word, justice.

Just as ancient peoples needed, above all, a common faith to live by, so we need justice, and we can be sure that this need will become ever more exacting if, as every fact presages, the conditions dominating social evolution remain the same.[41]

One might almost say that justice, the highest form of organic solidarity, *is* the new "common faith" or "common conscience," though Durkheim curiously avoids making that link. Without ever quite making this final connection, Durkheim does, however, develop a most interesting analysis of that form of mechanical solidarity or common conscience that survives in societies where organic solidarity predominates. He gives to this surviving form a positive though limited significance. The following passage from book I suggests the ambiguity and ambivalence of Durkheim's view:

This is not to say, however, that the common conscience is threatened with total disappearance. Only, it more and more comes to consist of very general and very indeterminate ways of thinking and feeling, which leave an open place for a growing multitude of individual differences. There is even a place where it is strengthened and made precise: that is the way in which it regards the individual. As all the other beliefs and all the other practices take on a character less and less religious, the individual becomes the object of a sort of religion. We erect a cult in behalf of personal dignity which, as every strong cult, already has its superstititions. It is thus, if one wishes, a common cult, but it is possible only by the ruin of all others, and, consequently, cannot produce the same effects as the multitude of extinguished beliefs. There is no compensation for that. Moreover, if it is common in so far as the community partakes of it, it is individual in its object. If it turns all wills towards the same end, this end is not social.[42]

However, toward the end of the book he returns to the cult of the individual with fewer qualifications. Indeed, he seems on the verge of linking it to justice, the essence of organic solidarity:

But it is not enough that there be rules; they must be just, and for that it is necessary for the external conditions of competition to be equal. If, moreover, we remember that the collective conscience is becoming more and more a cult of the individual, we shall see that what characterizes the morality of organized societies, compared to that of segmental societies, is that there is something more human, therefore more rational, about them. It does not direct our activities to ends which do not immediately concern us; it does not make us servants of ideal powers of a nature other than our own, which follow their directions without occupying themselves with the interests of men. It only asks that we be thoughtful of our fellows and that we be just, that we fulfill our duty, that we work at the function we can best execute, and receive the just reward for our services. The rules which constitute it do not have a constraining force which snuffs out free thought; but, because they are rather made for us, and in a certain sense, by us, we are free. We wish to understand them; we do not fear to change them.[43]

Durkheim's explanation of the causes of the division of labor, which is a development of a theory of Comte about the importance of demographic density for the emergence of the division of labor,[44] is complex and controversial. It is enough for our purposes to note that Durkheim sees the division of labor as the result of "naturalistic" social causes and not of deliberate rational foresight of individual men. This does not mean that the moral and ideal aspects of organic solidarity are unreal or purely epiphenomenal, nor does it mean that the processes described are unavailable for rational reflection and deliberate transformation. Both the above quotation and other passages in book 2, chapter 5 show the contrary. But Durkheim sees ideals as taking on meaning only relative to specific social forms and rational reflection as helpful only when it takes account of social realities. In this way Durkheim indicates his belief in real if limited human freedom.

In *The Division of Labor* Durkheim expressed a genuine but moderate optimism that the drift of social evolution was in the direction of the tendencies he approved. Nor were these tendencies of recent origin:

Individualism, free thought, dates neither from our time, nor from 1789, nor from the Reformation, nor from scholasticism, nor from the decline of Graeço-Latin polytheism or oriental theocracies. It is a phenomenon which begins in no certain part, but which develops without cessation all through history.[45]

The division of labor does not, however, inevitably occur in benign forms. There could be and are abnormal forms. Indeed the third book of *The Division of Labor* is devoted to these abnormal forms and suggestions for ameliorating them. The two chief abnormal forms are the anomic division of labor and the forced division of labor. The anomic form results from a lack of regulation of the social relations involved in the division of labor. The result is undue conflict between different groups and a loss of a sense of the meaning of the individual's contribution to a larger whole. The forced form results when stronger contracting parties use unjust means to enforce their will on weaker parties, thus undermining the genuine spontaneity characteristic of organic solidarity. The general tenor of the discussion of abnormal forms is concern without alarm.

Four years later, in 1897, Durkheim published a book called *Suicide,* but not simply because he found suicide statistics a useful source of data for a model exercise in sociological methodology. The book represents a marked increase in apprehensiveness about the moral health of modern society. It also contained the first published mention of Durkheim's most serious and comprehensive suggestion for social reform, the proposal for the establishment of professional groups, which would be developed considerably further in the preface to the second edition of *The Division of Labor* in 1902.

Durkheim's well-known typology of the social causes of suicide needs only brief mention here. He concentrates on two sociological variables, integration and regulation, and argues that too much or too little of either creates conditions in which suicide becomes more likely. Altruistic suicide results when an individual is too strongly integrated into his group, for example into a traditional religious group or into the army, so that he easily sacrifices himself either for the sake of the group or because he cannot face its disapproval. Egoistic suicide, on the other hand, results when an individual is not integrated very strongly into any group at all, when he recognizes nothing higher than himself and has few social supports in time or trouble. Excessive social regulation produces what Durkheim calls fatalistic suicide, and he gives the example of the suicide of slaves who are unable to influence at all the rules under which they must live. The opposite of excessive regulation, the case where regulation is weak or inadequate, is what he calls anomic suicide. Where inordinate desires and fears develop with no clear expectations or rules of conduct, the resulting disorientation can lead to anomic suicide.

There is a sense in which suicide is a normal phenomenon, and societies of different sorts will have the type of suicide which is related to their structures. Simple or segmental societies are more likely to have altruistic (and presumably fatalistic) suicide "precisely because [of] the strict subordination of the individual to the group."[46] More advanced societies will show a preponderance of the opposite types:

For opposite reasons, in societies and environments where the dignity of the person is the supreme end of conduct, where man is a God to mankind, the individual is readily inclined to consider the man in himself as a God and to regard himself as the object of his own cult. When morality consists primarily in giving one a very high idea of one's self, certain combinations of circumstances readily suffice to make man unable to perceive anything above himself. Individualism is of course not necessarily egoism, but it comes close to it; the one cannot be stimulated without the other being enlarged.

Thus, egoistic suicide arises. Finally, among peoples where progress is and should be rapid, rules restraining individuals must be sufficiently pliable and malleable; if they preserved all the rigidity they possess in primitive societies, evolution thus impeded could not take place promptly enough. But then inevitably, under weaker restraint, desires and ambitions overflow impetuously at certain points. As soon as men are inoculated with the precept that their duty is to progress, it is harder to make them accept resignation; so the number of the malcontent and disquieted is bound to increase. The entire morality of progress and perfection is thus inseparable from a certain amount of anomy.[47]

Realizing that a certain amount of suicide is perhaps an inevitable accompaniment of modern society, since individualism and relatively fluid rules are necessary for the very existence of that society, Durkheim nevertheless asks whether the rapid rise of suicide (and other forms of social pathology) in modern societies is normal or pathological. He concludes that the social conditions which underlie the rising suicide rate "result not from a regular evolution but from a morbid disturbance which, while able to uproot the institutions of the past, has put nothing in their place."[48] He takes as a sign of the sickness of modern societies not only the rising suicide rate but also the appearance of pessimistic philosophies such as those of Schopenhauer and Hartmann. And he adds, "The anarchist, the aesthete, the mystic, the social revolutionary, even if they do not despair of the future, have in common with the pessimist a single sentiment of hatred and disgust for the existing order, a single craving to destroy or to escape from reality."[49] Thus their appearance too is a sign of the pathological distress of modern society.

In the final chapter of *Suicide* Durkheim attempts to diagnose the ills of modern society and suggest a remedy. The suffering and alienation experienced so widely in modern society do not arise primarily because the struggle for existence has become more painful or because it is more difficult to satisfy our needs. They result rather because "we no longer know the limits of legitimate needs or perceive the direction of our efforts."[50] The problem is one of meaning, of knowing the purpose of existence and the legitimate standards for judging our actions. "The maladjustment from which we suffer does not exist because the objective causes of suffering have increased in number or intensity; it bears witness not to greater economic poverty, but to an alarming poverty of morality."[51] But of course for Durkheim a matter of morality is not a matter of mere sentiment and rhetoric:

By calling the evil of which the abnormal increase in suicides is symptomatic a moral evil, we are far from thinking to reduce it to some superficial ill which may be conjured away by soft words. On the contrary, the change in moral temperament thus betrayed bears witness to a profound change in our social structure. To cure one, therefore, the other must be reformed.[52]

The reform that he offered, of course, was his well-known idea of establishing occupational groups that would be intermediate between the state and the family and would provide a remedy for the lack of regulation in economic life to which he attributed the major disturbances and pathologies of modern society.

Even before the publication of *Suicide* Durkheim had alluded to the proposal concerning occupational groups (sometimes also referred to as professional groups or corporations) toward the end of a series of lectures on the early history of socialism given at Bordeaux during the academic year 1895–96, although not published until many years after his death.[53] Durkheim was offering his proposal in the first instance as an alternative to the socialist proposals of Saint-Simon, the chief subject of his lectures. But it is clear that more generally the occupational group was Durkheim's alternative to socialism or rather, in the words of one recent French writer, Durkheim's socialism.[54]

In order to understand the connection between Durkheim's proposal and socialism it might be well to begin with his definition of socialism:

We denote as socialist every doctrine which demands the connection of all economic functions, or of certain among them, which are at the present time diffuse, to the directing and conscious centers of society. It is important to note at once that we say connection, not subordination. In fact this bond between the economic life and the state does not imply, according to our belief, that every *action* would come from the latter. On the contrary, it is natural that it receive from it as much as it gives it.[55]

For Durkheim the various socialist doctrines and movements of the nineteenth century are to be taken primarily as symptoms of a serious social disturbance. This disturbance is primarily in the economic organization of society. The breakdown in social regulation of economic life has resulted in the anomic division of labor and the forced division of labor that he discussed in *The Division of Labor* and in the anomic and egoistic forms of suicide discussed in *Suicide*. Thus the same conditions which have called forth socialism are the ones to which he is responding in his proposal for the formation of occupational groups. His proposal even meets his own formal definition of socialism, for it is a means of connecting, though not subordinating, currently diffuse economic functions "to the directing and conscious centers of society."

The functions of the occupational group as detailed in the preface to the second edition of *The Division of Labor* are various. The groups would develop rules and regulations governing all aspects of the life of the occupation including working conditions, wages, and hours. The occupational group would be, in today's terms, a community, with a warm, intense group life of its own. This group life would include educational, recreational, and aesthetic dimensions as well as mutual aid. Durkheim cites the multifarious functions of some contemporary labor unions as examples of what he has in mind. This vigorous group life would provide the moral forces that would prevent the development of egoistic and anomic tendencies and would provide an environment of justice and equity so necessary if a highly differentiated society is to function without pathology.

Some critics have seen in Durkheim's views the precursor of the Italian fascist idea of the corporate state. In fact, there is very little similarity, and if anything Durkheim's views are closer to the French left-wing tradition of syndicalism before Sorel. For Durkheim, the occupational group was to be independent of the state, although in close communication with it. The Fascist conception of the corporation as a mere instrumentality of a totalitarian state or party would have been abhorrent to him. He argued that in the present state of industry employees and employers would have to be organized separately, since their interests are often "rival and antagonistic."[56] Both would independently elect representatives to the governing assembly of the group. Further, Durkheim envisioned the occupational group eventually taking over the ownership of productive property. Private ownership in individual families handed down through heredity he saw as a remnant of feudalism. Only collective ownership could ensure the new kind of regulation and morality within the economic sphere which could cure the current ills of society.

Granted that Durkheim's views lack specificity and do not deal extensively with how the present power structure would have to be changed to realize his goals, they are far from irrelevant even at present. His conception of worker representation in the control of industry parallels the spontaneous occurrence of councils in revolutionary conditions which Hannah Arendt has pointed to as a genuine model of participatory democracy.[57] Durkheim's insistence that the state cannot directly run the economy and that the ownership of productive property should be collective but decentralized seems to foreshadow such experiments as are now taking place in Yugoslavia. In any case some solution to the contemporary problems of the organization of economic life that can avoid the evils of despotic state control on the one hand and rampant economic individualism and normlessness on the other seems to be still very much the order of the day. Perhaps, especially in the advanced industrial nations, Durkheim's proposals have more to teach us than we have usually recognized.

In the writings Durkheim published during his lifetime there is not very much which could be called a political sociology sufficient to provide a context for his proposal concerning occupational groups. In the following passage from the 1902 preface to *The Division of Labor* he suggests such a context, but it remained undeveloped:

A society composed of an infinite number of unorganized individuals, that a hypertrophied State is forced to oppress and contain, constitutes a veritable sociological monstrosity. For collective activity is always too complex to be able to be expressed through the single and unique organ of the State. Moreover, the State is too remote from individuals; its relations with them too external and intermittent to penetrate deeply into individual consciences and socialize them within. Where the State is the only environment in which men can live communal lives, they inevitably lose contact, become detached, and thus society disintegrates. A nation can be maintained only if, between the State and the individual, there is intercalated a whole series of secondary groups near enough to the individuals to attract them strongly in their sphere of action and drag them, in this way, into the general torrent of social life.[58]

The occupational group was designed to be one of the secondary groups that could fulfill this function.

Durkheim developed a much more extensive political sociology in the section on civic morals in his lectures "The Nature of Morals and of Rights," given between 1898 and 1900. The manuscript of these lectures did not appear in published form until 1950, but it fills some important gaps in the earlier conceptions of his thought.[59]

In *The Division of Labor* Durkheim already had had a positive conception of the state and had seen it as increasingly important in modern society. In the lectures, he develops the notion of the state as the organized center of consciousness in society. Unlike the collective consciousness, which he saw as vague, diffuse, and not wholly conscious to anybody, the state, according to Durkheim, is the place for representative assemblies, debate, and conscious reflection. For Durkheim the state is not inherently opposed to the individual. On the contrary the growth of the state and the growth of individualism have been positively correlated. This has been because the state has acted to curtail the tyrannical authority of families, guilds, and "coteries of every kind" which have oppressed the individual. The growth of family law, for example, has continuously curtailed the arbitrary authority of parents over children and husbands over wives and enforced a more autonomous role for individuals within the family group. But Durkheim is also very much aware that the growth of the state could become malignant if there were nothing to counter the trend of the state's intervening in the operation of secondary groups.

In that case, as the sole existing collective force, it produces the effects that any collective force not neutralized by any counter-force of the same kind would have on individuals. The State itself then becomes a leveller and repressive. And its repressiveness becomes even harder to endure than that of small groups, because it is more artificial. The State, in our large-scale societies, is so removed from individual interests that it cannot take into account the special or local and other conditions in which they exist. Therefore when it does attempt to regulate them, it succeeds only at the cost of doing violence to them and distorting them. It is, too, not sufficiently in touch with individuals in the mass to be able to mould them inwardly, so that they readily accept its pressure on them.[60]

The inference that Durkheim draws from this is that if the state "is to be the liberator of the individual, it has need of some counterbalance; it must be restrained by other collective forces," in fact, by secondary groups appropriate to the structure of modern society. "It is not a good thing for the groups to stand alone, nevertheless they have to exist. And it is out of this conflict of social forces that individual liberties are born."[61]

The dialectic of differentiation and unity, conflict and consensus that was already apparent in *The Division of Labor* and *Suicide* becomes clearer and more explicit in the lectures on political sociology. A healthy political society needs a strong, conscious, responsive state to counteract the tyrannical propensities of particular groups and interests. But vigorous secondary groups are needed to counteract despotic tendencies in the state. Emphasizing the attribute of consciousness, Durkheim develops a communication theory of politics that seems quite contemporary. It is precisely the characteristic feature of democracy, the type of political organization most appropriate to an advanced society, that it maximizes the flow of communication. Its processes are open and accessible to the public eye, and it does not act without full consultation with interested parties. At least this is the ideal.

Finally, we may note that in the political lectures Durkheim once again brings in the idea of the common conscience, which cannot be absent even in the most advanced society. Since the state is the organ of consciousness of society, it must have a relation to that common conscience which is at the same time moral and religious. The state must be intimately related to the deepest level of value consensus in the society, what I have called in another connection, following Rousseau, the civil religion. And so here too, as he did in *The Division of Labor* and *Suicide*, Durkheim brings in the religion of humanity and the cult of the individual. Since the cult of the individual is the highest moral ideal of society and the state is society's organ of consciousness, Durkheim says that it is the role of the state "to organize the cult, to be the head of it and to ensure its regular working and development."[62] He is vague about structural details. In the sentence just quoted he seems very close to Rousseau when the latter spoke of civil religion in *The Social Contract*. But Durkheim's humanistic religion is by no means entirely fused with the state—it transcends the state. He says, "If the cult of the human person is to be the only one destined to survive, as it seems, it must be observed by the State as by the individual equally."[63] The new religion of humanity is not limited to particular nations but stands above them. As human society has evolved, men have become aware that there are universal values higher than any nation. "Thus," Durkheim says, "everything justifies our belief that national aims do not lie at the summit of this hierarchy—it is human aims that are destined to be supreme."[64] It might seem that there would be a tension between commitment to these universal values and patriotism toward one's own society, but Durkheim offers a way to reconcile the tension:

That is, for the national to merge with the human ideal, for the individual States to become, each in their own way, the agencies by which this general idea is carried into effect. If each State had as its chief aim, not to expand, or to lengthen its borders, but to set its own house in order and to make the widest appeal to its members for a moral life on an ever higher level, then all discrepancy between national and human morals would be excluded. If the State had no other purpose than making men of its citizens, in the widest sense of the term, then civil duties would be only a particular form of the general obligations of humanity.[65]

It might be imagined that such notions as the moral role of the state appeared in Durkheim's mind as memories of classical political thought or as hopes for a utopian future but that they had little to do with his practical response to his own society. Such is not the case. In the most dramatic instance in which he involved himself in the life of his society, the Dreyfus case, he based himself precisely on the ideas, moral and even religious, that we have just been considering.

Durkheim chose to publicly enter the controversy arising from the Dreyfus case not, as we have already noted, because of the element of anti-Semitism and not, certainly, because of any matter of party politics, but because the case raised the fundamental moral issues at the heart of modern society. What moved him to make his major statement in the controversy, the article "Individualism and the Intellectuals,"[66] was the appearance of an article by Ferdinand Brunetière, called "After the Trial," published in March 1898 in the *Revue des deux mondes*.[67] Brunetière, a conservative Catholic literary critic, attacked the critical intellectuals for undermining the moral bases of French society. This they did, he said, by trying to undermine the army and by supporting the socially corrosive doctrine of individualism. Said Brunetière, "the army of France, today as of old, is France itself."[68] Durkheim replied, in terms with which we have become familiar, that individualism in its true form—the religion of humanity, the cult of the dignity of the individual—is the true moral basis of modern society and that a trial which denies justice to the individual is the really subversive social force undermining modern society.

Durkheim involved himself vigorously in the Dreyfusard cause.[69] He was active in committees of intellectuals demanding that the conviction be overturned. His lectures were rallying points for the student supporters of Dreyfus. He took advantage of his old friendship with Jean Jaurès to persuade him to bring the socialists into the coalition in defense of the republic and to abandon the earlier socialist view that the controversy was merely an internal struggle of the bourgeoisie and as such of no interest to the workers.[70] And yet Durkheim never involved himself in party politics.

Some of Durkheim's closest collaborators were not only sympathizers of the socialist party but militantly active. Marcel Mauss, Durkheim's nephew, and François Simiand, one of his closest colleagues, were involved in the founding of the socialist newspaper *L'humanité*, and others of his students were frequent contributors to it. Mauss, Simiand, and Fauconnet taught at the Ecole socialiste, established for the instruction of workers. Durkheim himself ostentatiously carried his copy of *L'humanité* in the courtyard of the Sorbonne and invited Jean Jaurès to the tenth anniversary celebration of *L'année sociologique*.[71] How are we to understand the fact that he never joined the socialist party?

Perhaps the best explanation for Durkheim's aloofness from party politics is contained in his brief essay "The Intellectual Elite and Democracy,"[72] published in 1904. A scholar is a citizen and may be an active and vigorous one. But that does not mean he should necessarily be a politician. "Just as a great physiologist is generally a mediocre clinician, a sociologist has every chance of being a very incomplete statesman."[73] It is not through direct political action that Durkheim thinks the intellectual best makes his contribution to society but through "books, seminars, and popular education."

Above all, we must be *advisors, educators*. It is our function to help our contemporaries know themselves in their ideas and in their feelings, far more than to govern them. And in the state of mental confusion in which we live, what is a more useful role to play?[74]

Durkheim was not saying that the role of the scholar is to carry out his research without regard to his society, but he did argue for the autonomous worth and vitality of the intellectual role. The intellectual is called to hold a mirror to his society, to make conscious its deepest values. The sociologist today must be what Plato's Socrates was in times past, the educator of his society.

In this connection it is worth noting how closely Durkheim was involved with education from the very beginning of his career, in a society where education was acutely sensitive politically. Even before his appointment at Bordeaux in 1887 Durkheim had been sent to Germany to study the teaching of philosophy and to make recommendations for the reform of French education in that field. During his years at Bordeaux pedagogy remained one of his concerns, and he wrote an important article on the teaching of philosophy in 1895.[75] When he was called to Paris in 1902 it was as a *chargé de cours* in the science of education and it was to the chair of the science of education that he succeeded in 1906. Not until 1913 was Durkheim's chair changed to "Science of Education and Sociology."[76] Two of Durkheim's most important works are the posthumously published lecture series "The Evolution of Pedagogy in France" and "Moral Education." Durkheim's course, presumably "Moral Education," was the only course in the Sorbonne required of all prospective teachers in the French secondary schools. During his Paris years Durkheim was influential in academic appointments throughout the country.[77]

All of this activity was not by any means politically and morally "neutral." The anticlericalism endemic in the Third Republic was greatly exacerbated by the Dreyfus affair. There was a conscious effort by liberal and left republicans, politicians and intellectuals, to replace the conservative moral teachings of Catholicism with a secular ethic of a modern democracy. Durkheim's sociology was the most conscious and sophisticated body of thought which could play this role, and Durkheim himself made the necessary application. Many opponents of these trends were thoroughly aware of Durkheim's role and attacked him accordingly. Clerical intellectuals opposed his sociology as fundamentally atheistic and immoral.[78] Durkheim was attacked as a leader of *"le parti politico-scolastique"* by Sorel and *"le parti intellectuel"* by Peguy. Both of these highly individual thinkers rejected Durkheim's effort to provide a new foundation to the Third Republic or to erect a new state religion.[79] Whatever he would have said to these critics,

Durkheim would not have denied that his teachings and their dissemination thoughout the national educational system were intended to have important consequences for the reconstruction of French society. Indeed, that was the purpose with which he took up sociology in the first place.

Durkheim's opening course of lectures at Paris in 1902 was on the subject of moral education. In the inaugural lecture[80] he made a by now familiar distinction. He divided education into that which is the same for all and that which is different for various individuals and groups. With the rise of the division of labor the latter grows at the expense of the former; specialization becomes ever more necessary. But that which is common to all becomes no less important. Without it, men would tend to relapse into provincial and particular loyalties and the great modern societies would fall apart. The course was concerned precisely with what was most important in the common elements of education: morality.

It is clear from the beginning that the moral education Durkheim had in mind was not a mere warmed-over serving of the timeless moral maxims of the ages. His course was aimed to introduce a new secular morality based on his understanding of individualism as the core value of modern society. He wanted to maintain the element of respect toward authority, almost religious in quality, that he felt was essential to the nature of morality in all times and places. Discipline—the ability to restrain one's egoistic impulses and do one's moral duty—was always something that Durkheim admired, and he made it the first of the elements of morality.[81] But he did not see morality as simply a matter of external obligation and authority operating mainly through prohibition and repression, however important some element of control may be. His second element in morality is attachment to social groups—the warm, voluntary, positive aspect of group commitment—not out of external duty but out of willing attraction. Filloux has pointed out the perennial dialectic of *nomos* and *eros* in Durkheim's conception of morality.[82]

But in the elements of discipline and attachment to social

groups there is nothing particularly modern. They are the eternal aspects of morality in all societies. It is only in connection with the third element, autonomy or self-determination, that the modern secular morality comes fully into view. And the element of critical autonomy reflects back on the way the elements of discipline and attachment to social groups are to be understood. The new secular moral discipline is to be divested of the religious myths and symbols with which traditional systems covered themselves in an effort to avoid any critical inspection. The new morality is not to be accepted blindly and without question. Rather, rational criticism is to be part of its very essence:

Rationalism is only one of the aspects of individualism: it is the intellectual aspect of it. We are not dealing here with two different states of mind; each is the converse of the other. When one feels the need of liberating individual thought, it is because in a general way one feels the need of liberating the individual. Intellectual servitude is only one of the servitudes that individualism combats. All development of individualism has the effect of opening moral consciousness to new ideas and rendering it more demanding. Since every advance that it makes results in a higher conception, a more delicate sense of the dignity of man, individualism cannot be developed without making apparent to us as contrary to human dignity, as unjust, social relations that at one time did not seem unjust at all. Conversely, as a matter of fact, rationalistic faith reacts on individualistic sentiment and stimulates it. For injustice is unreasonable and absurd, and, consequently, we are the more sensitive to it as we are more sensitive to the rights of reason. Consequently, a given advance in moral education in the direction of greater rationality cannot occur without also bringing to light new moral tendencies, without inducing a greater thirst for justice, without stirring the public conscience by latent aspirations.[83]

In this paragraph and elsewhere in his later writings Durkheim seems finally to have closed the gap between justice, the highest aspect of the morality of organic solidarity, and individualism, the sole surviving form of mechanical solidarity in modern society. Perhaps this is why he abandoned the terms mechanical and organic solidarity after the publication of *The Division of Labor*. It is certain that he never abandoned the basic structural typology of simple segmental societies and advanced differentiated societies. But the contrast of the two types of society at the moral level has become the contrast of two types of common conscience rather than the contrast between strength or weakness of the common conscience.

But not only does the secular morality with its element of rational autonomy change the conception of the rules which are the essence of moral discipline, it also changes the meaning of attachment to social groups. This attachment too is no longer to be blind and uncritical. The nation or political society is to enjoy a certain moral primacy in the new secular morality (in this way replacing the church).

However, it [the nation] can enjoy moral primacy only on the condition that it is not conceived of as an unscrupulous self-centered being, solely preoccupied with expansion and self-aggrandizement to the detriment of similar entities; but as one of many agencies that must collaborate for the progressive realization of the conception of mankind.[84]

Thus Durkheim outlined the morality he had developed for a secular France. Disciplined, firm, with a definite sense of authority, it was nonetheless to be based on a critical, rational individualism.

It is not surprising that an effort to hold so many things together in a new synthesis should show signs of tension. Two major difficulties in the analysis presented in the lectures on moral education recurred throughout Durkheim's later work, particularly in connection with his analysis of religion and morality.

One of the major tasks of the new secular morality is to express moral reality in rational terms. "We must discover," he says, "those moral forces that men, down to the present time, have conceived of only under the form of religious allegories. We must disengage them from their symbols, present them in their rational nakedness."[85] The "purely empirical reality" which lies behind these allegories and symbols is, as Durkheim says so many times, society. But we would be mistaken if we imagine that this society is nonsymbolic:

It is a complex of ideas and sentiments, of ways of seeing and of feeling, a certain intellectual and moral framework distinctive of the entire group. Society is above all a consciousness of the whole.[86]

What we must above all cherish in society—that to which above all we must give ourselves—is not society in its physical aspects, but its spirit. And what is this thing that people call society's soul or spirit but a complex of ideas, of which the isolated individual would never have been able to conceive, which go beyond his mentality, and which come into being and sustain themselves only through the interaction of a plurality of associated individuals?[87]

Society too turns out to be a set of ideas and sentiments. Behind the reality which traditional morality and religion disguised with symbols seems to be not a nonsymbolic reality but another set of symbols.

The second difficulty, not unrelated to the first, arises from Durkheim's insistence that the new morality be rational—be composed of clear and distinct ideas. Already in *Suicide* he had argued that religion as it becomes more rational loses its power to constrain individual consciences, and he gives Protestantism as an example.[88] In the lectures on moral education he recognizes the inadequacy of purely theoretical ideas to gain sufficient influence in the life of the child.

we can only become attached to things through the impressions or images we have of them. To say that the idea we acquire of these social groups is a part of our consciousness is really to say that it cannot disappear without creating a painful void. Not only must we repeat this representation, but in repeating it, give the idea enough color, form, and life to stimulate action. It must warm the heart and set the will in motion. The point here is not to enrich the mind with some theoretical notion, a speculative conception; but to give it a principle of action, which we must make as effective as necessary and possible. In other words, the representation must have something emotional; it must have the characteristic of a sentiment more than of a conception.[89]

The difficulty is that though Durkheim makes it clear where the theoretical notions are to come from he does not tell us how to derive the warm, living, colorful images and sentiments which he also finds necessary. By downgrading art[90] as not sufficiently grounded in reality to play a primary moral role, he cuts himself off from one possible source of a solution to this problem.

The closest he comes to a solution to either difficulty is his conception that it is the very intensity of group interaction itself that produces social ideas and ideals and that it is from the warmth of group life that they become compelling and attractive to individuals. Once again he laments the decline of group life in modern France. The old groupings that have died or are dying cannot be revived as such. New groups appropriate to new conditions must arise, and the "spirit of association" must be born again. "We can only reanimate collective life, revive it from this torpor, if we love it; we cannot learn to love it unless we live it, and in order to do so it must exist."[91] In the lectures on moral education Durkheim sees the schools as virtually the only actually functioning secondary group in which the new secular morality could have a vital collective basis. The idea of intense collective experience as the basis of society would later reappear in a context far from that of the French school. In his great work on the sociology of religion he developed the central concept of "collective effervescence" as it was expressed in the life of the primitive Australians.

In spite of all the excellent and persuasive reasons Durkheim gave in the introduction to *The Elementary Forms of the Religious Life* for choosing the Australian aborigines as the subject of his greatest book, one must still wonder at this choice. Why did this highly rational, secular, positivistic Frenchman decide sometime after 1895 to devote nearly fifteen of the most productive years of his life to the exotic cults, dancing, and blood-letting of a primitive people? His earlier work is not without reference to primitives. Indeed, the *Division of Labor* takes as a fundamental reference point an ideal type of primitive society which the *Elementary Forms* fleshes out in detail. But always before the primitive example was rather quickly disposed of as a kind of background contrast against which to analyze the complexities of highly differentiated "advanced" societies. This is the case with his economic sociology, his sociology of law, his political and educational sociologies, and his analysis of suicide. Formally, the same argument is given in the *Elementary Forms*. The analysis of primitive religion is presented as one big background to what comes later. But the background this time has become so immense and has so swallowed up the foreground that we must consider the possibility that in some way the analysis of Australian religion was for Durkheim an end in itself and even, perhaps, a partially veiled expression of aspects of existence largely repressed in his formal thought.

Once in his later years when he was at home in Epinal, Durkheim, in order to please his mother, went to the holiday service at the synagogue. To his acute embarrassment the rabbi, his father's successor, took the occasion to preach that the Jewish religion would always live, since a Sorbonne professor, "a very enlightened person," remained a worshiper.[92] How much more embarrassed would this famous professor and proponent of the "secular" religion of humanity have been to be caught among the naked intoxicated celebrants of Australian totemic rituals; and yet there, through some six hundred pages of the masterwork of his mature years, he was, in a sense, to be found.

There is a fundamental distinction in the *Elementary Forms* that bears a striking similarity to the basic dichotomy between organic and mechanical solidarity in the *Division of Labor*. This is the distinction between the two phases through which the life of the Australian tribes cyclically oscillates. "Sometimes the population is broken up into little groups who wander about independently of one another, in their various occupations. . . . Sometimes, on the contrary, the population concentrates and gathers at determined points . . . and on this occasion they celebrate a religious ceremony."[93] What he treated as a massive evolutionary shift from one type of society to another in the *Division of Labor* is here treated as two alternating phases of a single society. This is not inconsistent with the earlier view, since Durkheim originally argued only for a shift in predominance from one type to the other, admitting that all societies had both kinds of solidarity to some extent. The interesting change in Durkheim's thought, however, is the very considerable shift in valence between the two types. In the *Division of Labor* all the metaphors combined to make the life of mechanical solidarity uniform, routine, and repressive, whereas organic solidarity brought out exfoliating energies, differentiations, and advances. But in the *Elementary Forms* we find that the dispersed economic activity is "of a very mediocre intensity." It does not "awaken lively passions." Its life is "uniform, languishing and dull."[94] But when the tribe gathers together and "a corrobbori takes place, everything changes."

The very fact of the concentration acts as an exceptionally powerful stimulant. When they are once come together, a sort of electricity is formed by their collecting which quickly transports them to an extraordinary degree of exaltation. . . . This effervescence often reaches such a point that it causes unheard-of actions. The passions released are of such an impetuosity that they can be restrained by nothing. They are so far removed from their ordinary conditions of life, and they are so thoroughly conscious of it, that they feel that they must set themselves outside of and above their ordinary morals. The sexes unite contrarily to the rules governing sexual relations. Men exchange wives with each other. Sometimes even incestuous unions, which in normal times are thought abominable and are severely punished, are now contracted openly and with impunity. If we add to all this that the ceremonies generally take place at night in a darkness pierced here and there by the light of fires, we can easily imagine what effect such scenes ought to produce on the minds of those who participate.[95]

And, we might add, on the minds of highly civilized sociologists of religion.

Durkheim himself has left us an important clue to the time when his interests began to shift. In a letter published in 1907 he dates his new interest in religion to the first course he gave on that subject in Bordeaux in 1895.

It was only in 1895 that I had a clear sense of the capital role played by religion in social life. . . . It was for me a revelation. This course of 1895 marks a line of demarcation in the development of my thought, so that all my earlier researches had to be revised anew in order to be put in harmony with these new views.[96]

The *Division of Labor* was published in 1893. It was the last unadulterated celebration of the glories of progress in Durkheim's writing. It was the last time he would unambiguously applaud the decline of the common conscience and of religion. After 1895 he was, as we have seen, more doubtful of many aspects of modern society and increasingly concerned with a new moral basis which would allow it to rise from its malaise. It is therefore not surprising that Durkheim would return imaginatively, especially in the years after 1900, to the profound depths of social life expressed in primitive society, where the common conscience was vividly, disturbingly alive.

It would be a mistake to overdramatize the transition. In his earliest writings he recognized the importance of religion. Even in the *Division of Labor* organic solidarity is not depicted without shadows. In a world of increasing specialization we are told that it is necessary to get the child "to like the idea of circumscribed tasks and limited horizons."[97] This chilling admonition is a premonition of the "dull" and "mediocre" quality of the dispersed economic life of the Australians. Nor does Durkheim in his late years ever give up entirely a sort of stoic acceptance of the cost in inner tension and suffering of an ever more differentiated society. This somber note is struck with particular clarity in the 1914 essay "The Dualism of Human Nature."

It seems that . . . human malaise continues to increase. The great religions of modern man are those which insist the most on the existence of the contradictions in the midst of which we struggle. These continue to depict us as tormented and suffering, while only the crude cults of inferior societies breathe forth and inspire a joyful confidence.[98]

But that essay is exceptional. Repeatedly during his later years he hopes for a revival of the profound collective experience, the experience of fusion and ecstasy, which is the essence of primitive religion and the womb out of which the renewal of society at any period can take place.

Near the end of the *Elementary Forms* he says:

In a word, the old gods are growing old or already dead, and others are not yet born. This is what rendered vain the attempt of Comte with the old historic souvenirs artificially revived: it is life itself, and not a dead past which can produce a living cult. But this state of incertitude and confused agitation cannot last forever. A day will come when our societies will know again those hours of creative effervescence, in the course of which new ideas arise and new formulae are found which serve for a while as a guide to humanity; and when these hours shall have been passed through once, men will spontaneously feel the need of reliving them from time to time in thought, that is to say, of keeping alive their memory by means of celebrations which regularly reproduce their fruits.[99]

Even more striking, perhaps, is a passage from 1914, the same year as "The Dualism of Human Nature."

The old ideals and the divinities which incarnate them are dying because they no longer respond sufficiently to the new aspirations of our day; and the new ideals which are necessary to orient our life are not yet born. Thus we find ourselves in an intermediary period, a period of moral cold which explains the diverse manifestations of which we are, at every instant, the uneasy and sorrowful witnesses.

But who does not feel—and this is what should reassure us— who does not feel that, in the depths of society, an intense life is developing which seeks ways to come forth and which will finally find them. We aspire to a higher justice that no existing formulas express to our satisfaction. But these obscure aspirations which agitate us will finally, one day or another, reach a clearer self-consciousness and translate themselves into definite formulas around which men will rally and which will become a center of crystallization for new beliefs. . . .

All that matters is to feel below the moral cold which reigns on the surface of our collective life the sources of warmth that our societies bear in themselves. One may even go farther and say with some precision in what region of society these new forces are particularly forming: it is in the popular classes.[100]

Whether Durkheim was a good or a bad prophet remains to be seen, since the incertitude and moral cold of which he speaks are still with us. Not in France and not in the United States, but in many parts of the world, the twentieth century has seen the emergence of great charismatic revolutions which resemble the collective transformations of which Durkheim wrote. But his attitude toward the results of most of them would have been highly skeptical. We have yet to see the revival of associational life Durkheim hoped for, which would curtail both bureaucratic centralization and individual atomization. In a word, we have yet to see a genuinely democratic socialism.

As an analyst of social process, however, Durkheim was without a peer. The analysis of society, personality, and symbolism and their interpenetration in the *Elementary Forms* remains a fundamental reference point for present understanding of these problems. In his theory of ritual Durkheim attempts to show how a new level of consciousness comes about and supersedes the isolated, fragmented individual consciousnesses which operate in the dispersed conditions of everyday life. The new consciousness could be called a social consciousness or even a symbolic consciousness—for it cannot occur without symbolism—but it penetrates into the interior of the personality and even strongly affects physiology. Durkheim's analysis depends heavily on his conception of the symbol or the "emblem," as he calls the symbolic indications of totemic identity in Australia:

That an emblem is useful as a rallying-centre for any sort of a group is superfluous to point out. By expressing the social unity in a material form, it makes this more obvious to all, and for that very reason the use of emblematic symbols must have spread quickly once thought of. But more than that, this idea should spontaneously arise out of the conditions of common life; for the emblem is not merely a convenient process for clarifying the sentiment society has of itself; it also serves to create this sentiment; it is one of its constituent elements.

In fact, if left to themselves, individual consciousnesses are closed to each other; they can communicate only by means of signs which express their internal states. If the communication established between them is to become a real communion, that is to say, a fusion of all particular sentiments into one common sentiment, the signs expressing them must themselves be fused into one single and unique resultant. It is the appearance of this that informs individuals that they are in harmony and makes them conscious of their moral unity.

It is by uttering the same cry, pronouncing the same word, or performing the same gesture in regard to some object that they become and feel themselves to be in unison.[101]

In the conclusion of *Elementary Forms* Durkheim argues that religion is not some historic phenomenon destined soon to fade away. The existence of society itself depends on the recurrence of periodic ritual, and only through such events can the sentiments of individuals be united:

Thus there is something eternal in religion which is destined to survive all the particular symbols in which religious thought has successively enveloped itself. There can be no society which does not feel the need of upholding and reaffirming at regular intervals the collective sentiments and the collective ideas which make its unity and its personality. Now this moral remaking cannot be achieved except by the means of reunions, assemblies and meetings where the individuals, being closely united to one another, reaffirm in common their common sentiments; hence come ceremonies which do not differ from regular religious ceremonies, either in their object, the results which they produce, or the processes employed to attain these results. What essential difference is there between an assembly of Christians celebrating the principal dates of the life of Christ, or of Jews remembering the exodus from Egypt or the promulgation of the decalogue, and a reunion of citizens commemorating the promulgation of a new moral or legal system or some great event in the national life?[102]

As Durkheim's examples indicate, religious ritual often points back to some founding experience, some archetypal moment, when the basic symbols came into existence. He tends to analyze such events as great historic outbursts of collective effervescence, fundamentally similar in the forces involved to the ritual situation, except that whereas the ritual repeats some previous symbolism the historic moments of collective enthusiasm create new ones.

It is, in fact, at such moments of collective ferment that are born the great ideals upon which civilizations rest. The periods of creation or renewal occur when men for various reasons are led into a closer relationship with each other, when reunions and assemblies are most frequent, relationships better maintained and the exchange of ideas most active. Such was the great crisis of Christendom, the movement of collective enthusiasm which, in the twelfth and thirteenth centuries, bringing together in Paris the scholars of Europe, gave birth to Scholasticism. Such were the Reformation and the Renaissance, the revolutionary epoch and the Socialist upheavals of the nineteenth century. At such moments this higher form of life is lived with such intensity and exclusiveness that it monopolizes all minds to the more or less complete exclusion of egoism and the commonplace. At such times the ideal tends to become one with the real, and for this reason men have the impression that the time is close when the ideal will in fact be realized and the Kingdom of God established on earth.[103]

With the inevitable return of everyday considerations enthusiasm recedes, but unless it is periodically recreated, at least to some extent, through collective ritual, society cannot survive at all. Such is Durkheim's analysis.

A major problem for Durkheim is the nature of the emblems, symbols, or representations which are so central to this theory of ritual and of society. At times he argues that the religious symbols are merely the confused precursors of scientific concepts. Since he believed that scientific thinking is itself a direct development out of religious thought, he had to hold out for some degree of homogeneity or continuity between the two spheres and to oppose Lévy-Bruhl's sharp dichotomy between "primitive" and "scientific" thinking. And yet Durkheim recognized that the speculative side of religion, that which produced the great cosmologies and world classifications, is always secondary. The chief aim of religious symbolism is to reproduce society—social forces, not the cosmos. It is this line of thinking which led him to adopt at moments what appears to be a straightforward representational or objective theory of religious symbols: religious symbols stand for society; particular symbols stand for particular groups.

We have already noticed that this objective representational conception of symbols runs into difficulty if society is not defined as a physical group inhabiting a given territory. We have had occasion to see that Durkheim often indicates that society is by no means to be defined in such a physical way. In the *Elementary Forms* he explicitly says that religious symbols do not merely give an intellectual conception of society, they create it: "for the emblem is not merely a convenient process for clarifying the sentiment society has of itself; it also serves to create this sentiment; it is one of its constituent elements."[104] A little later he says, "Thus social life, in all its aspects and in every period of its history, is made possible only by a vast symbolism."[105] Yet within the *Elementary Forms* Durkheim never seems to ask whether a constitutive symbol and a concept standing for some external reality can be treated in the same way. In the conclusion he gives two bases for the survival of religious symbols once science has become advanced. One is that we still need the symbols of faith which arouse sentiments and impel to action even when religious speculation about the cosmos is outmoded. The other is that even though science is advanced it can never solve all problems, or at least there will be many cases where we need to have some cognitive guide before the results of scientific investigation are in. In these circumstances we may consult religious ideas.[106] But he does not face the possibility that constitutive symbols may have their own reality which is neither merely emotional nor a residual category of what science has not yet solved. Only in the essay "Value Judgements and Judgements of Reality," published in 1911 but not followed up in the *Elementary Forms,* does he indicate another possibility. He has argued that both judgments of reality and judgments of value involve ideals, or standards of judgment. Yet the two types of judgment are not the same:

We have, nevertheless, indicated a difference that still persists. If all judgements involve ideals we have different species of ideals. The function of some is to express the reality to which they adhere. These are properly called concepts. The function of others is, on the contrary, to transfigure the realities to which they relate, and these are the ideals of value. In the first instance the ideal is a symbol of a thing and makes it an object of understanding. In the second the thing itself symbolizes the ideal and acts as the medium through which the ideal becomes capable of being understood. Naturally the judgements vary according to the ideals involved. Judgements of the first order are limited to the faithful analysis and representation of reality, while those of the second order express that novel aspect of the object with which it is endowed by the ideal. This aspect is itself real, but not real in the same way that the inherent properties of the object are real.[107]

"To transfigure the realities to which they relate." That seems to indicate a more active, forming, imaginative role for religious symbolism than Durkheim's usual epistemology admits. It is my belief that at many points in his late work he is on the verge of, or, as in the above quotation, actually obscurely states, a position which I have come to call "symbolic realism."[108] This position openly asserts the autonomous creative function of religious symbolism operating in a different way from the cognitive symbolism of science.

There are probably several reasons why Durkheim never fully made this last step in the implications of his argument. For one thing he quite rightly perceived deep lines of continuity between religious and scientific symbolism, lines of continuity which have by no means been satisfactorily analyzed to this day. Another is his deep aversion to the aesthetic-literary tradition for which the word "imagination" was central. He felt that clever verbalists could all too easily conjure up their private visions, claiming for them the status of profound insights into reality, while never bothering to investigate any facts. Durkheim's devotion to science was steadfast throughout his life. It was part of his piety toward the real.

But perhaps Durkheim did not mean by science quite what present-day philosophers of science mean. For him science itself is a living thing, evolving through various stages. Comte's influence on him was still strong enough that he did not conceive of sociology as merely another form of natural science whose object happened to be society. Since the object was different from physical nature, so had the science to be.

Society is also of nature and yet dominates it. Not only do all the forces of the universe converge in society, but they also form a new synthesis which surpasses in richness, complexity and power of action all that went to form it. In a word, society is nature arrived at a higher point in its development, concentrating all its energies to surpass, as it were, itself.[109]

Since society is capable of transcending itself, the role of sociology is not just to predict inevitably determined trends. It is to serve as a creative reflection and guide for the process of social thought itself. Even though Durkheim never explicitly defined his role in this way, he did so clearly in his action. He was not simply sociologist *and* citizen. His sociology was the chief contribution of his citizenship, not of France alone but of mankind.

There were two periods in Durkheim's life when he felt the revivifying currents of collective enthusiasm in his own society. One was the period of the Dreyfus affair, when social energies were mobilized to prevent injustice and advance the cause of the secular republic. Durkheim's brief assessment of this experience can be seen in his article "The Intellectual Elite and Democracy."[110]

The second experience was the First World War. Never before in his life, not even in the Dreyfus affair, had Durkheim thrown himself into public activity as he did then. He joined innumerable committees, attended many public functions, and abandoned almost all his research in order to write pamphlets and letters on behalf of the French war effort. At first he experienced the same elation that Weber did. Courage, heroism, and self-sacrifice seemed at last to have replaced the dreadful pettiness, the "chaotic and colorless public life" which had continued to the eve of the war. Durkheim was impressed with "the unsuspected moral forces which slumbered for want of a definite object to which to devote themselves."[111]

Weber soon became disillusioned with the war and went into active, even dangerous, opposition. Durkheim, viewing the war not as a power struggle, as Weber saw it, but as a moral struggle against rampant egoistic nationalism, never opposed it. Yet the war crushed him. Just before Christmas in 1915 he received word of the death of his only son and promising disciple, André, during the retreat from Serbia. He went on indefatigably with his patriotic duties while the list of his young followers killed in the war grew ever longer. Perhaps he even sensed the deathblow the war was giving to the ideals of the Third Republic, which, though it survived the war for twenty years, never recovered from it. He carried on with his stern exterior and the almost feminine sensitivity which Georges Davy tells us was hidden behind it until he too, on 15 November 1917, became "though far from the field of battle, a victim of the war."[112]

The Durkheimian tradition of sociology in France did not survive the physical and moral losses of the war.[113] This is not the place to trace Durkheim's worldwide influence during the years after his death. It would be a story of partial misunderstanding, of appropriation of what was perceived as important in one place or another without any necessary recognition of the function of what was appropriated in the total structure of his work. This perhaps was inevitable.[114] Yet he has not been forgotten. His works are appearing in new editions and the secondary literature is steadily expanding. Perhaps we can hope that a more adequate understanding of the whole of his work and of the role he projected for it in the moral crisis of modern society will before long become general.

Today Durkheim appears not only as a founder of scientific sociology but as one of the classical figures in the history of social thought. His imaginative vision of society will take its place alongside those of Plato, Machiavelli, Montesquieu, and Rousseau as one which not only analyzes society but provides the tools for its renewal. Very few modern social thinkers rank in the same class— perhaps only Marx and Weber.

Each great thinker has his own angle of vision and his own blind spots. It is fashionable to read Durkheim to discover the ways he is not Marx or not Weber. From such a reading there will be very little instruction. In Durkheim there is to be found a moral vision, a return to the depths of social existence, which is in some ways more radical than that of either of his rivals. There are significant parallels with Freud, since Durkheim was trying to understand the unconscious sources of social existence as Freud was the unconscious sources of personal existence. His extended imaginative sojourn among the primitive Australians was perhaps Durkheim's equivalent to Freud's work on dreams. He wanted to bring together in contemporary society a deep respect for the dignity of the individual and a profound social solidarity, to find a way out of the impasse of *Gemeinschaft* and *Gesellschaft*. His means were rational reflection and science; yet he created no lifeless set of abstractions, but a profound imaginative vision, a partially autonomous symbol structure, which is not only an aid to the intellect but a source of life. Durkheim's work has itself become a great collective representation.

I. The French Tradition
of Social Thought

SOCIOLOGY IN FRANCE
IN THE NINETEENTH CENTURY

First Period: Saint-Simon and Auguste Comte

To DETERMINE France's part in the progress made by sociology during the nineteenth century is to review, in large part, the history of that science. For it is in our country and in the course of this century that it was born, and it has remained an essentially French science.

It is true that, if we call all speculation about the life of peoples "sociology," it appears much earlier than the word which today is used to designate it. Indeed, in that case the theories of Plato and Aristotle on the diverse forms of political organization could be regarded as a first attempt at sociology (*science sociale*), and they are often presented in this light. In fact it cannot be disputed that they constituted an important innovation; for they were part of an historical development in the course of which sociology one day had to appear. They are a first application of reflection to things of a social order. However, it is not enough that reflection be applied to an order of facts for a science to result; beyond that, it is necessary that it be applied in a certain way. Medicine existed for centuries before anyone had the idea of physiology and, just the same, whatever its errors, it cannot be doubted that medicine already involved reflection and that it had as its object, just as

This article was one of a series which appeared in the *Revue bleue* of 1900, reviewing the accomplishments of the 1800s in various fields. Translated by Mark Traugott.

did human physiology, the phenomena which occur in the human body.

The fact is that art, even methodical and reflective art, is one thing and science is another. Science studies facts just to know them, indifferent to the applications to which its ideas can be put. Art, on the contrary, deals with them only in order to know what can be done with them, for what useful ends they can be employed, what harmful effects they must be prevented from producing, and how one or another result can be obtained. Even to resolve these problems it is no doubt absolutely necessary to form some idea of the objects on which one wishes to act. To know what function a thing can perform one must to some degree be acquainted with it. There is therefore no art which does not contain theories immanent in itself. But these theories are not the immediate end of art; for the practitioner they are only a means to arrive at his end, which is to act. Now, to be able to reflect methodically, that is, in such a way as to diminish the chance of error, one must have time before one. Action, on the contrary, is always more or less urgent and cannot wait. The exigencies of life oblige us to reestablish the vital equilibrium without delay as soon as it is upset and consequently to take sides immediately. The theories which are thus subordinated to practical exigencies are therefore hastily and summarily constructed. To the extent that reflection is awakened, one is doubtless forced to use it, and, moreover, of itself it requires that it be taken into account. But on the other hand it cannot be allowed to go against the end it is supposed to serve and to suspend pressing action indefinitely. It is therefore more or less reduced to its proper proportions. Unable to proceed with the prudence required by sound methodology, it easily contents itself with reasons and proofs. Most often, the proofs are only adduced in order to take the form of arguments. They are instincts, passions, prejudices disguised in the form of dialectic. They fool our need for awareness more than they satisfy it.

Science appears only when the mind, setting aside all practical concerns, approaches things with the sole end of representing them. Then, no longer being hurried by the exigencies of life, it can take its time and surround itself with all possible precautions against unreasonable suggestions. But this dissociation of theory and practice always assumes a relatively advanced mentality. For, to arrive at the study of facts only with a view to knowing what they are, one must come to understand that they are of one definite sort and not another; that is to say, they have a constant mode of existence, a nature from which necessary relationships are derived. In other words, one must have arrived at the notion of laws; the sense that there are laws is the determining factor of scientific thought. Now, we know with what slowness the notion of natural law was formed and was progressively extended to the different spheres of nature. There was a time, and not so long ago, when it was still inconsistent and confused even as regards the mineral realm. It has only recently been introduced into speculations about life. It is still only imperfectly acclimated in psychology. We can imagine, then, that it was only able to penetrate the world of social facts with the greatest difficulty, and that is why sociology could appear only at a late moment of scientific evolution.

This new extension even encountered quite special resistances. It was first necessary that a sufficiently well elaborated notion of law appear in the natural sciences proper. This condition was necessary but not sufficient. For centuries the mind has been accustomed to imagine such an abyss between the physical world and what is called the human world that for a long time we refused to admit that the principles, even the fundamental principles, of one are also those of the other. Hence the general tendency to put men and societies outside nature, to make separate disciplines of the sciences of human life, whether individual or social, without analogies among the physical sciences, even the highest. That is to say that people see in them not true sciences but indecisive speculations in which the linking of events has always concealed obscure contingencies, for which literary description was more suitable than systematic analysis. To overcome this obstacle, it was necessary to push aside the dualist prejudice. And the only way to do that was to acquire and to give a lively feeling for the unity of human knowledge.

At the end of the last century, these conditions seemed to be fulfilled. The disruption of the old social system, challenging reflection to seek out a remedy for the evils from which society suffered, incited it by this alone to apply itself to collective things. On the other hand, the unity of science no longer had to be discovered, since the enterprise of the encyclopedists had as its object precisely to proclaim it. Moreover, from then on such attempts were made, evidently inspired by a vague feeling for the science which was still to be founded. It is Montesquieu and Condorcet who appear to have had the sharpest awareness of the gap and who made the most noteworthy effort to fill it in. But neither of them approached the problem in all its scope. They were quite aware that the succession of social phenomena presented a certain order, but they did not have a very definite conception of this order, of its nature, or of the processes most suitable for discovering it. Also, they limited themselves to offering ingenious or novel views on social facts rather than seeking to create an entirely new discipline, at least in its principles and method. Their attempts remain brilliant personal works which, however, cannot serve as a point of departure for a scientific tradition. It is doubtless because the practical concerns of the time upset men's minds too much to leave them the composure and the serenity without which there can be no scholars. What is certain is that from the day when the revolutionary tempest had passed, the notion of sociology (*la science sociale*) was formed as if by magic.

The honor of having first formulated it belongs to Saint-Simon. It was his faith in the all-powerfulness of science which inspired the conception in him. Starting from the idea that the uneasiness with which European societies were afflicted derived above all from their state of intellectual disorganization, he took upon himself the task of ending it by replacing the system on which the *ancien régime* rested and which the French Revolution had definitively destroyed with a new system which was in harmony with the new order of things. And he considered it obvious that the elements could only be derived from the sciences, source of all truth. But for such a project it was not the natural sciences which could furnish the most useful contribution. In order to

create a new consciousness (*conscience*) for societies, it is societies above all that one must know about. Now this science of
societies, the most indispensable of all, did not exist. It was therefore necessary, from a practical viewpoint, to found it without
delay. A creative and adventurous mind, desirous of using his
imaginative faculties and the ardors of his genius for some great
work, Saint-Simon was naturally seduced by the idea of discovering, like a new Christopher Columbus, a still unknown world and
conquering it for science.

He gave this new science a new name: he called it *social
physiology*. It considers social organisms in their development
and thereby is clearly distinguished from what he called "ordinary" or "special" physiology, which deals only with individual
organisms. For society is not for Saint-Simon "a simple agglomera-
tion of living beings whose actions have no cause other than the
arbitrariness of individual wills"; it is "a veritable being whose
existence is more or less vigorous or faltering according to whether
its organs more or less regularly fulfill the functions entrusted
to them."[1] Social physiology, then, soars "above individuals who
are for it thenceforth only organs of the social body whose organic
functions it must study as special physiology studies those of individuals."[2] But if human societies constitute a unique reality—
a reality sui generis—they do not avoid being subjected to the
same determinism as the rest of nature. There is in particular
one law which dominates their development with the same ruth-
lessness with which the law of gravity dominates the physiochemical world: that is the law of progress. "For it, men are only
instruments. It is no more within our power to remove ourselves
from its influence or to master its action than to change at will
the primitive force which makes our planet revolve around the
sun."[3] To formulate this law in such a way as to obey it by realizing the course of action it prescribes for us—that is the grand
objective of social physiology. To reach this goal we must proceed
as in the natural sciences; that is to say, by observation. Since
this law is not of our making, we can never discover it by self-
examination, but only by examining the facts which manifest it.
Social physiology must therefore have a rigorously positive char-

acter. Political questions must come to be "treated in the same manner that those related to other phenomena are treated today."[4] It is a science of observation. It is by establishing series of historical facts, as extensive as possible, that we will succeed in perceiving the direction in which humanity is evolving. The method of the new science will therefore be essentially historical. In order to perform this function, however, history will have to be transformed and become scientific. Now in this respect it is still a babe in swaddling clothes, a pure collection of facts unrelated to any theory; "it cannot give men the means of concluding what will happen from what has happened."[5] It must therefore raise itself above a national point of view which can only be descriptive and no longer consider one or another people in particular but humanity in its entirety, in its progressive and continuous advance.

Here we are no longer dealing with fragmentary considerations on one or another aspect of social phenomena but with an attempt at opening an entirely new career to scientific research. Even the two most essential qualities which this as yet to be created science would subsequently maintain were, as of then, expressly affirmed: its positivity and its specificity. The social realm was connected to the other realms, all the while preserving its own physiognomy. However, Saint-Simon did more to formulate this vast program than to execute it. There is nothing in his work that can be regarded as a methodical attempt to succeed in discovering this law of progress which he made the keystone of the whole social system. The views he set forth on the question are scattered in all directions; they are rapid intuitions, very imperfectly coordinated and unaccompanied by any proper proof. It is only with Auguste Comte that the great project conceived by Saint-Simon begins to become a reality.

In one sense it could be said that all the fundamental ideas of Comtist sociology were already to be found in Saint-Simon. But Comte did not limit himself to giving glimpses of how they could serve as a basis for a whole science; he wished to create this science. He defined its method and established its framework. Whereas until then it appeared to be only a very confused nebula at whose heart distinct parts could not yet be perceived, he introduced into it useful divisions which have in part survived. Two great sections were thenceforth constituted which, although closely related one to another, nonetheless require that they be dealt with separately: they are the static and the dynamic. Social statics has as its object the connecting relations which link together the diverse elements of one and the same social system considered at a determinate phase of its evolution. Dynamics seeks the law according to which the succession of human societies which constitutes humanity has evolved through time. Comte was not content to trace this plan for the science; he undertook the integral execution of this colossal project with his own unaided activity. In statics he barely indicated the problems and outlined the solutions. But in dynamics he intended to leave us a complete and, to his mind, definitive treatise: the two final volumes of the *Course of Positive Philosophy* are consecrated to it.

What remains today of this doctrine? To be sure, there are to be found very few propositions which could be integrally retained by present-day science. It is perhaps in the two-little-known chapter on statics that the propositions are the most suggestive. But as for the famous law of three states or stages which dominates the whole system, it can no longer be defended. Moreover, Comte did not have at his disposal enough knowledge to deal with a problem of such scope. What is more, the terms in which he posed it rendered it insoluble. Indeed, Comte undertook to determine the law according to which the development not of societies but of human society in general occurred. He reasons as though humanity formed an actual whole, as though mankind in its totality were one and the same society which always develops in the same direction, following a rectilinear advance. But, in fact, humanity is only a creation of reason, a generic term which designates the whole of human societies. It is the particular tribes, nations, and states which are the only and the true historical realities with which sociology (*la science sociale*) can and must concern itself. It is these diverse collective individualities which are born and die, which progress and regress, and the evolution of mankind is only the complex system of these specific evolutions. Further, they do not all develop in the same direction or come together exactly like

the segments of a single straight line. Humanity is moving simultaneously along different paths and, consequently, any doctrine
which posits as a principle that it always and everywhere pursues
the same end reposes on a radically erroneous postulate.

But though the positive conclusions at which Comte arrived are
rarely the kind that can be preserved, the grandeur of his work
is nonetheless undeniable. Indeed, the fact remains that he was
the first to make a coherent and methodical effort to establish
the positive science of societies. Saint-Simon doubtless had very
clearly glimpsed what was possible and knew some of the characteristics it should present. But it is one thing to affirm the possibility of a science and another to undertake it. The best way to
overcome the resistance opposed to the establishment of a new
science is to attempt it resolutely. Once it has been undertaken,
imperfect though it necessarily is, it already has begun to live.
And this demonstration by doing testifies to its vitality more
than all the reasonings of dialectic. And that is the difficult thing
to do; for the truly creative act consists not in expressing in passing a few fine ideas with which the intellect can amuse itself,
but in seizing upon them to bring them to fruition by placing
them in contact with things, by coordinating them, by supporting
them with a beginning of proofs in such a way as to render them
at once logically able to be assimilated and controlled by others.
That is what Comte did for sociology. It is thanks to him that it
became a factor in scientific life. This is why it is just that he be
considered its father and that the name of *sociology* which he gave
to the newborn science has been definitively retained. Add to this
that throughout his doctrine, amid many errors, runs a very lively
feeling for what is properly characteristic of it, the state of mind
in which one must enter upon its study. For this reason, reading
the last three volumes of the *Course of Positive Philosophy* constitutes, to our mind, the best initiation into the study of sociology.
No doubt, in order to properly understand Comte, we must go
back to Saint-Simon. But whatever Comte may owe to his master,
he remains for us the master par excellence.

It is remarkable that such a project should have remained

without an immediate tomorrow. The movement begun with Saint-Simon ended, at least temporarily, with Auguste Comte and the *Course of Positive Philosophy*. Neither Comte himself nor his disciples added much to it. Practical and political preoccupations became once again predominant for them, to the detriment of scientific preoccupations. Moreover, from the moment when the master died, all intellectual activity ended. Thus sociology, barely born, disappeared from the horizon, and the eclipse lasted no less than thirty years.

Since most of this period corresponds to the Second Empire, it is tempting to think that it was the imperial despotism which created an obstacle to the progress of the science. But it is not clear how purely administrative procedures could have such an influence on the mind of scholars. Moreover, the slowing down of properly sociological activity occurred before the Empire, since the last volume of the *Course* appeared in 1842. The cause of this stagnancy, which is in reality a retreat, must be sought elsewhere. It must be admitted that the profound causes which gave birth to sociology and which alone could sustain its life had finally lost their force. A veritable thrust of rationalist enthusiasm occurred during the first years of the Restoration. It was from reason alone, that is to say from science, that the means of remaking the moral organization of the country were expected. It was from this intellectual effervescence that Saint-Simonism, Fourierism, Comtism, and sociology simultaneously resulted. But from the beginning of the July Monarchy this whole restlessness began to calm down. It might be said that the taste for reflection, especially as applied to social things, tended more and more to be lost. A sort of mental torpor occurred which the events of 1848 interrupted only for an instant. The revolution of 1848 was probably only a last and necessarily feeble echo of the intellectual movement which had rendered illustrious the first part of the century. This explains why it was so quickly and easily vanquished.

Nonetheless, during this long period of drowsiness, a single work appeared which could be considered, in certain regards, as a sociological contribution: that of Cournot. In his *Essay on the Foundation of Our Knowledge* Cournot deals with the historical method, and what he says about it can be applied to sociology; what is more, the entire second volume of his *Chain of Fundamental Ideas* is devoted to the study of the social milieu. But Cournot's objective was not to establish a new science or to make it progress. He simply intended to coordinate the notions which the existing sciences furnished him. He seeks from history, linguistics, and political economy the elements of a philosophy of history and does not try to superimpose on these different disciplines a new discipline which envelops them, dominates them, and transforms them by restoring their unity. These philosophical considerations obviously could not suffice to renew the sociological tradition. Moveover, curiosity was so little roused in this direction that they did not attract attention and did not even have the suggestive influence which they could have and should have exerted.

Second Period: From 1870 to 1900

It was only after the war [of 1870] that the reawakening took place. The shock produced by events was the stimulant that reanimated men's minds. The country found itself faced with the same question as at the beginning of the century. The organization, or rather the facade, which constituted the imperial system had just collapsed; it was a matter of remaking another, or rather of making one which could survive other than by administrative artifice—that is, one which was truly grounded in the nature of things. For that, it was necessary to know what this nature of things was; consequently, the urgent need for a science of societies made itself felt without delay.

Although the growth of sociology was checked in the country of its birth, it was being pursued in England, and not without brilliance. At the base of Comtist sociology, like any sociology, was the principle that societies are natural entities and not machines created by men according to a preconceived plan. But for Comte this was a scientific postulate which did not need proof. He affirmed that societies were part of nature without showing how they were connected to other natural things. It was this connection which Spencer thought to accomplish by relating social organization to living organization and by thus making societies a species of the genus *organism*. To be sure, today it is agreed that the comparison is in no way rigorous or specific. Between the biological realm and the social realm, the differences are as marked as the resemblances. However, the comparison had the temporary advantage of making us more aware of all the spontaneity there is in social life and that it, like all forms of life, results from internal causes and not from external and mechanical impulsion. As disputable and imprecise as this idea may be, it could therefore usefully serve to guide the initial research in this science and to rid us of the artificialist conception which still so obstinately haunts our minds.

The idea was introduced into France by Espinas. His *Animal Societies* tends, above all, to leave us with the impression that societies are born, live, die, and are organized after the fashion of animals—that sociology is a branch of biology. But Espinas, in deepening the thought of Spencer, pushed it and disposed it in a psychological direction. If societies are organisms, they are distinguished from purely physical organisms in that they are essentially consciousnesses (*consciences*). They are nothing if not systems of representations. One has not, therefore, sufficiently characterized them when one has said that they are living beings; one must add that "they are living consciousnesses, organisms of ideas." To be sure, sociology has its roots deep in biology, but it differs from it from the moment when it is truly itself, to the extent that a representation differs from a mechanical movement. The consciousness of society, moreover, is not of a different nature from that of the individual. The latter is also produced by a coalescence of elementary consciousnesses (*consciences*), of representations or impressions which are concentrated in a more or less definite self (*moi*); it is a "coalesced whole" like the social consciousness. The entire difference is that the distinctions among the integrating elements are more apparent in society than in the individual; but they are equally genuine in both cases. The individual self (*moi*) is, in fact, a we (*un nous*); that permits us to understand why the social we (*le nous social*) can be considered a self (*un moi*). Sociology and psychology thus appear as two branches off a single trunk, biology, which diverge after a certain point but preserve all the while a sort of parallelism in their development. They are both representations, emotions, impulses which are grouped and organized. The object of sociology was better determined in this way than by the biological analogies with which Spencer contented himself. For societies can only be compared to living beings because they are organized entities; but organization is only the external framework of social life. It was therefore important to create for ourselves a representation of what the contents consist in. It is this representation that Espinas offers us when he shows us society as an organization of ideas. No doubt, when he likens this organization to that observed in individuals, he invites precisely the reproach which has been addressed to him by Fouillée, that of ignoring the differences which separate these two classes of facts. But this comparison, if not taken literally, served at least to make perceptible all that is real in the life of society, since it so much recalls the life of the individual, and to show what the nature of this reality is: it is of a psychic order and the essential object of sociology is to study how collective representations are formed and combined.

Thus, the notion of sociology was progressively confirmed and determined more and more. However, it is impossible not to feel to what extent these conceptions of social reality remained general and schematic. All possible comparisons between organisms and societies, between individual consciousnesses and collective consciousnesses, could never of themselves give us the least law. They are preparatory procedures which sciences make use of in their heroic period but of which they must subsequently rid themselves. Until then, sociologists reduced the science to a single and unique question which was supposed to encompass all others, the question of progress, of evolution, the question of knowing what beings social beings most resembled, and so on. It was time to deal more directly with the facts—to acquire their specificity in order to diversify the problems themselves and to determine them and apply to them a method which was immediately suited to the special nature of collective things.

It is to this task that we have earnestly consecrated ourselves.

Instead of considering sociology in general, we have methodically confined ourselves to a sharply limited order of facts: except for necessary excursions into domains adjacent to the one we are exploring, we have only been concerned with judicial or moral rules studied either in their genesis or development[6] by means of comparative history and ethnography, or in their functioning by means of statistics.[7] Even within this circumscribed circle, we have more and more fixed upon limited problems. In a word, we have endeavored to open, as far as regards sociology in France, what Comte would have called the era of specialization.

This specialization was the more indispensable because, along the way, special disciplines were formed outside sociology, some of them even older, which had undertaken the study of different orders of social phenomena: among them were the comparative history of law and of religions, demography, and political economy. Because these researches were thus removed from the influence of sociology, they largely fell short of its goal. For thus losing sight of what constitutes the very nature of the phenomena with which they dealt—namely, their social character—they studied them without knowing where they came from or where they were going, on what milieus they depended, and, leaving them thus suspended in the void, also left them without explanation. For they can only be understood if they are related to the collective milieus in the heart of which they are elaborated and which they express. Moreover, the very notion of law was too often absent from these works, which sprang from literature and erudition rather than from science. The various studies relative to social phenomena thus presented themselves to us in the following form: on the one hand was a fairly incoherent group of sciences or quasi-sciences which, although they had the same object, were unaware of their relatedness, the profound unity of the facts they were studying, and only vaguely sensed their rationality; and on the other hand was sociology, which was aware of this unity, but which soared too high above the facts to have any effect on the way they were studied. The most urgent reform was therefore to make the sociological idea come down into these special techniques, and by that very fact to transform them by truly making of them social sciences. It was on this condition that sociology could cease to be an abstract metaphysic and the works of specialists could cease being monographs without connection among themselves and without explanatory value.[8]

But for this specific research a method was needed which was related to the complexity of the things from which the science was to be created. The very general procedures with which Comte was content to treat the very general problem he posed could not suffice to resolve these particular questions; they bore, moreover, the mark of the errors which vitiate his sociology. For all these reasons, the methodological problem demanded reexamination; this was the best way to subject to criticism a certain number of prejudices which opposed progress in our discipline. It is in this spirit that we wrote our *Rules of the Sociological Method*. To be sure, the logic of a science is worthless if the logician who attempts it has not himself practiced this science; nothing is as vain as the abstract treatises of those philosophers who daily legislate the sociological method without ever having had dealings with social facts. Also, it was only after having tested ourselves in a certain number of studies, sufficiently varied, that we dared translate into precepts the technique we created for ourselves. The method we put forth is only a summary of our practical experience.

As for this method itself, if we dispense with the detailed rules, it quite entirely depends on two propositions:

1. Social facts exist sui generis; they have their own nature. There truly exists a social realm, as distinct from the psychic realm as the latter is from the biological realm and as this last, in its turn, is from the mineral realm. Without doubt, collective life is only made of representations, and collective representations for their part are only made of individual representations, since individuals are all that society is made of. But the first present specific characteristics which the second do not have. The syntheses from which they result are chemical syntheses which develop properties whose existence would never have been suspected if the constitutive elements had remained isolated. Individual consciousnesses (*consciences particulières*), by uniting, by acting and reacting on one another, by fusing, give birth to a new reality

which is the consciousness (*conscience*) of society. The mentality of groups is not that of individuals (*particuliers*), precisely because it assumes a plurality of individual minds joined together. A collectivity has its own ways of thinking and feeling to which its members bend but which are different from those they would create if they were left to their own devices. The individual by himself would never have been able to form anything that resembled the idea of the gods, the myths and dogmas of the religions, the idea of duty and moral discipline, and so on. And what shows that all these beliefs and practices are not the simple extension of individual ideas is that they are invested with an ascendancy by virtue of which they impose themselves on the individual: proof that they do not derive from him but come to him from a source which is external and superior to him. This is why we have made this ascendancy the characteristic of social phenomena. The method for studying them therefore must not be a copy of any other scientific method. *It must be strictly sociological.*

2. But for that very reason it must be objective. Social facts must be studied from the outside like other phenomena of nature. *The anthropocentric viewpoint is no better grounded in sociology than in the other natural sciences.* When it was believed that social evolution was only the progressive realization of certain notions which every man carried within himself (the notion of humanity as Comte thought; the notion of cooperation as Spencer said), to create this science one had only to fall back upon oneself, to become aware of this fundamental concept and draw from it by deduction all that it contained. From this point of view, the consideration of facts was of only secondary importance; they could serve to illustrate one's reasoning, but were not essential to the proof. But if social phenomena are not the work of the isolated individual, if they result from combinations—in which he participates, no doubt, but into which enter many things other than himself—to know what these syntheses consist of and what their efforts are the scholar must observe, since they take place outside himself. He must face these things in the same state of mind in which the physicist or the chemist faces physiochemical phe-

nomena. That is to say, he must see in them not the expression of individual ideas or sentiments but the product of unknown forces, the nature and mode of whose composition it is precisely a question of determining. In this sense, consequently, this method is naturalistic, since it prescribes for sociology a mental attitude which is the rule in the natural sciences. But it is not naturalistic in the ordinary sense of the word, since it does not tend to absorb the social realm in the other realms of nature but, on the contrary, requires that it maintain its uniqueness, the naturalism which it practices is essentially sociological.

All the preceding doctrines are like phases in a single course of evolution. In effect, they all originate from the same thought— that social phenomena are natural, that is to say, rational, like the other phenomena of the universe. By that we simply mean that they are bound one to another according to definite relations called laws. At the same time, all the scholars of whom we have just spoken had the feeling that to discover these laws, one had to use a positive method—to substitute the patient observation of facts for the summary procedures of ideological dialectic. We have still to discuss the work which, by its orientation, contrasts with all those mentioned above and which, in one sense, constitutes a sort of scientific reaction. This is the work of Tarde.

In the presence of the results at which the comparative history of institutions has as of now arrived, there can no longer be any question of purely and simply denying the possibility of a scientific study of societies; Tarde, moreover, himself intends to create a sociology. Only he conceives of it in such a way that it ceases to be a science properly so-called and becomes a very particular form of speculation in which imagination plays the preponderant role, in which thought is not considered to be constrained to the regular obligations of proof or to the control of facts. One can no longer contend today that there is not a certain order among social phenomena; but it is believed to be so contingent, and so much place is given to the unintelligible accident, that the mind could hardly be united by so indecisive—that is, so unreal—a reality, and distinct concepts do not appear to be able to express so fluctuating and inconstant a matter.

For Tarde, indeed, all social facts are the product of individual inventions, propagated by imitation. Every belief, just like every practice, would have its origin in an original idea, born in the brain of some individual. Thousands of inventions of this type occur daily. However, although most abort, a few succeed; they are adopted by the other members of the society either because they seem useful or because their originator is invested with special authority which is transmitted to all that comes from him. Once generalized, the invention ceases to be an individual phenomenon and becomes a collective phenomenon. There is no science of inventions as Tarde envisions it. For they are possible only thanks to the inventors; and the inventor—the genius—is the "supreme accident," the result of pure chance. As long as these two elements of fertilization "shall meet without understanding and acknowledging each other from a distance, shall couple without being selected for each other in an intelligent way, and, from this blind and random coupling shall be born individual singularities of which a few will be brilliant, the source of discoveries and inventions . . . just that long *it will be said that the role of chance in sociology is considerable, incomparable.*"[9]

No doubt, once genius is given, one can investigate the causes which favor in genius the mental combinations from which new ideas result, and that is doubtless what Tarde calls the *laws of invention.* But the essential factor of any novelty is genius itself, its creative nature, and this is the product of entirely fortuitous causes. On the other hand, since it is in it that the mysterious source "of the social flow" (p. 172) is found, chance is thus placed at the root of social phenomena. There is no absolute necessity that this belief or that institution should appear only at this moment of history or in that determinate social milieu; accordingly as chance has the innovator born sooner or later, the same idea may take centuries to germinate or may burst forth all at once. Moreover, there is a whole category of inventions which can succeed one another in a haphazard order; they are those

which are not contradictory, but are, on the contrary, of a sort
to aid each other. No matter if they "often appear in about the
same order in two different countries out of communication, their
succession in an inverse order always remains conceivable and
possible" (p. 181). It would no doubt be an "error to think that
they follow one another in no particular order"; but it is equally
false "that they be subjected to an invariable order, nay, even
to a single normal order" (p. 162). In conformity to his principle, Tarde devoted the whole of his book on the *Transformations
of the Law* to demonstrating that in fact judicial evolution presented the most unexpected oddities. Contrary to the teachings of
the comparative history of the law, he attempted to establish that
the family, for example, could as easily have begun by promiscuity
as by monogamy; that matrilineality was not a necessary phase
of historical development, and so on. Thus the notion of law
which Comte had finally succeeded in introducing into the sphere
of social phenomena, which his successors had managed to specify
and consolidate, is here obscured and veiled; and caprice, because
it is found within things, by that very token is permitted in
thought.

This review of systems is necessarily incomplete; we have
limited ourselves to those which seemed to us to represent a more
or less important phase in sociological development. We have
even left out works which are at least important for their physical
dimensions, like that of Letourneau. The numerous volumes he
published on the evolution of the family, the law, property, education, literature, and so on attest to an assiduous labor, and useful
information can sometimes be found in them. But the facts are
accumulated in a confused way—unsystematically and, what is
more, uncritically. They are placed in the service of very simplistic
conceptions. Moreover, all this work has remained without perceptible influence on contemporary thought. For other reasons,
we have not spent time on Lapouge and anthroposociology. First,
we may wonder whether this school has even a place in a history
of the progress of sociology, since it has as its object to make this
science vanish into anthropology. Then, too, the scientific bases

on which this system rests are far too suspect, as Manouvrier has recently shown.[10]

But, even thus filled in, the list of doctrines would only give a cursory idea of what sociological activity in France has become in these past years. All sorts of debates have taken place either about these theories or about related questions and have given rise to a number of books and articles which we cannot study here. We shall be content to recall the work of Dumont on *Depopulation;* Richard on *The Origin and the Idea of Law;* Worms on *Organism and Society;* Coste on *Objective Sociology;* Bouglé on *Egalitarian Ideas;* Bernès on *The Sociological Method,* and so on. Productivity is, moreover, stimulated by the general curiosity recently excited by this research. Whereas less than fifteen years ago the word "sociology" was almost unused and the thing itself stamped with a sort of discredit, today the word is on everyone's lips; it is even used excessively often, and the thing itself has become ordinary. All eyes are fixed on the new science, and much is expected of it. In this way there was produced at the end of the century an intellectual movement completely analogous to that which we observed in the beginning and which, moreover, depends upon the same causes. And one can doubtless find, and not without reason, that the life which has thus developed is a little tumultous and not without regrettable waste of energy. But, after all, it is life. If it is disciplined and regulated, if the passions thus aroused are grouped and organized instead of spent unsystematically, if everyone puts himself to a definite task, we may permit ourselves the hope that this movement will count in the history of ideas in general and in sociology in particular.

Moreover, everything predestines our country to play an important role in the development of this science. Two causes have determined its appearance and, consequently, are likely to favor its progress. The first is a sufficiently marked weakening of traditionalism. Wherever the religious, political, and legal traditions have retained their rigidity and their authority, they restrain all inclination to change and by that very fact prevent the awakening of reflection; when one is raised to believe that things should remain in the state they are in, one has no reason to wonder what they should be or, consequently, what they are. The second factor is what could be called the rationalist state of mind. One must have faith in the power of reason in order to dare submit to its laws this sphere of social facts where the events, by their complexity, seem to escape the formulations of science. Now, France fulfills these two conditions to the highest degree. Of all the countries of Europe, it is the one where the old social organization has been most completely uprooted; we have made of it a tabula rasa, and on the field thus laid bare we must raise an entirely new edifice, an enterprise whose urgency we have felt for a century but which, always announced and always put off, is hardly more advanced now than at the time of the Revolution. On the other hand, we are and we remain, whatever we do, the country of Descartes: we have the irresistible need to bring things back to definite notions. Without doubt, Cartesianism is an archaic and narrow form of rationalism and we must not cling to it. But if it is important to go beyond it, it is even more important to preserve its principle. We must accommodate ourselves to more complex ways of thinking but retain this cult of distinct ideas which is the very root of the French spirit as well as the basis of all science.

Nonetheless, if the hope is legitimate, the danger is great. We are passing through a particularly critical period. Because much is expected of our science, it will be discredited if it does not live up to its promises. If this commotion remains sterile, public opinion will soon grow tired, withdraw, and lose interest, and the intellectual lull which dishonored the middle of the century and which would be a disaster for reason will return. No doubt, we can never impose silence upon science for long; sooner or later, it finishes by having the last word. But as temporary as its defeats may be, everything must be done to avoid them, for they are at the very least a useless loss of time. A reaction against science could well defer the problems; but, as it does not resolve them, the moment always comes when they are posed anew and everything is begun again.

II. Sociology and Social Action

2

ADDRESS TO THE
LYCEENS OF SENS

WHATEVER THE COST to our pride, we must recognize that God created two quite different sorts of men: the great and the little. The role of the small and humble here on earth has never been much discussed. Alas! We know only too well, for the most part, that our only function is to live, to perpetuate the race, to furnish material for new creations, to occupy the stage while other events and new actors prepare themselves. But the others—what purpose do they serve? To what ends are they destined? Here is where the doctrines and the variety of opinions begin. Whereas some nations place themselves entirely in the hands of their great men, others, on the contrary, distrust them as they would the greatest dangers. In one place, they are persistently persecuted and made miserable; in another they are exalted and glorified. Athens made a martyr of Socrates; Rome made a God of Augustus. Who, then, is correct and where does the truth lie? Are men of genius necessarily and always a threat to our mediocre individualities? Or, on the contrary, is it from them and from them alone that we must expect our salvation? In a word, what is their role in modern societies? Such is, gentlemen, the grave question I would like to try to debate before you.

According to one of the most illustrious writers of our century,[1]

Address delivered at prize-day ceremonies on 6 August 1883 at the Lycée of Sens, where Durkheim taught before going to Bordeaux. Translated from "Discours aux lycéens de Sens," *Cahiers internationaux de sociologie* 43 (1967) : 25–32 (Paris: Presses universitaires de France). Translated by Mark Traugott.

great men constitute the ultimate purpose of humanity. To produce great men, he says, is the goal toward which the whole of nature tends. To it the happiness of the masses is of no concern. How could it be conceded that, in effect, this immense universe has no other raison d'être than to furnish the obscure mass of individuals with convenient means to tranquilly enjoy their petty destinies? How could it be conceded that the earth was made solely to nourish and the sun to warm a few million worthless and nameless beings? Truly, this would be a very poor outcome of such prodigious efforts. But nature is far from having so clumsily squandered her forces. Quite the contrary; at every instant and in the most striking manner she affirms her profound disdain for individuals. She has made them all mortal; what does it matter to her as long as the species does not die? Thus, after exhausting us in the service of her mysterious ends, when she sees us without strength and judges us useless, she suppresses us; and then she calls upon others to continue our labors and to profit from the work we have done. Ah! It can doubtless seem cruel to us that those who plant do not reap! But what does it matter to her as long as the work never ceases, as long as progress continues?

That is, in effect, the only thing which concerns her, the only end which she pursues and toward which she pushes us all, no matter what we do. What she wishes is that progress be made, that the ideal be realized. Now what can this ideal be if not the accession of reason and the reign of truth? How, then, will reason manage to establish its reign on earth? Must it conquer one by one every individual intellect? But such a task would be impossible. There are too many minds invincibly resistant to science, there are too few souls sufficiently elevated to be able to attain the truth. Truth, therefore, can reveal itself only to a small number of privileged intellects; reason will be incarnated only in a few superior men who will realize the ideal and who constitute, for this reason, the final goal of human evolution.

But, no doubt, these superior men, once formed, will return to the masses from which they emanate to elevate them to their own level, to permit them to participate in the treasure which they possess, to teach them a life in conformity with reason? To what good end, our author asks? What purpose would be served by this immense apostolate? This would be a useless waste of effort. For the essential is that truth be known and not that it be known by all men. Why should the highest culture be accessible to everyone? It is sufficient that it establish itself and that it reign. Science is disdainful and does not need to have a great number of faithful. What good is it to pare down the ideal in order to place it within the reach of little minds? Thus, humanity would be divided into two great classes between which there would exist an abyss. On the very *top* would be this elite, favored by the caprice of nature. On the very bottom, the masses would vegetate in their lack of consciousness (*l'inconscience*). The first would think for the second. They would be like the consciousness (*conscience*) of the whole of humanity. As for the others, they would content themselves with admiring and adoring these extraordinary beings, with serving them, happy, moreover, to serve them and to sacrifice themselves. What is more, we are told, they would not have the greatest cause for complaint. For they would at least have the pleasures of the family, the joys reserved for simple souls, and the gentle illusions of the ignorant. Let us pity, rather, those obliged to see the truth face to face! For it may well be that the truth is sad.

You see, gentlemen, that for progress to be possible, it is necessary, according to our philosopher, that nature place on one side all happiness and on the other all intelligence, pushing the division of labor to its final limits and separating that which we would like to think indissolubly united. It is necessary that some renounce enjoyment and that others renounce thought. What a somber tableau, gentlemen. What a desolate dream! But is it after all the truth? Is this in fact the future which awaits us and must we resign ourselves to it without hope? I believe, gentlemen, that we have good reasons to reassure ourselves; and I hope to make you see now that we have the right to count on a less dismal destiny.

Indeed, why would nature take so little account of individuals? Why should this better suit her majesty? Is there not, on the contrary, a sort of hateful meanness in so brutally sacrificing the many to the few for reasons of economy? No doubt I understand all the beauty in those exceptional men who embody in themselves the whole life of a century or of a people. Let us admire them and be proud of them; for they express and realize our humanity in its perfection. But why should it be unworthy of nature to concern herself with the small and mediocre in order to render them more and more capable of understanding and loving her? In what way would her wisdom and her power be diminished if, not content to concentrate herself from time to time in the form of one of these eminent beings, she ceaselessly radiated in all directions, illuminating, vitalizing, spiritualizing more and more the mass of individuals?

It is said that truth does not love crowds. But why lend it this aristocratic disdain? For myself, I consider truth to have a single reason for and a single mode of existing: that is to be known. The more it is known, the more it will be. Therefore, to wish for it only the restricted cult of a few initiates is to diminish it, just as the sun would appear less magnificent to us if it illuminated only a small portion of the globe. If it has often inspired poets to enthusiastic hymns of gratitude, and if certain peoples have made of it a god, it is because it generously emits its heat and its light in all directions, scorning nothing and no one.

It will be objected, it is true, that most intellects are not and will never be capable of receiving truth. Ah, gentlemen, let us not so quickly despair of the human spirit! When we see in history the innumerable ideas which it has already gone through, rejecting in turn all those whose falseness was demonstrated and making its way, laboriously, no doubt, but with consistency and perseverence, toward the truth—I tell you that we have no right to be discouraged. Without doubt, every apostolate brings its disillusionments and its bitterness. Without doubt, when we encounter invincible obstacles, when we feel temporarily powerless, we must endure difficult moments of defeat and disgust. But if we have a passion for truth, if we have for others less disdain and more love, we soon gain ascendency. For at such moments we know how to find in ourselves the warmth which ends by softening the most resistant hearts.

Thus, the world is not made solely with great men in mind. The rest of humanity is not simply the humus from which spring these rare and exquisite flowers. All individuals, however humble, have the right to aspire to the higher life of the spirit. It is possible that such a life may be less tranquil and less easy than the common existence. It is possible that truth is sad. What does it matter? Even at such a price, everyone has a right to desire it. Everyone has the right to aspire to this noble sadness, which, moreover, is not without charm; for once having tasted it one no longer desires the other pleasures, which henceforth are without savor or attraction.

But, gentlemen, if great men are not the whole of humanity, should we conclude that they are useless to it? Must we grant to genius a sort of value and interest which are only aesthetic? Must we, as is too often done, reduce it to a mere ornament, a luxury which wise societies would do well to do without?

Here we no longer have to do with an actual system made illustrious by a great name. But we are dealing with all sorts of ideas and sentiments, hardly formulated as theories, which one barely admits to oneself, but which many cherish in the depths of their minds (*consciences*). Everything for genius and by genius, we were told a moment ago. And now we are told we must sacrifice everything for the happiness of individuals. For what makes a nation is not one or two great men born by chance here and there, who can suddenly fail to appear; it is the compact mass of citizens. It is therefore only they who should concern us: it is only their interests which we should consult. What does it matter to them that from their midst rises from time to time a superior man? It is not for them that the poet writes, that the arist works, that the philosopher thinks, but for a tiny aristocracy, jealous and closed. What interest do they have, therefore, in the formation of a society far above their heads where people live a life apart, where people taste pleasures and even sufferings which are refused to them? What should they care about a progress which is achieved neither by them nor for them? Everything which surpasses them is superfluous. The only thing which interests them is the average culture of the spirit which they are in a position to absorb: it alone, therefore, should reign. The ideal must be on their scale and within their reach.

Still, if we could produce at the same time men of genius and enlightened masses! But, we are told, one of these goals excludes the other. All genius is, in effect, a sort of monster which cannot be brought forth without profoundly upsetting the natural order of things. Nothing comes of nothing. If some possess too much intelligence, others necessarily possess too little. To mold a man of genius, it is necessary to "drain, distill, condense" millions of lesser intellects. Should a nation wish to enrich itself in great men, it gathers and concentrates all its vital forces in a single point of territory. Then, on the territory thus prepared, it soon sees divine intellects blossom. But the life which it has accumulated in a single spot and which a few individuals have absorbed has been withdrawn from the rest of the nation. This is why the body of the society languishes and soon dies of inanition. Here, then, is the price paid for the glory of having great men!

To all these reasons, we also add that to give birth to men of genius means creating within the nation dangerous inequalities; it means preparing one's masters. How can these beings who infinitely surpass the common level be subjected to the common law? Beside them, the mass of citizens would seem not to exist. It is therefore better that all citizens keep in step; that those most in a hurry wait for the slowest. Without doubt, truth must succeed in conquering the world; but let it begin its conquests at the bottom and not at the top. Let it unveil itself little by little to the masses instead of revealing itself entirely and all at once to the privileged few.

That, gentlemen, is what we often hear in everyday conversations. Well! I do not hesitate to declare that this theory, as false as the preceding one, seems to me perhaps more dangerous. Assuredly, it is contrary to nature to systematically sacrifice the masses to genius. But, on the other hand, a society where genius is sacrificed to the masses and to some blind love of a sterile equality would condemn itself of its own accord to an immobility not much different from death. Why would it seek out new enterprises? All the individuals which compose it resemble each other: they would therefore not even conceive of changing. As they know of no other beings than themselves, nor of any other state than their own, it would appear to them that their goal has been attained and that they have nothing more to do than fall asleep amid their self-satisfied mediocrity. But suppose a great man should appear. Immediately, the equilibrium is dissolved. Humanity perceives that it has not arrived at the end of its course. Here is a superior form of existence which was unknown until now and which it will now work to realize. Here is a new goal offered for its efforts. Now a thousand sentiments which lay dormant are awakened all at once; a sort of unrest invades hearts; and this mass, just previously immobile, begins to tremble and carry itself forward. And do not fear that this movement should stop. Do not fear that the masses would ever definitively overtake the great men who precede and guide them. For when the first have been reached, others will appear farther along the route of progress, and after these latter still others, always dragging humanity in their wake toward the ideal goal which it will never attain.

Is it true that a great man consumes, without any possibility of return, what is best in the nation? Ah! It would no doubt be this way if the man of genius, once created, cut himself off from society and shut himself up in a proud solitude. But, unfortunately, as great and as disdainful as he may be, he is no less a man and cannot easily do without his fellowmen. He needs the sympathy, the respect, and the admiration of the very people whose inferiority he disdains. In vain he scorns popularity; it is not good to feel alone. The artist likes to hear himself applauded, the poet to know he is admired; the thinker especially insists on rallying to himself the greatest possible number of intellects. To do this, he must renounce isolation. He must return to the masses which have remained behind him; he must hold out his hand in order to be followed, must instruct in order to be understood. He thereby repays, a hundred times over, all that has been loaned him.

Ah, gentlemen, is it not in this way that events have taken place in France? For a long time our kings labored to bring forth greatness in order to create a sort of retinue. It was therefore not to instruct and mold the spirit of the people, but to give the monarchy added prestige. And yet, what happened? We can say without national vanity that in all Europe there is perhaps no country where the level of average intelligence is higher than in France. All the glory reverts to our great men who served ends which were hardly foreseen by their royal protectors. The fine lords of Versailles believed that Racine wrote and Molière thought only for them: but all of France benefited thereby.

Thus, great men are not tyrants of some sort who, living in our place, live at our expense. Far from being able to grow larger only through our abasement, their greatness brings forth ours. Without doubt, there is always between them and us a great distance, but we have the means of diminishing it, and they have an interest in supporting our efforts. We can therefore leave behind the one-sided theories which we have just set forth and refuted one after another. No, nature does not require that great men be egoists. But, on the other hand, humanity was not made to taste easy and vulgar pleasures forever. It is therefore necessary that an elite be formed to make humanity scorn this inferior life, to tear it from this mortal repose, to urge it to move forward. That, gentlemen, is the purpose served by great men. They are not solely destined to be the crowning of the universe, at once grandiose and sterile. If theirs is the privilege to incarnate the ideal here on earth, it is in order to make it visible to all eyes in a palpable form; it is in order to make it understood and loved. If, therefore, there are those among them who do not deign to look down upon the rest of their fellowmen, who busy themselves exclusively with the contemplation of their own grandeur, or who isolate themselves in the enjoyment of their superiority, let us condemn them without a second thought. But for the others—and this is the greater number—for those who give themselves entirely to the masses, for those whose sole concern is for sharing with them their minds and their hearts, for those who, in whatever century they may have lived, whether they were once the servants of the great king or are now citizens of our free republic, whether named Bossuet or Pasteur, for those, I beg of you, may we have only words of admiration and love. Let us respectfully proclaim them the benefactors of humanity.

Dear students, perhaps at this moment you are reproaching me in whispers for having forgotten you a bit too much today. And yet that is not true at all. While I was speaking, it was of you that I was thinking. Especially of you with whom I have just spent all this past year and who are now going to leave us to try your hand at life. If you will closely examine this speech, you will see that it contained a final lesson addressed to you, a sort of lesson in extremis. Could not all that I have said be summarized as follows: My dear friends, I would be most happy if you would carry away with you from this school two feelings which seem contradictory, but which strong minds know how to reconcile. On the one hand, maintain a very vivid sense of your own dignity. However great a man may be, never abdicate into his hands and in an irremediable fashion your liberty. You do not have that right. But also, do not believe that you will become much greater by never permitting anyone to raise himself above you. Do not glory in being self-sufficient, in owing nothing to anyone; for then, in order to humor a false pride, you would condemn yourself to sterility. Whenever you sense that a man is your superior, do not be ashamed to evince a just deference for him. Without false shame, make him your guide. There is a certain way of letting yourself be guided which takes nothing away from your independence. In a word, know how to respect natural superiority without ever losing your self-respect. This is what the future citizens of our democracy must be.

3

THE PRINCIPLES OF 1789

AND SOCIOLOGY

FOR BETTER OR FOR WORSE, the French Revolution, once an object of faith, is more and more becoming an object of science. The revolutionary doctrine no longer appears to us as a faultless gospel or as a tissue of monstrous aberrations; we are little by little getting used to seeing in it nothing but a social fact of the greatest importance, whose origins and import we seek to know. The time is just about ripe for an objective and impartial study of its history, even though it is still very much involved in today's disputes. It would be interesting to investigate the origins of this change. Is it simply a result of the remoteness of these events in time? Is it weariness of fighting against irresistible tendencies, or disappointment caused by unexpected failures? It is probable that all these causes coincided to produce this movement; in any case, it exists. The very interesting book *The Principles of 1789 and Social Science*[1] which Ferneuil has just given us is a new and important manifestation of this state of mind.

The question posed by Ferneuil cannot be summarized in a word, for the principles of '89 can be considered from quite different points of view. They are a historical event, a political fact, at the same time that they are a scientific theory of society. Forget the social conditions in which they were produced in order to appreciate them for themselves, and you will see only a succes-

---

Originally published as "Les principes de 1789 et la sociologie," *Revue internationale de l'enseignement* 19 (1890) : 450–56. Translated by Mark Traugott.

sion of abstract propositions, definitions, axioms, and theorems which are presented like a summary of a definitive science: a sort of breviary of sociology, or at least of a certain "type of" sociology. But place them back in their historical milieu and the point of view changes. The men of the Revolution were not scholars who contrived a system in the silence of the study but men of action who believed themselves called upon to reconstruct society on new foundations. And it is all too clear that such a reconstruction could not be accomplished according to a scientific method. In reality, it was the needs, the aspirations of all sorts that were tormenting French society which guided the statesmen of the age and which determined the outline of the work, both destructive and restorative, they undertook. The famous principles express only these tendencies rather than the actual relations of things. Their authority comes not from their being in accord with reality but from their conformity to national aspirations. They are believed in not as theorems but as articles of faith. They were created neither by science nor for science; rather, they result from the very practice of life. In a word, they have been a religion which has had its martyrs and apostles, which has profoundly moved the masses, and which, after all, has given birth to great things.

It is important to make the distinction: for, depending on whether one adopts one or another point of view, the judgment one brings to bear on the principles of 1789 changes completely.

If they are seen as a scientific doctrine, they must be treated as such and consequently must have applied to them the critical method which alone is suited to science. We must see whether they are adequate to the facts they claim to express. And if they are presented as an explication of the principal social phenomena, do they really account for them? Is it in fact true that "men live and die free and equal in their rights," that "liberty consists in being able to do whatever does not harm others," and so on and on? The only way to answer these questions is to confront the reality of facts with the prescriptions which are supposed to include them.

But this problem is not the only one which poses itself. Even admitting that the principles of 1789 were definitively refuted as theoretical truths, they still subsist as social facts, as an expression of the state of mind of an age and of a society. To appreciate them from this point of view, it is no longer enough to consider the letter of the formulation to gauge its objective truth. On the contrary, it is necessary to set them aside in order to reach back to the needs from which they sprang and which they sum up, and it is the latter which must be judged. Simplistic minds may, it is true, believe that to know these tendencies and these aspirations one must merely develop the formulation which makes them known and to understand well its literal meaning. But such a method is open to grave errors. In fact, these prescriptions are the conscious outcome of an entire unconscious process. The distant causes on which it depends escape us because of their remoteness and their complexity; only the nearest and simplest consequences penetrate the field of consciousness (*conscience*). Perceiving them thus detached from the conditions which explain them, we are obliged to elaborate and rearrange them to make them intelligible. By means of analogies or of any other process of reasoning, we invent reasons for them, lacking the real ones which we do not see, and it is the result of all this work that we translate into simple and clear propositions. These latter, then, can reflect the underlying reality only in a very inexact way. They are symbols, but imperfect and deceptive ones. For example, multiple causes, which the inner sense is powerless to disentangle, which even scientific analysis has trouble sorting out, have long led societies to prohibit marriages between relatives. Today, of all these past experiences there has survived nothing in our consciousnesses (*consciences*) but the horror this sort of union inspires. If we look for reasons for this horror, those we find vary by country and national temperament—religious reasons here, physiological ones elsewhere—but, it is understood, they bear no relation to the true causes of the phenomenon. If, therefore, there is no direct relation between these explanatory formulations and the social needs to which they correspond, it cannot be enough to refute the first in order to demonstrate the unhealthy nature of the second. There are no religions which, considered as scientific doctrines, resist critical analysis. From a scientific point of view, most postulate veritable heresies. But we have no right to conclude that they have played or still play today a harmful or evil role in history. For it is quite possible and even infinitely probable that, as inadequate as they may be in their cosmological or sociological explanations, they respond to real and legitimate needs which otherwise would not have been satisfied.

There are therefore two totally distinct and independent problems, and this double aspect of the question has not escaped Ferneuil. He has understood perfectly that the principles of '89 do not depend purely and simply on scientific examination; that they are not only doctrines more or less correct, but social facts to which our entire national development for the past century is linked. "Science," he says quite rightly, "will crush the principles of 1789 in vain; the strict duty of our contemporaries will still be to piously cull from the heritage of the Revolution those inestimable treasures of patriotic faith, of devotion to the public realm, of national solidarity which our fathers deposited as an example for their descendants." However, as the title of the work indicates, it is above all as a scholar that he examines them, and that is why his conclusions may have appeared a little severe to certain critics.

For the men of the Revolution are not the only ones alluded to by his book; on every page we sense from the tone of the polemics that the adversaries he is combating are not so old as we might think at first glance, and that they have not all had time to become part of history. Abstract the principles of 1789 from the circumstances of time and place in which they occurred, disengage their general spirit, and you will recognize that they still inspire most French moralists and economists. It is true that many of them protest against relating them in this way. They deny their masters, but only because they are inconsequential or ungrateful disciples. All of them, in effect, reduce sociology (*la science sociale*) to a simple ideological analysis. They start from the abstract concept of the individual in himself and from it develop the contents. Given the notion of an absolutely autonomous individual, depending only on himself, without historical antecedents, without a social milieu, how should he conduct himself either in his economic relations or in his moral life? Such is the question which they pose themselves and which they seek to resolve by reasoning.

Now, as our author demonstrates, such a method cannot give objective results. By proceeding in such a manner, it is quite possible to connect concepts among themselves; but such a system cannot be expected to express the real relations among things. For the individual thus conceived does not exist in reality. The actual man has nothing in common with this abstract entity. He partakes of an age and a country; he has ideas and feelings which come not from himself but from those around him; he has prejudices and beliefs; he is subject to rules of action which he did not make but which he nevertheless respects. He has aspirations of all sorts and many concerns other than keeping his budget economically. And all these heterogeneous motives intersect and crisscross in their action, so much so that most often it is not easy to distinguish them and to recognize the role of each one. One might answer that every science lives from abstractions, that the real and complete man is doubtless not simply an isolated and egoistic individual, but that we can agree to study him exclusively from that point of view. Assuredly. But for the result of such an investigation to have some value, it is necessary that the abstraction be made experimentally. It would have been necessary, if not for all social types, at least for the one to which we belong, to establish by observation what are the practical principles which govern the economic and moral conduct of man, then to isolate among the latter, by means of suitable experiments, those which correspond to the egoistic side of our nature. Thus we would have a truly adequate notion of what the economists call the individual (*l'individu*), of what the moralists call the person (*la personne*), and of the sphere of action proper to him. One could study it and, after having determined what it is, seek what it ought to be. But our theoreticians do not proceed in this way. They construct from nothing and all at once this concept of the individual, which in reality can be formed only after very laborious analyses which presuppose that some part of the science already exists. They see in it one of those very simple, very clear notions

which the scholar postulates and does not demonstrate, whose
accuracy everyone can easily verify by introspection and without
any further procedure. That is to say that it can have only a very
subjective value.

This methodological error in the doctrine leads to another—
one of the deepest gravity. If we proceed with the slowness whose
necessity we have just demonstrated, we observe that the sphere
within which the individual depends only on himself is in fact
extremely restricted. When, on the contrary, we begin by assuming the problem already resolved, as do the moralists and economists of this school, we believe and assume in principle that this
tiny part of man is the whole of man. This is, to tell the truth,
the source idea of all these systems. If we do not deem it necessary to proceed to the experiments and analysis of which we have
just spoken in order to isolate this region of the human soul from
other regions, we admit as a postulate that there is not much of
anything beyond it. This is the source of the intransigent individualism which is the common faith of all these thinkers. This individualism has never been demonstrated and cannot be. It has
never been shown in detail and by a truly experimental comparison that the rules and practices which dominate and govern our
legal, moral, and economic life had any other aim or raison d'être
than the material and moral well-being of individuals. This is,
however, an axiom—a matter of faith or, to use a word in favor
among the economists even though it has a rather unscientific
connotation, an *orthodoxy*. But if it is truly this way, it becomes
entirely impossible to reintegrate man into the social milieu in
which he nonetheless takes part. If man is essentially a whole, an
individual and egoistic being—no matter whether a material or
moral egoism—if he has no other objective than the development
of his moral personality (Kant) or the satisfaction of his needs
with the least possible effort (Bastiat), society appears as something against nature, as a violence wreaked upon our most fundamental propensities. Rousseau avows this, or rather proclaims it.
Bastiat fights Rousseau, but their disagreement is only apparent.
Both, in effect, agree in that they see something forced, artificial,
monstrous in society such as it actually exists with its traditions,

its hereditary prejudices, and the limits it imposes on the individual by placing on him the weight of public opinion, of mores, of customs, of laws, and so on. No doubt, our economists tell us, man is naturally made for social life. But they understand thereby a social life which would be absolutely different from the one we have before our eyes, one where there would be no traditions, no past, where everyone would live on his own without worrying about others, where there would be no public action except to protect each individual from the encroachments of his neighbor, and so on. As for society as it has been constituted historically, it is in their eyes a product of compression, a machine of war against individuals, a remnant of barbarism which is maintained only by the force of prejudices and which is destined sooner or later to disappear.[2] Rousseau never used a different language.

Such is the double error which Ferneuil has very courageously pointed out and fought against. I say that some courage was necessary because it meant rebelling against an opinion which, though it is losing ground, is still quite general in France. There is therein a way of looking at and experiencing social matters that our exclusively literary education has strongly impressed on our intellects. A purely aesthetic culture does not place the mind (*l'esprit*) in direct enough contact with reality to enable it to create a sufficiently adequate representation of it. It is not by learning to appreciate the masterpieces of classical literature that one acquires a feeling for the organic development of society, for the dependence we have upon previous generations and the milieus of all sorts which surround us. These multiple ties which link us to each other and to the group in which we take part are not so obvious that all we need to perceive them is a somewhat developed taste. Having received, therefore, no other education, we are necessarily led to deny their existence; that is to say, to see in the individual an autonomous power which depends only on itself and to see in society a simple framework of relations of all these independent forces. This is why whoever undertakes to react against this superficial simplism and to recall the true place of the individual in society runs up against rather lively feelings and prejudices. Since such a conception of collective life does not lead to one of those systems of clear ideas which our French tempera-

ment loves, we feel we have dealt with it justly when we disdain-
fully accuse it of being a German import. It cannot be demonstrated that the sphere of social action extends itself to the degree
that societies develop without being accused of state socialism
and treated as an enemy of liberty. Assuredly, even on this point,
our temperament is changing. We are little by little doing away
with this narrow individualism devoid of generosity. However,
this regressive movement is only beginning. We hope that Ferneuil's book will contribute to its acceleration. There is in it such
a sincerity, such a seriousness of purpose, that the reader can
keep from being won over only with difficulty.

On the second question raised by the principles of 1789 his
book seemed to us less complete and less profound. While recog-
nizing, as we have said, the legitimacy of the two points of view,
he has examined the ideas of the Revolution as a theory of society,
not as a social fact. He seems not to see anything specific in the
revolutionary spirit except for an immoderate taste for the absolute which is explained by the exceptional circumstances in which
France then found itself. But this taste for the absolute is not
peculiar to the Revolution. It is found in all creative eras, in all
centuries of new and hardy faith. Ferneuil knows this and says it
himself in his book. Every time we undertake some great enterprise, we like to believe that we work for eternity. It is possible
in this way to take account of only the most general character of
the famous principles, namely their categorical and absolute form.
All their own special characteristics remain unexplained. Moreover, they have survived over time and have extended themselves
far beyond the countries where they were born. A good part of
Europe believed in them, and believes in them still. They therefore depend not on accidental and local circumstances but on
some general change which occurred in the structure of European societies.

It is only when this change is known with some precision that
we will be able to definitively qualify the principles of 1789 and
to say whether they constitute a pathological phenomenon or, on
the contrary, simply represent a necessary transformation of our
social conscience. Above all, it is only then that we will be able
to resolve this other question: what is the destiny of the revolu-

tionary religion? What is it called upon to become? Assuredly this is a grave problem, and we find it quite natural that it attracted a writer preoccupied with the future of the country. There is in fact no question which absorbs more of the attention of legislators and statesmen, for do not all the difficulties on which nations founder at the present time come from the trouble we encounter in adapting the traditional structure of societies to these new and unconscious aspirations which have afflicted them for a century? But once again, to know the meaning and the source of these aspirations it cannot suffice to meditate on the formulations which translate it into consciousness, for nothing is less certain than the exactness of this translation.

We must add, moreover, that this question depends more on the political art (*l'art politique*) than on sociology (*la science sociale*). In presenting Ferneuil's book to the public, Albert Sorel indicated some uneasiness with the excessive ambitions of our young science. "What!" he cried, "are we going to convoke a council of sociologists to resolve all these problems?" Saint-Simon or Comte perhaps deserved such reproaches, but today they can be addressed to none. To the extent that sociology actually exists, it is more and more sharply separated from what is called, rather inappropriately, the political sciences, those bastard speculations, half theoretical and half practical, half science and half art, which are sometimes still confused, but wrongly, with sociology. The latter, like any science, studies what is and what has been, seeks laws, but is not interested in the future. Ferneuil may well have abused on occasion the expressions "sociology admits," and "sociology rejects." But these are errors of formulation which badly translate his thought. It is enough to read his chapter on art and science to perceive that he does not confuse their domains. The practical difficulties can be definitively solved only by practice, by everyday experience. This is not a sociologist's advice—it will be the societies themselves which will find the solution. But it can only be beneficial for a man acquainted with the results of science, as is Ferneuil, to apply his reflection to these matters, and that is why men of action will be no less interested in reading this book than men of science.

4

INDIVIDUALISM AND THE

INTELLECTUALS

THE QUESTION that has so painfully divided our country
for the past six months is in the process of being transformed:
originally a simple factual question, it has been generalized little
by little. The recent intervention of a well-known man of letters[1]
has greatly contributed to this result. It seems that the moment has
arrived to renew in a brilliant move a polemic which was bogged
down in repetitiveness. This is why, instead of resuming once
again the discussion of facts, we have passed on, in a single bound,
to the level of principles: it is the mental state of the "intellectuals,"[2] the basic ideas they profess, and no longer the details of
their reasoning which are being attacked. If they obstinately refuse "to bend their logic before the word of an army general," it
is evidently because they presume the right to decide the question
for themselves; it is because they place their reason above authority, because the rights of the individual seem to them inalienable.
It is therefore their individualism which has determined their
schism. But then, it is said, if we wish to restore peace in our
minds and to prevent the return of similar discord, this individualism must be fought tooth and nail. This inexhaustible source of
internal division must be dried up once and for all. And so a veritable crusade has begun against this public scourge, against "this
great sickness of the present age."

We gladly accept the debate in these terms. We also believe

Originally published as "L'individualisme et les intellectuels," *Revue
bleue*, 4e série, 10 (1898) : 7–13. Translated by Mark Traugott.

that the controversies of yesterday only gave superficial expression to a more profound disagreement, and that opinion was divided far more over a question of principle than over a question of fact. Let us therefore leave aside the arguments over circumstances which have been exchanged on both sides. Let us forget the matter itself and the sad spectacles we have witnessed. The problem before us goes infinitely beyond the present incidents and must be distinguished from them.

There is one ambiguity that must be cleared up before all else.

In order to prosecute individualism more easily, they confuse it with the strict utilitarianism and the utilitarian egoism of Spencer and the economists. But that is to make the contest too easy. It is indeed an easy game to denounce as an ideal without grandeur this crass commercialism which reduces society to nothing more than a vast apparatus of production and exchange. For it is exceedingly clear that all communal life is impossible without the existence of interests superior to those of the individual. We quite agree that nothing is more deserved than that such doctrines be considered anarchical. But what is inadmissable is that they should reason as though this form of individualism were the only one which existed or was even possible. Quite the contrary—it is more and more becoming a rarity and an exception. The practical philosophy of Spencer is morally so impoverished that it can hardly claim any adherents anymore. As for the economists, though they formerly allowed themselves to be seduced by the simplicity of this theory, for some time they have sensed the necessity of tempering the rigor of their primitive orthodoxy and of opening themselves to more generous sentiments. Molinari is just about alone in France in remaining intractable, and I do not believe he has exercised a great influence on the ideas of our epoch. In truth, if individualism had no other representatives, it would be quite useless thus to move heaven and earth to combat an enemy who is in the process of quietly dying a natural death.

But there exists another sort of individualism which is less easily overcome. It has been professed, for the past century, by the vast majority of thinkers: this is the individualism of Kant and Rousseau, of the idealists—the one which the Declaration of the Rights of Man attempted, more or less happily, to formulate and which is currently taught in our schools and has become the basis of our moral catechism. They hope to deal a blow to this form of individualism by striking instead at the former type; but this one is profoundly different, and the criticisms which apply to the one could hardly suit the other. Far from making personal interest the objective of conduct, this one sees in all personal motives the very source of evil. According to Kant, I am sure of acting properly only if the motives which determine my behavior depend not on the particular circumstances in which I find myself, but on my humanity in the abstract. Inversely, my actions are bad when they can be logically justified only by my favored position or by my social condition, by my class or caste interests, by my strong passions, and so on. This is why immoral conduct can be recognized by the fact that it is closely tied to the actor's individuality and cannot be generalized without manifest absurdity. In the same way, if, according to Rousseau, the general will, which is the basis of the social contract, is infallible, if it is the authentic expression of perfect justice, it is because it is the sum of all individual wills; it follows that it constitutes a sort of impersonal average from which all individual considerations are eliminated, because, being divergent and even antagonistic, they neutralize each other and cancel each other out.[3] Thus, for both these men, the only moral ways of acting are those which can be applied to all men indiscriminately; that is, which are implied in the general notion of "man."

Here we have come a long way from that apotheosis of well-being and private interest, from that egoistic cult of the self for which utilitarian individualism has been rightly criticized. Quite the contrary, according to these moralists, duty consists in disregarding all that concerns us personally, all that derives from our empirical individuality, in order to seek out only that which our humanity requires and which we share with all our fellowmen. This ideal so far surpasses the level of utilitarian goals that it seems to those minds who aspire to it to be completely stamped with religiousity. This human person (*personne humaine*), the definition of which is like the touchstone which distinguishes good from evil, is considered sacred in the ritual sense of the word. It partakes of the transcendent majesty that churches of all time lend to their gods; it is conceived of as being invested with that mysterious property which creates a void about sacred things, which removes them from vulgar contacts and withdraws them from common circulation. And the respect which is given it comes precisely from this source. Whoever makes an attempt on a man's life, on a man's liberty, on a man's honor, inspires in us a feeling of horror analogous in every way to that which the believer experiences when he sees his idol profaned. Such an ethic is therefore not simply a hygenic discipline or a prudent economy of existence; it is a religion in which man is at once the worshiper and the god.

But this religion is individualistic, since it takes man as its object and since man is an individual by definition. What is more, there is no system whose individualism is more intransigent. Nowhere are the rights of the individual affirmed with greater energy, since the individual is placed in the ranks of sacrosanct objects; nowhere is the individual more jealously protected from encroachments from the outside, whatever their source. The doctrine of utility can easily accept all sorts of compromises without belying its fundamental axiom; it can admit of individual liberties' being suspended whenever the interest of the greater number requires that sacrifice. But no compromise is possible with a principle which is thus placed outside and above all temporal interests. There is no political reason which can excuse an attack upon the individual when the rights of the individual are above those of the state. If then, individualism is, in and of itself, the catalyst of moral dissolution, we should see it here manifest its antisocial essence. Now we understand the gravity of the question. For this eighteenth-century liberalism which is at bottom the whole object of the dispute is not simply a drawing-room theory, a philosophical construct; it has become a fact, it has penetrated our institutions and our mores, it has blended with our whole life, and if, truly, we had to give it up, we would have to recast our whole moral organization at the same stroke.

Now it is already a remarkable fact that all those theoreticians of individualism are no less sensitive to the rights of the collectivity than to those of the individual. No one has insisted more strongly than Kant upon the supraindividual character of ethics and of law; he makes of them a sort of commandment that man must obey without any discussion simply because it is a commandment. And if he has sometimes been reproached for having exaggerated the autonomy of reason, one could equally well say, and not without foundation, that he placed at the base of his ethics an irrational act of faith and submission. Moreover, doctrines are judged above all by what they produce—that is, by the spirit of the doctrines to which they give birth. Now Kantianism gave rise to the ethics of Fichte, which are already quite impregnated with socialism, and the philosophy of Hegel, of whom Marx was the disciple. As for Rousseau, we know how his individualism is complemented by his authoritarian conception of society. Following him, the men of the Revolution, even while promulgating the famous Declaration of Rights, made of France an indivisible and centralized entity. Perhaps we should see in the work of the Revolution above all a great movement of national concentration. Finally, the principal reason the idealists have fought against the utilitarian ethic is that it appeared to them incompatible with social necessities.

This eclecticism, it is said, is not without contradictions. To be sure, we do not dream of defending the way these different thinkers went about fusing these two aspects of their systems of thought. If, with Rousseau, we begin by making of the individual a sort of absolute which can and must suffice unto itself, it is evidently difficult then to explain how it was possible for the civil state to be established. But the present question is to know not whether this or that moralist succeeded in showing how these two tendencies are reconciled, but whether or not they are, in and of themselves, reconcilable. The reasons given for establishing their unity may be worthless, and yet this unity may be real; and already the fact that they generally coincide in the same minds leads us to believe that they go together; from all this, it follows that they must depend on a single social state of which they are probably only different aspects.

And, in fact, once we have stopped confusing individualism with its opposite—that is, with utilitarianism—all these supposed contradictions disappear like magic. This religion of humanity has everything it needs to speak to its faithful in a no less imperative tone than the religions it replaces. Far from limiting itself to flattering our instincts, it fixes before us an ideal which infinitely surpasses nature. For ours is not naturally a wise and pure reason which, purged of all personal motives, would legislate in the abstract its own conduct. Doubtless, if the dignity of the individual came from his personal characteristics, from the peculiarities which distinguish him from others, we might fear that it would shut him off in a sort of moral egoism which would make any solidarity impossible. But in reality he receives dignity from a higher source, one which he shares with all men. If he has a right to this religious respect, it is because he partakes of humanity. It is humanity which is worthy of respect and sacred. Now it is not all in him. It is diffused among all his fellowmen and consequently he cannot adopt it as the aim of his conduct without being obliged to come out of himself and relate to others. The cult, of which he is at once both object and agent, does not address itself to the particular being which he is and which bears his name, but to the human person (*la personne humaine*) wherever it is to be found, and in whatever form it is embodied. Impersonal and anonymous, such an aim, then, soars far above all individual minds (*consciences particulières*) and can thus serve them as a rallying point. The fact that it is not alien to us (by the simple fact that it is human) does not prevent it from dominating us. Now, the only thing necessary for a society to be coherent is that its members have their eyes fixed on the same goal, concur in the same faith. But it is in no way necessary that the object of this common faith be unrelated to individual natures. After all, individualism thus extended is the glorification not of the self but of the individual in general. It springs not from egoism but from sympathy for all that is human, a broader pity for all sufferings, for all human miseries, a more ardent need to combat them and mitigate them, a greater thirst for justice. Is there not herein what is needed to place all men of good will in communion? Without doubt, it can happen that individualism is practiced in a completely different spirit. Some use it for their personal ends, as a means of disguising their egoism and of more easily escaping their duties to society. But this abusive exploitation of individualism proves nothing against it, just as the utilitarian falsehoods about religious hypocrisy prove nothing against religion.

But I am anxious to come to the great objection. This cult of man has as its primary dogma the autonomy of reason and as its primary rite the doctrine of free inquiry. But, we are told, if all opinions are free, by what miracle will they be in harmony? If they are formed without mutual awareness and without having to take one another into account, how can they not be incoherent? Intellectual and moral anarchy would thus be the inevitable result of liberalism. Such is the argument, always refuted and always renewed, to which the eternal adversaries of reason periodically return with a perseverance which nothing discourages, every time a momentary lassitude of the human spirit places it more at their mercy. Yes, it is quite true that individualism implies a certain intellectualism; for freedom of thought is the first of the freedoms. But where has it been seen to have as a consequence this absurd infatuation with oneself which shuts everyone up in his own feelings and creates a vacuum between intellects? What it requires is the right for each individual to know the things he legitimately can know. But it in no way consecrates some sort of right to incompetence. On a question on which I can form no knowledgeable opinion, it costs my intellectual independence nothing to follow more competent opinions. The collaboration of learned men is possible only thanks to this mutual deference; every science constantly borrows from its neighboring disciplines propositions that it accepts without further verification. However, my reason requires reasons before it bows before someone else's. Respect for authority is in no way incompatible with rationalism as long as the authority is rationally grounded.

This is why, when it comes to calling upon certain men to rally themselves to an opinion which is not their own, it is not enough, in order to convince them, to recall to them that commonplace of banal rhetoric that society is not possible without mutual sacrifices and without a certain spirit of subordination. The docility which is asked of them must still be justified for the particular case by demonstrating their incompetence. For if, on the contrary, it were one of those questions which, by definition, come under the jurisdiction of common judgment, a similar abdication would be contrary to all reason and, consequently, to their duty. To know whether a tribunal can be permitted to condemn an accused man without having heard his defense requires no special intelligence. It is a problem of practical ethics for which every man of good sense is competent and to which no one should be indifferent. If, therefore, in recent times, a certain number of artists, and especially scholars, believed they had to refuse to concur in a judgment whose legality appeared to them suspect, it was not because, in their capacity as chemists or philologists, as philosophers or historians, they attributed to themselves some sort of special privilege and a sort of eminent right of control over the thing being judged. It is because, being men, they intend to exercise all their human rights and retain before them a matter which is amenable to reason alone. It is true that they have shown themselves to be more jealous of that right than has the rest of the society; but it is simply because in consequence of their professional practices they take it more to heart. Since they are accustomed by the practice of the scientific method to reserve their judgment as long as they do not feel themselves enlightened, it is natural that they should yield less easily to the sway of the masses and the prestige of authority.

Not only is individualism not anarchical, but it henceforth is the only system of beliefs which can ensure the moral unity of the country.

We often hear it said today that religion alone can produce this harmony. This proposition, which modern prophets believe they must develop in mystic tones, is essentially a simple truism about which everyone can agree. For we know today that a religion does not necessarily imply symbols and rites, properly speaking, or temples and priests. This whole exterior apparatus is only the superficial part. Essentially, it is nothing other than a body of collective beliefs and practices endowed with a certain authority. As soon as a goal is pursued by an entire people, it acquires, in consequence of this unanimous adherence, a sort of moral supremacy which raises it far above private aims and thus gives it a religious character. From another viewpoint, it is apparent that a society cannot be coherent if there does not exist among its members a certain intellectual and moral community. However, after recalling once again this sociological truism, we have not gotten very far. For if it is true that religion is, in a sense, indispensable, it is no less certain that religions change—that the religion of yesterday could not be the religion of tomorrow. What is important therefore is to say what the religion of today should be.

Now everything converges in the belief that this religion of humanity, of which the individualistic ethic is the rational expression, is the only one possible. Hereafter, to what can the collective sensitivity cling? To the extent that societies become more voluminous and expand over vaster territories, traditions and practices, in order to accommodate themselves to the diversity of situations and to the mobility of circumstances, are obliged to maintain themselves in a state of plasticity and inconstancy which no longer offers enough resistance to individual variations. These variations, being less well restrained, are produced more freely and multiply; that is to say, everyone tends to go off in his own direction. At the same time, as a result of a more developed division of labor, each mind finds itself oriented to a different point on the horizon, reflecting a different aspect of the world, and consequently the contents of consciousness (*conscience*) differs from one person to another. Thus, we make our way, little by little, toward a state, nearly achieved as of now, where the members of a single social group will have nothing in common among themselves except their humanity, except the constitutive attributes of the human person (*personne humaine*) in general. This idea of the human person, given different nuances according to the diversity of national temperaments, is therefore the only idea which would be retained, unalterable and impersonal, above the changing torrent of individual opinions. And the feelings it awakens would be the only ones which could be found in almost every heart. The communion of spirits can no longer be based on definite rites and prejudices, since rites and prejudices are overcome by the course of events. Consequently, nothing remains which men can love and honor in common if not man himself. That is how man has become a god for man and why he can no longer create other gods without lying to himself. And since each of us incarnates something of humanity, each individual consciousness contains something divine and thus finds itself marked with a character which renders it sacred and inviolable to others. Therein lies all individualism; and that is what makes it a necessary doctrine. For in order to halt its advance it would be necessary to prevent men from differentiating themselves more and more from each other, to equalize their personalities, to lead them back to the old conformism of former times, to contain, as a result, the tendency for societies to become always more extended and more centralized, and to place an obstacle in the way of the unceasing progress of the division of labor. Such an enterprise, whether desirable or not, infinitely exceeds all human capability.

Moreover, what are we offered in place of this despised individualism? The merits of Christian morality are praised and we are discreetly invited to embrace them. But are we to ignore the fact that the originality of Christianity consisted precisely in a remarkable development of the individualistic spirit? Whereas the religion of the ancient city-state was quite entirely made of external practices, from which the spiritual was absent, Christianity demonstrated in its inner faith, in the personal conviction of the individual, the essential condition of piety. First, it taught that the moral value of acts had to be measured according to the intention, a preeminently inward thing which by its very nature escapes all external judgments and which only the agent could competently appraise. The very center of moral life was thus transported from the external to the internal, and the individual was thus elevated to be sovereign judge of his own conduct, accountable only to himself and to his God. Finally, in consumating the definitive separation of the spiritual and the temporal, in abandoning the world to the disputes of men, Christ delivered it at once to science and to free inquiry. This explains the rapid progress made by the scientific spirit from the day when Christian societies were established. Individualism should not, then, be denounced as the enemy which must be combated at any cost! We combat it only to return to it, so impossible is it to escape it. We can oppose to it only itself; but the whole question is to know its proper bounds and whether there is some advantage in disguising it beneath symbols. Now if it is as dangerous as we are told, how can it become inoffensive or beneficial by simply having its true nature dissimulated with the help of metaphors? And looking at it from another point of view, if this restrained individualism which is Christianity was necessary eighteen centuries ago, there is a good chance that a more fully developed individualism is indispensable today. For things have changed. It is therefore a singular error to present the individualistic ethic as the antagonist of Christian morality. Quite the contrary—the former derived from the latter. By attaching ourselves to the first, we do not deny our past; we only continue it.

We are now in a better position to understand why certain minds believe they must oppose an opinionated resistance against everything that seems to threaten the individualistic creed. If every enterprise directed against the rights of an individual revolts them, it is not only out of sympathy for the victim; nor is it from fear of having to suffer similar injustices. Rather, it is because such attempts cannot remain unpunished without compromising the national existence. Indeed, it is impossible for them to occur freely without weakening the feelings they transgress against. And since these feelings are the only ones we hold in common, they cannot be weakened without disturbing the cohesion of society. A religion which tolerates sacrilege abdicates all dominion over men's minds (*consciences*). The religion of the individual therefore cannot let itself be scoffed at without resistance, under penalty of undermining its authority. And since it is the only tie which binds us all to each other, such a weakness cannot exist without a beginning of social dissolution. Thus the individualist who defends the rights of the individual defends at the same time the vital interests of society, for he prevents the criminal inpoverishment of that last reserve of collective ideas and feelings which is the very soul of the nation. He renders to his country the same service the aged Roman once rendered to his city in defending the traditional rites against foolhardy innovators. And if there is a country among all others where the cause of individualism is truly national, it is our own; for there is no other which has created such rigorous solidarity between its fate and the fate of these ideas. We have given them their most recent formulation, and it is from us that other peoples have received them. And this is why even now we are considered their most authoritative representatives. Therefore we cannot disavow them today without disavowing ourselves, without diminishing ourselves in the eyes of the world, without committing a veritable moral suicide. Not long ago, people wondered whether it would not perhaps be convenient to consent to a temporary eclipse of these principles, in order not to disturb the functioning of a public administration which everyone recognized to be indispensable to the security of the state. We do not know if the antinomy really poses itself in this acute form; but, in any case, if a choice truly is necessary between these two evils, to thus sacrifice what has been to this day our historical raison d'être would be to choose the worst. An organ of public life, however important, is only an instrument, a means to an end. What purpose does it serve to maintain the means with such care if the end is dispensed with? And what a sad way of figuring to renounce everything that makes life worthwhile and lends it dignity in order to live,

Et propter vitam vivendi perdere causes!

In truth, I fear there may have been some frivolity in the way this campaign was undertaken. A verbal similarity has permitted the belief that "individualism" necessarily derived from "individual" and therefore egoistic feelings. In reality, the religion of the individual was socially instituted, as were all known religions. It is society which fixes for us this ideal as the sole common goal which can rally our wills. To take it away from us when we have nothing else to put in its place is, then, to precipitate us into that moral anarchy which is precisely what we wish to combat.[4]

Yet we have almost considered the eighteenth-century formulation of individualism perfect and definitive and have made the mistake of preserving it almost without modification. Although it was sufficient a century ago, it now needs to be enlarged and made complete. It presents individualism only in its most negative light. Our fathers undertook exclusively the task of freeing the individual from the political shackles which impeded his development. The freedom to think, the freedom to write, the freedom to vote were therefore placed by them in the ranks of the primary benefits to be obtained, and this emancipation was certainly the necessary precondition of all subsequent progress. However, quite completely carried away by the fervor of the struggle toward the objective they pursued, they ended by no longer seeing beyond it and by erecting as a sort of final goal this proximate term of their efforts. Now political freedom is a means, not an end; its worth lies in the manner in which it is used. If it does not serve some end which goes beyond itself, it is not simply useless; it becomes dangerous. It is a battle weapon; if those who wield it do not know how to use it in fruitful struggles, they soon end by turning it against themselves.

And this is precisely the reason why today it has fallen into a certain disrepute. Men of my generation recall how great our enthusiasm was when, twenty years ago, we finally saw the fall of the last barriers which restrained our restlessness. But alas! Disenchantment quickly followed. For we soon had to admit that we did not know what to do with this hard-won freedom. Those to whom we owed this freedom used it only to tear each other to pieces. And from that moment on, we felt that wind of sadness and discouragement rise over the land which daily grew stronger and eventually finished by disheartening the least resistant spirits.

Thus, we cannot limit ourselves to this negative ideal. We must go beyond the results achieved, if only to preserve them. If we do not finally learn to put to work the means of action we have in our hands, they will inevitably lose their worth. Let us therefore make use of our liberties to seek out what we must do and to do it, to smooth the functioning of the social machine, still so harsh on individuals, to place within their reach all possible means of developing their abilities without hindrance, to work finally to make a reality of the famous precept: to each according to his labor! Let us even recognize that in a general way liberty is a delicate instrument which one must learn to handle; and let us train our children accordingly. All moral education should be oriented to this end. Clearly, we have no lack of matters on which to take action. However, though it is certain that we will hereafter have to set up new goals beyond those already attained, it would be senseless to renounce the latter in order to better pursue the former. For the necessary progress is possible only thanks to progress already achieved. It is a matter of completing, extending, and organizing individualism, not of restraining and combating it. It is a matter of using reflection, not of imposing silence upon it. Reflection alone can help us emerge from our present difficulties. We do not see what could replace it. It is not, however, by meditating upon *Politics in the Holy Scriptures* that we will ever find the means of organizing economic life and of introducing greater justice in contractual relations!

In these circumstances, is our duty not clear? All those who believe in the utility or simply in the necessity of the moral transformations accomplished in the past century have the same interest: they must forget the differences which separate them and unite in their efforts to preserve the already acquired position. Once the crisis has passed, there will certainly be cause to recall the teachings of experience, so that we do not again fall into that sterile inaction for which we are now paying the penalty. But that is tomorrow's task. Today, the urgent task which must come before all others is to save our moral patrimony; once it is secure, we will see that it prospers. Let the common danger at least shake us from our torpor and give us back a taste for action! And already, indeed, we see across the country initiative wakening and men of good will seeking each other out. If someone would come to group them together and lead them into battle, then victory might not be far off. For what should reassure us to a certain extent is that our adversaries are strong only because of our own weakness. They have neither the profound faith nor the generous impulses which irresistibly lead peoples to great reactions, as to great revolutions. We certainly would not dream of questioning their sincerity! But how could we fail to sense to what extent their conviction is improvised? They are neither apostles who let their anger or their enthusiasm overflow nor scholars who bring us the product of their research and reflections; they are men of letters seduced by an interesting theme. It would therefore seem impossible that these dilettantes' games could long succeed in holding back the masses if we know how to act. But also, what a humiliation it would be if reason, dealing with so weak an opponent, should end by being worsted, even if only for a time!

5

THE INTELLECTUAL ELITE
AND DEMOCRACY

WRITERS AND SCHOLARS are citizens. It is therefore obvious that they have a strict duty to participate in public life. It remains to be seen in what form and to what extent.

Men of thought and imagination, they would not seem to be particularly predestined to a properly political career. For that demands, above all, the qualities of a man of action. Even those whose profession is to contemplate societies, even the historian and the sociologist, do not seem to me more fit for these active functions than the man of letters or the naturalist; for it is possible to have a genius for discovering the general laws which explain social facts of the past without necessarily having the practical sense which allows one to divine the course of action which the condition of a given people at a given moment in its history requires. Just as a great physiologist is generally a mediocre clinician, a sociologist has every chance of making a very incomplete statesman. It is no doubt good that intellectuals be represented in deliberative assemblies. Aside from the fact that their culture permits them to bring to deliberations elements of information which are not negligible, they are more qualified than anyone to defend before the public powers the interests of the arts and sciences. But it is not necessary that they be numerous in the parliament in order to perform this task. Moreover, we may wonder whether—except for a few exceptional cases of eminently

Originally published as "L'élite intellectuelle et la démocratie," *Revue bleue*, 5e série, 1 (1904) : 705–6. Translated by Mark Traugott.

gifted geniuses—it is possible to become a deputy or senator without ceasing, to the same degree, to be a writer or a scholar, since these two types of functions imply so different an orientation of mind (*esprit*) and will!

What I mean is that above all our action must be exerted through books, seminars, and popular education. Above all, we must be *advisers, educators*. It is our function to help our contemporaries know themselves in their ideas and in their feelings, far more than to govern them. And in the state of mental confusion in which we live, what is a more useful role to play? Moreover, we will perform it that much better for having thus limited our ambition. We will gain the confidence of the people all the more easily if we are attributed fewer selfish, hidden motives. The lecturer of today must not be suspected to be the candidate of tomorrow.

It has, however, been said that the mob was not made to understand the intellectuals, and it is democracy and its so-called dull-witted spirit that have been blamed for the sort of political indifference scholars and artists have evinced during the first twenty years of our Third Republic. But what shows how groundless this explanation is, is that this indifference was ended as soon as a great moral and social problem was posed before the country. The lengthy abstention which previously existed, therefore, came quite simply from the absence of any question likely to impassion. Our political life was languishing miserably in questions of personalities. We were divided over who should have the power. But there was no great impersonal cause to which to consecrate ourselves, no lofty goal to which our wills could cling. We therefore followed, more or less distractedly, the petty incidents of daily politics without experiencing the need to intervene. But as soon as a grave question of principle was raised, the scholars were seen to leave their laboratories, the learned to leave their libraries to draw nearer the masses, to involve themselves in life; and the experience has proved that they know how to make themselves heard.

The moral agitation to which these events gave rise has not been extinguished, and I am among those who think that it must not be extinguished. For it is necessary. It was our former apathy that was abnormal and which constituted a danger. For better or for worse, the critical period begun with the fall of the *ancien régime* has not ended. It is better to recognize it than to abandon ourselves to a deceptive security. Our hour of repose has not struck. There is too much to do for us not to keep our social energies perpetually mobilized. That is why I believe the course of political events in the last four years preferable to those which preceded them. They have succeeded in maintaining a lasting current of collective activity of considerable intensity. To be sure, I am far from thinking that anticlericalism is enough; indeed, I hope to see society soon attach itself to more objective ends. But the essential thing is not to let ourselves fall back into the state of moral stagnation in which we so long tarried.

III. The Evolution of Morality

6

PROGRESSIVE PREPONDERANCE
OF ORGANIC SOLIDARITY

I

THUS, it is an historical law that mechanical solidarity which first stands alone, or nearly so, progressively loses ground, and that organic solidarity becomes, little by little, preponderant. But when the way in which men are solidary becomes modified, the structure of societies cannot but change. The form of a body is necessarily transformed when the molecular affinities are no longer the same. Consequently, if the preceding proposition is correct, there ought to be two social types which correspond to these two types of solidarity.

If we try to construct intellectually the ideal type of a society whose cohesion was exclusively the result of resemblances, we should have to conceive it as an absolutely homogeneous mass whose parts were not distinguished from one another. Consequently, they would have no arrangement; in short, it would be devoid of all definite form and all organization. It would be the veritable social protoplasm, the germ whence would arise all social types. We propose to call the aggregate thus characterized, *horde*.

From *The Division of Labor in Society,* translated and with an introduction by George Simpson (New York: Macmillan Co., 1933), pp. 174–99. Originally published as *De la division du travail social: Etude sur l'organisation des sociétés supérieures* (Paris: Félix Alcan, 1893); 2d ed. with a new preface entitled "Quelques remarques sur les groupements professionels," 1902.

It is true that we have not yet, in any completely authentic fashion, observed societies which, in all respects, complied with this definition. What gives us the right to postulate their existence, however, is that lower societies, those which are most closely akin to primitivity, are formed by a simple repetition of aggregates of this kind. We find an almost perfectly pure example of this social organization among the Indians of North America. Each Iroquois tribe, for example, contains a certain number of partial societies (the largest ones comprise eight) which present all the characteristics we have just mentioned. The adults of both sexes are on a plane of equality. The sachems and chiefs, who are at the head of these groups and by whose council the common affairs of the tribe are administered, do not enjoy any superiority. Kinship itself is not organized, for we cannot give this name to the distribution of the mass in generations. In the late epoch when we observed these peoples, there were, indeed, some special obligations which bound the child to its maternal relatives, but these relations come to very little and are not sensibly distinguishable from those which bind the child to other members of society. Originally, all persons of the same age were kin in the same degree.[1] In other cases, we are even nearer the horde. Fison and Howitt describe Australian tribes which consist of only two such divisions.[2]

We give the name *clan* to the horde which has ceased to be independent by becoming an element in a more extensive group, and that of *segmental societies with a clan-base* to peoples who are constituted through an association of clans. We say of these societies that they are segmental in order to indicate their formation by the repetition of like aggregates in them, analogous to the rings of an earthworm, and we say of this elementary aggregate that it is a clan, because this word well expresses its mixed nature, at once familial and political. It is a family in the sense that all the members who compose it are considered as kin of one another, and they are, in fact, for the most part consanguineous. The affinities that the community of blood brings about are principally those which keep them united. Moreover, they sustain relations with one another that we can term domestic, since we also find them in societies whose familial character is uncontested: I mean collective punishment, collective responsibility, and, as soon as private property makes its appearance, mutual inheritance. But, on the other hand, it is not a family in the proper sense of the word, for, in order to partake of it, it is not necessary to have any definite relations of consanguinity with other members of the clan. It is enough to present an external criterion which generally consists in using the same name. Although this sign is thought to denote a common origin, such a civil state really constitutes a proof which is not very demonstrative and very easy to imitate. Thus, the clan contains a great many strangers, and this permits it to attain dimensions such as a family, properly speaking, never has. It often comprises several thousand persons. Moreover, it is the fundamental political unity; the heads of clans are the only social authorities.[3]

We can thus qualify this organization as politico-familial. Not only has the clan consanguinity as its basis, but different clans of the same people are often considered as kin to one another. Among the Iroquois, they treat each other, according to circumstances, as brothers or as cousins.[4] Among the Jews, who present, as we shall see, the most characteristic traits of the same social organization, the ancestor of each of the clans which compose the tribe is believed to be descended from the tribal founder, who is himself regarded as one of the sons of the father of the race. But this denomination has the inconvenience, in comparison with the preceding, of not putting in relief that which gives the peculiar structure to these societies.

But, in whatever manner we name it, this organization, just as the horde, of which it is only an extension, carries with it no other solidarity than that derived from likenesses, since the society is formed of similar segments and these in their turn enclose only homogeneous elements. No doubt, each clan has its own features and is thereby distinguished from others, but also the solidarity is proportionally more feeble as they are more heterogeneous, and inversely. For segmental organization to be possible, the segments must resemble one another; without that, they would not be united. And they must differ; without this, they would lose themselves in each other and be effaced. According to the societies, the two contrary necessities are satisfied in different proportions, but the social type remains the same.

Now we are leaving the domain of pre-history and conjecture. Not only is there nothing hypothetical about this social type, but it is almost the most common among lower societies, and we know that they are the most numerous. We have already seen that it was general in America and in Australia. Post shows that it is very frequent among the African negroes.[5] The Hebrews remained in it to a late date, and the Kabyles never passed beyond it.[6] Thus, Waitz, wishing to characterize the structure of these peoples in a general way, people whom he calls *Naturvoelker*, gives the following picture in which will be found the general lines of the organization that we have just described: "As a general rule, families live one beside the other in great independence, and little by little develop a grouping of small societies [clans][7] which have no definite constitution, so long as internal conflicts or an external danger, such as war, does not lead one or several men to disengage themselves from the mass and become leaders. Their influence, which rests peculiarly on their personal titles, only extends and has sway within marked limits set forth by the confidence and patience of the others. Every adult remains in the eyes of such a chief in a state of complete independence. That is why such people, without any other internal organization, are held together only by external circumstances and through the habit of common life."[8]

The disposition of the clans in the interior of the society, and, accordingly, its configuration, can, of course, vary. Sometimes, they are simply juxtaposed so as to form a linear series; such is the case among many of the Indian tribes of North America.[9] Sometimes—and this is a mark of a more elevated organization— each of them is involved in a much greater group which, formed by the union of several clans, has its own life and a special name. Each of these groups, in its turn, can be involved with several others in another aggregate still more extensive, and from this series of successive involvements there results the unity of the total society. Thus, among the Kabyles, the political unity is the clan, constituted in the form of a village (*djemmaa or thaddart*); several *djemmaa* form a tribe (*arch'*), and several tribes form the confederation (*thak' ebilt*), the highest political society that the Kabyles know. The same is true among the Hebrews; the clan (which is so erroneously translated as the *family*) is a vast society which encompasses thousands of persons, descended, according to tradition, from the same ancestor.[10] A certain number of *families* composed the tribe and the union of the twelve tribes formed the totality of the Hebrew people.

These societies are such typical examples of mechanical solidarity that their principal physiological characteristics come from it.

We know that, in them, religion pervades the whole social life, but that is because social life is made up almost exclusively of common beliefs and of common practices which derive from unanimous adhesion a very particular intensity. Retracing by analysis of only classical texts until an epoch completely analogous to that of which we are speaking, Fustel de Coulanges has discovered that the early organization of these societies was of a familial nature, and that, moreover, the primitive family was constituted on a religious base. But he has mistaken the cause for the effect. After setting up the religious idea, without bothering to establish its derivation, he has deduced from it social arrangements,[11] when, on the contrary, it is the latter that explain the power and nature of the religious idea. Because all social masses have been formed from homogeneous elements, that is to say, because the collective type was very developed there and the individual type in a rudimentary state, it was inevitable that the whole psychic life of society should take on a religious character.

Thus does communism arise, a quality so often noted among these peoples. Communism, in effect, is the necessary product of this special cohesion which absorbs the individual in the group, the part in the whole. Property is definitive only of the extension of the person over things. Where the collective personality is the only one existent, property also must be collective. It will become individual only when the individual, disengaging himself from the mass, shall become a being personal and distinct, not only as an organism, but also as a factor in social life.[12]

This type can even be modified without the nature of social solidarity undergoing any change. In fact, primitive peoples do not all present this absence of centralization that we have just observed. There are some, on the contrary, subservient to an absolute power. The division of labor has then made its appearance among them. But in this case, the tie which binds the individual to the chief is identical with that which in our days attaches the thing to the person. The relations of a barbarous despot with his subjects, as that of a master with his slaves, of a father of a Roman family with his children, is not to be distinguished from the relations of an owner with the object he possesses. In these relations there is none of the reciprocity which the division of labor produces. They have with good reason been called unilateral.[13] The solidarity that they express remains mechanical. The whole difference is that it links the individual, not more directly to the group, but to the image of the group. But the unity of the whole is, as before, exclusive of the individuality of its parts.

If this early division of labor, important as it otherwise is, does not result in making social solidarity tractable, as might be expected, that is because of the particular conditions in which it is realized. It is a general law that the eminent organ of every society participates in the nature of the collective being that it represents. Where society has a religious and, so to speak, superhuman character, whose source we have just shown to lie in the constitution of the common conscience, it necessarily transmits itself to the chief who directs it and who is thus elevated above the rest of men. Where individuals are in simple dependence upon the collective type, they quite naturally become dependent upon the central authority in which it is incarnated. Indeed, the right of property which the community exercises over things in an undivided way passes intact into the superior personality who finds himself thus constituted. The properly professional services which the latter renders are little things in comparison with the extraordinary power with which he is invested. If, in some types of society, the directive power has so much authority, it is not, as has been said, because they have a more special need of energetic direction, but this authority emanates entirely from the common conscience, and it is great because the common conscience itself is highly developed. Suppose that the common conscience is very feeble or that it only embraces a small part of social life; the necessity for a supreme regulative function will not be less. The rest of society, however, will not be stronger than he who is entrusted with inferior authority. That is why solidarity is still mechanical where the division of labor is not highly developed. It is, indeed, under these conditions that mechanical solidarity reaches its maximum power, for the action of the common conscience is stronger when it is exercised, not in a diffuse manner, but through the medium of a defined organ.

There is, then, a social structure of determined nature to which mechanical solidarity corresponds. What characterizes it is a system of segments homogeneous and similar to each other.

II

Quite different is the structure of societies where organic solidarity is preponderant.

They are constituted, not by a repetition of similar, homogeneous segments, but by a system of different organs each of which has a special role, and which are themselves formed of differentiated parts. Not only are social elements not of the same nature, but they are not arranged in the same manner. They are not juxtaposed linearily as the rings of an earthworm, nor entwined one with another, but co-ordinated and subordinated one to another around the same central organ which exercises a moderating action over the rest of the organism. This organ itself no longer has the same character as in the preceding case, for, if the others depend upon it, it, in its turn, depends upon them. No doubt, it still enjoys a special situation, and, if one chooses so to speak of it, a privileged position, but that is due to the nature of the role that it fills and not to some cause foreign to its functions, nor to some force communicated to it from without. Thus, there is no longer anything about it that is not temporal and human. Between it and other organs, there is no longer anything but differences in degree. It is thus that, in the animal kingdom, the pre-eminence of the nervous system over the other systems is reduced to the right if one may speak thus, of receiving a choicer nourishment and of having its fill before the others. But it has need of them, just as they have need of it.

This social type rests on principles so different from the preceding that it can develop only in proportion to the effacement of that preceding type. In effect, individuals are here grouped, no longer according to their relations of lineage, but according to the particular nature of the social activity to which they consecrate themselves. Their natural milieu is no longer the natal milieu, but the occupational milieu. It is no longer real or fictitious consanguinity which marks the place of each one, but the function which he fills. No doubt, when this new organization begins to appear, it tries to utilize the existing organization and assimilate it. The way in which functions are divided thus follows, as faithfully as possible, the way in which society is already divided. The segments, or at least the groups of segments united by special affinities, become organs. It is thus that the clans which together formed the tribe of the Levites appropriated sacerdotal functions for themselves among the Hebrew people. In a general way, classes and castes probably have no other origin nor any other nature; they arise from the multitude of occupational organizations being born amidst the pre-existing familial organization. But this mixed arrangement cannot long endure, for between the two states that it attempts to reconcile there is an antagonism which necessarily ends in a break. It is only a very rudimentary division of labor which can adapt itself to those rigid, defined moulds which were not made for it. It can grow only by freeing itself from the framework which encloses it. As soon as it has passed a certain stage of development, there is no longer any relation either between the immutable number of segments and the steady growth of functions which are becoming specialized, or between the hereditarily fixed properties of the first and the new aptitudes that the second calls forth.[14] The social material must enter into entirely new combinations in order to organize itself upon completely different foundations. But the old structure, so far as it persists, is opposed to this. That is why it must disappear.

The history of these two types shows, in effect, that one has progressed only as the other has retrogressed.

Among the Iroquois, the social constitution with a clan-base is in a state of purity, and the same is true of the Hebrews as we see them in the Pentateuch, except for the slight alteration that we have just noted. Thus, the organized type exists neither in the first nor in the second, although we can perhaps see the first stirrings of it in Jewish society.

The case is no longer the same among the Franks in their Salic law. It presents itself with its own characteristics, disengaged from all compromise. We find among these people, besides a central authority, stable and regular, a whole system of administrative functions, as well as judicial. Moreover, the existence of a contract-law, still, it is true, very poorly developed, is proof that economic functions themselves are beginning to be divided and organized. Thus, the politico-familial constitution is seriously undermined. To be sure, the last social molecule, the village, is still only a transformed clan. The proof of this is that, among the inhabitants of the same village, there are relations which are evidently of a domestic nature and which, in every case, are characteristic of the clan. All the members of the village have, in the absence of relatives, properly so designated, an hereditary right over one another.[15] A text found among the *Capita extravagantia legis salicae* (art. 9) tells us, indeed, that in case of murder committed in the village, the neighbors were collectively solidary. Moreover, the village is a much more hermetically closed system to the outside and more sufficient unto itself than would be a simple territorial circumscription, for nothing can be established there without unanimous consent, express or tacit, from all the inhabitants.[16] But, under this form, the clan has lost some of its essential characteristics. Not only has all remembrance of a common origin disappeared, but it has been almost completely stripped of any political importance. The political unit is the *Hundred*.

"The population," says Waitz, "lived in villages, but it divided itself into Hundreds which, in peace and in war, formed the unity which served as a foundation for all relations."[17]

In Rome, this double movement of progression and retrogression also takes place. The Roman clan is the *gens*, and it is certain that the *gens* was the basis of the old Roman constitution. But, from the founding of the Republic, it has almost completely ceased to be a public institution. It is no longer either a definite territorial unity, as the village among the Franks, or a political unit. We find it neither in the configuration of territory, nor in the structure of the assemblies of the people. The *comitia curiata*, where it played a social role,[18] are replaced by the *comitia centuriata*, or by the *comitia tributa*, which were organized on quite different lines. It is no longer anything but a private association which is maintained by force of habit, but which is destined to disappear, because it no longer corresponds to anything in Roman life. But also, since the time of the Twelve Tables, the division of labor was much further advanced in Rome than among the preceding peoples and the organized structure more highly developed. There are already to be found there important corporations of functionaries (senators, equites, a pontifical college, etc.), workman's groups,[19] at the same time that the notion of the lay state gets clear.

Thus, we find justification for the hierarchy that we have just established according to other criteria, less methodical, between the social types that we have previously compared. If we could say that the Hebrews of the Pentateuch appeared to be a social type less elevated than the Franks of the Salic law, and that the latter, in their turn, were below the Romans of the Twelve Tables, then there is a general law: the more the segmental organization with a clan-base is manifest and strong among a people, the more inferior is their social type. It can elevate itself to a higher state only after freeing itself from this first stage. It is for the same reason that the Athenian city, while appearing to be exactly the same type as the Roman city, is, however, a more primitive type. The politico-familial organization disappeared much less quickly there. It persisted there almost until Athens' decadence.[20]

But the organized type cannot subsist alone in a pure state once the clan has disappeared. The organization with a clan-base is really only a species of a larger genus, the segmental organization. The distribution of society into similar compartments corresponds to persisting necessities, even in new societies where social life is being established, but which produce their effects in another form. The bulk of the population is no longer divided according to relations of consanguinity, real or fictive, but according to the division of territory. The segments are no longer familial aggregates, but territorial circumscriptions.

It is through a slow evolution, however, that the passage from one to another is made. When remembrance of common origin is extinct, when the domestic relations which derive from it—but as we have seen, often survive it—have themselves disappeared, the clan no longer has any conception of itself other than as a group of individuals who occupy the same territory. It becomes, properly speaking, the village. Thus it is that all peoples who have passed beyond the clan-stage are organized in territorial districts (counties, communes, etc.) which, just as the Roman *gens* came to take part in the curia, connected themselves with other districts of similar nature, but vaster, sometimes called the Hundred, sometimes the assembly, sometimes the ward, which, in their turn, are often enveloped by others, still more extensive (shire, province, department), whose union formed the society.[21] The envelopment can, however, be more or less hermetic; the ties which bind the widest districts can be more or less strong, as in the centralized countries of contemporary Europe, or loose, as in simple confederations. But the structural principle is the same, and that is why mechanical solidarity persists even in the most elevated societies.

But even as it is no longer preponderant, the arrangement by segments is no longer, as in the preceding, the unique framework, nor even the essential framework of society. In the first place, territorial divisions have something artificial about them. The ties which result from cohabitation are not as profoundly affective of the heart of men as are those arising from consanguinity. Thus, they have a much smaller resistive power. When a person is born into a clan, he can in no way ever change the fact of his parentage. The same does not hold true of changing from a city or a province. No doubt, the geographical distribution generally coincides, in the large, with a certain moral distribution of population. Each province, each territorial division, has its peculiar customs and manners, a life peculiar unto itself. It therefore exercises over the individuals who are affected by it an attraction which tends to keep itself alive, and to repel all opposing forces. But, in the case of the same country, these differences would be neither very numerous, nor very firmly marked out. The segments are each more exposed to the others. And in truth, since the Middle Ages, "after the formation of cities, foreign artisans moved about as easily and as far as did merchants."[22] The segmental organization lost its distinction.

It loses more and more ground as societies develop. It is a general law that partial aggregates which participate in a larger aggregate see their individuality becoming less and less distinct. With the disappearance of the familial organization, local religions disappear without returning. Yet they persist in local customs. Little by little, they join together and unite at the same time that dialects and jargons begin to resolve themselves into one and the same national language, at the same time that regional administration loses its autonomy. Some have seen in this fact a simple consequence of the law of imitation.[23] But it is rather a levelling analogous to that which is produced between liquid masses put into communication. The partitions which separate the various cells of social life, being less thick, are more often broken through. Their permeability becomes greater as they are traversed more. Accordingly, they lose their cohesion, become progressively effaced, and, in the same measure, confound themselves. But local diversities can maintain themselves only in so far as diversity of environments continues to exist. Territorial divisions are thus less and less grounded in the nature of things, and, consequently, lose their significance. We can almost say that a people is as much more advanced as territorial divisions are more superficial.

On the other hand, at the same time that the segmental organization is thus effaced, occupational organization comes out of its torpor more and more completely. In the beginning, it is true, it establishes itself only within the limits of the simplest segments without extending beyond them. Each city and its immediate environs form a group in the interior of which work is divided, but seeks to be sufficient unto itself. "The city," says Schmoller, "becomes as far as possible the ecclesiastical centre, the political and military centre of the surrounding villages. It tries to develop all the industries necessary for the supplying of the country, by seeking to concentrate commerce and transportation in its territory."[24] At the same time, in the interior of the city, the inhabitants are grouped according to their occupations. Each body of workers is like a city which leads its own life.[25] This is the state in which the cities of antiquity remained until a comparatively late date, and where Christian societies started. But the latter grew out of this stage very early. Since the fourteenth century, the inter-regional division of labor has been developing: "Each city, in its beginnings, had as many drapers as it needed. But the makers of grey cloth of Basle succumbed, even before 1362, to the competition of the Alsatians. In Strasburg, Frankfort, Leipzig, the spinning of wool is ruined about 1500. . . . The character of industrial universality of cities of former times found itself irreparably destroyed."

Since then the movement has been extended. "In the capital, today more than heretofore, the active forces of the central government, arts, literature, large credit-operations concentrate themselves; in the great seaports are concentrated, more than ever, all importing and exporting. Hundreds of small commercial places, trafficking in cattle and wheat, prosper and grow. Whereas previously each city had its ramparts and moats, now great fortresses are erected for the protection of the whole country. Like the capital, the chief places of each province grow through the concentration of provincial administration, by provincial establishments, collections, and schools. The insane and the sick of certain types, who were heretofore dispersed, are banded together from every province and every department into a single enclosure. Different cities always tend towards certain specialties, so that we now distinguish university-cities, government-cities, manufacturing cities,

cities of commerce, of shipping, of banking. In certain points or certain regions, large industries are concentrated: machine-construction, spinning, textile-manufacture, tanneries, furnaces, a sugar industry supplying the whole country. Special schools have been established, the working-class population adapts itself there, the construction of machines is concentrated there, while the means of communication and the organization of credit accommodate themselves to particular circumstances."[26]

To be sure, in certain measure, this occupational organization was forced to adapt itself to the one which had existed before it, as it had earlier adapted itself to the familial organization. That is apparent from the description which has preceded. It is, moreover, a very general fact that new institutions first fall into the mould of old institutions. Territorial circumscriptions tend to specialize themselves like tissues, organs, or different parts, just as the clans before them. But, just like the latter, they are incapable of continuing this role. In fact, a city always circumscribes either different organs or parts of different organs; and inversely, there are not many organs which may be completely comprised within the limits of a determined district, no matter how far it extends. It almost always runs beyond them. Indeed, although very often the most highly solidary organs tend to come closer to each other, nevertheless, in general, their material proximity very inexactly reflects the more or less great intimacy of their relations. Certain of them are very distant, although they are directly dependent upon each other. Others are near, yet their relations are only mediate and distant. The manner of human grouping which results from the division of labor is thus very dfferent from that which expresses the partition of the population in space. The occupational environment does not coincide with the territorial environment any more than it does with the familial environment. It is a new framework which substitutes itself for the others; thus the substitution is possible only in so far as the others are effaced.

If this social type is nowhere observable in its absolute purity; if, indeed, organic solidarity is nowhere come upon wholly alone, at least it disengages itself more and more from all mixture, just as it becomes more and more preponderant. This predominance is much more rapid and complete at the very moment when this structure affirms itself more strongly, the other having become more indistinct. The very defined segment that the clan formed is replaced by territorial circumscription. In its origin, at least, the latter corresponded, although in a vague and only proximate way, to the real moral division of the population. But it slowly loses this character and becomes an arbitrary, conventional combination. But in the degree that these barriers are broken down, they are rebuilt by systems of organs much more highly developed. If, then, social evolution rests upon the action of these same determinate causes—and we shall later see that this hypothesis is the only one conceivable—we may be permitted to predict that this double movement will continue in the same path, and that a day will come when our whole social and political organization will have a base exclusively, or almost exclusively, occupational.

Moreover, the investigations which are to follow[27] will prove that this occupational organization is not today everything that it ought to be; that abnormal causes have prevented it from attaining the degree of development which our social order now demands. We may judge by that what importance it must have in the future.

III

The same law holds of biological development.

We know today that lower animals are formed of similar segments, composed either of irregular masses, or in linear series. Indeed, at the lowest rung of the ladder, the elements are not only alike, they are still in homogeneous composition. We generally call them *colonies*. But this expression, which is certainly not without equivocation, does not signify that these associations are not individual organisms, for "every colony whose members have a continuity of tissues is, in reality, an individual."[28] What characterizes the individuality of any given aggregate is the existence of operations effectuated in common by all parts. Thus, among the members of a colony, nutritive materials are taken in

common, making impossible any movement except through movements of the totality, in order for the colony not to be dissolved.
Moreover, the egg, issuing from one of the associated segments,
reproduces, not this segment, but the entire colony of which it is
a part. "Between colonies of polyps and the most elevated animals, there is, from this point of view, no difference."[29] What
makes such a total, radical separation impossible is that there
are no organisms, as centralized as they may be, which do not
present, in different degrees, some colonial constitution. We find
traces up through the vertebrates, in their skeletal composition, in
their urogenital make-up, etc. Particularly is proof rendered by
their embryonic development of their being nothing else than
modified colonies.[30]

There is, thus, in the animal world an individuality "which is
produced apart from a whole combination of organs."[31] But it
is identical with that of societies that we have termed segmental.
Not only is the structural plan evidently the same, but the solidarity
is of the same kind. Since the parts which make up an animal
colony are mechanically attached to each other, they can act only
as a whole, at least if they remain united. Activity is here collective. In a society of polyps, since all stomachs work together, an
individual cannot eat without other individuals eating. It is, says,
Perrier, communism in every meaning of the word.[32] A member
of a colony, particularly when it is irresolute, cannot contract itself
without dragging into its movement the polyps to which it is
joined, and the movement communicates itself from place to
place.[33] In a worm, each annule depends upon the others very
rigidly, and that is so even though it can detach itself without
danger.

But, even as the segmental type becomes effaced as we advance in the scale of social evolution, the colonial type disappears
in so far as we go up in the scale of organisms. Already impaired
among the earthworms, although still very apparent, it becomes
almost imperceptible among the molluscs, and ultimately only the
analysis of a scholar can find any traces of it among the vertebrates. We do not have to show the analogies between the type
which replaces the preceding one and that of organic societies.

In one case as in the other, the structure derives from the division of labor and its solidarity. Each part of the animal, having become an organ, has its proper sphere of action where it moves independently without imposing itself upon others. But, from another point of view, they depend more upon one another than in a colony, since they cannot separate without perishing. Finally, in organic evolution as in social evolution, the division of labor begins by utilizing the framework of segmental organization, but ultimately frees itself and develops autonomously. If, in fact, the organ is sometimes only a transformed segment, that is an exception.[34]

In sum, we have distinguished two kinds of solidarity; we have just learned that there exist two social types which correspond to them. Even as the solidarities develop in inverse ratio to each other, of the two corresponding social types, one regresses while the other progresses, and the latter is that fixed by the division of labor. Besides confirming what has preceded, this result succeeds in showing us the total importance of the division of labor. Just as it is it which, for the most part, makes coherent the societies in which we live, so also does it determine the constitutive traits of their structure, and every fact presages that, in the future, its role, from this point of view, will become even greater.

IV

The law that we have established in the last two chapters has been able by a quality, but by a quality only, to recall to us the dominating tendency in Spencer's sociology. With him, we have said that the place of the individual in society, of no account in its origins, becomes greater with civilization. But this incontestable fact is presented to us under an aspect totally different from that of English philosophy, so that, ultimately, our conclusions are opposed to his more than they are in agreement.

First of all, according to him, this absorption of the individual into the group would be the result of force and of an artificial organization necessitated by the state of war in which lower societies chronically live. It is especially in war that union is neces-

sary to success. A group can defend itself against another group
or subject it to itself only by acting together. It is necessary for
all the individual forces to be concentrated in a permanent manner
in an indissoluble union. But the only means of producing this
concentration instantaneously is by instituting a very strong authority to which individuals are absolutely submissive. It is necessary that, as the will of a soldier finds itself suspended in executing
the will of his superior, so too does the will of citizens find itself
curtailed by that of the government.[35] Thus, it is an organized despotism which would annihilate individuals, and since this organization is essentially military, it is through militarism that Spencer
defines these types of society.

We have seen, on the contrary, that this effacement of the
individual has as its place of origin a social type which is characterized by a complete absence of all centralization. It is a product
of that state of homogeneity which distinguishes primitive societies. If the individual is not distinct from the group, it is because the individual conscience is hardly at all distinguishable
from the collective conscience. Spencer and other sociologists
with him seem to have interpreted these distant facts in terms
of very modern ideas. The very pronounced contemporary sentiment that each of us has of his own individuality has led them
to believe that personal rights cannot be restrained to this point
except by a coercive organization. We cling to them so firmly that
they find it inconceivable for man to have willingly abandoned
them. In fact, if in lower societies so small a place is given to
individual personality, that is not because it has been restrained
or artificially suppressed. It is simply because, at that moment
of history, *it did not exist.*

Moreover, Spencer himself realizes that, of these societies,
many have a constitution so little military and authoritarian that
he qualifies them as democratic.[36] He wishes, however, to see in
them the first symptoms of the future which he calls industrial.
To that end, it is necessary for him to misconceive the fact that
here as in those where there is submission to a despotic government, the individual has no sphere of action proper to him, as the
general institution of communism proves. Indeed, the traditions,

prejudices, the collective usages of all sorts are not any the less burdensome to him than would be a constituted authority. Thus, we can term them democratic only by distorting the ordinary sense of the word. Moreover, if they were really impressed with the precocious individualism that is attributed to them, we would come to the strange conclusion that social evolution has tried, from the very first, to produce the most perfect types, since, as he says, no governmental force exists at first except that of the common will expressed in the assembled horde.[37] Would not the movement of history then be circular and would progress consist in anything but a return to the past?

In a general way, it is easy to understand why individuals will not be submissive except to a collective despotism, for the members of a society can be dominated only by a force which is superior to them, and there is only one which has this quality: that is the group. Any personality, as powerful as it might be, would be as nothing against a whole society; the latter can carry on in spite of it. That is why, as we have seen, the force of authoritarian governments does not come from authorities themselves, but from the very constitution of society. If, however, individualism was at this point congenital with humanity, we cannot see how primitive peoples could so easily subject themselves to the despotic authority of a chief, wherever necessary. The ideas, customs, institutions would have opposed such a radical transformation. But all this is explained once we have taken cognizance of the nature of these societies, for then the change is no longer as great as it seems. Individuals, instead of subordinating themselves to the group, were subordinated to that which represented it, and as the collective authority, when it was diffuse, was absolute, that of the chief, who is only its organized incarnation, naturally took on the same character.

Rather than dating the effacement of the individual from the institution of a despotic authority, we must, on the contrary, see in this institution the first step made towards individualism. Chiefs are, in fact, the first personalities who emerge from the social mass. Their exceptional situation, putting them beyond the level of others, gives them a distinct physiognomy and accordingly confers individuality upon them. In dominating society, they are no longer forced to follow all of its movements. Of course, it is from the group that they derive their power, but once power is organized, it becomes autonomous and makes them capable of personal activity. A source of initiative is thus opened which had not existed before then. There is, hereafter, someone who can produce new things and even, in certain measure, deny collective usages. Equilibrium has been broken.[38]

Our insistence upon this point was made in order to establish two important propositions.

In the first place, whenever we find ourselves in the presence of a governmental system endowed with great authority, we must seek the reason for it, not in the particular situation of the governing, but in the nature of the societies they govern. We must observe the common beliefs, the common sentiments which, by incarnating themselves in a person or in a family, communicate such power to it. As for the personal superiority of the chief, it plays only a secondary role in this process. It explains why the collective force is concentrated in his hands rather than in some others, but does not explain its intensity. From the moment that this force, instead of remaining diffuse, becomes delegated, it can only be for the profit of the individuals who have already otherwise evinced some superiority. But if such superiority suggests the sense in which the current is directed, it does not create the current. In Rome if the father of a family enjoys absolute power, it is not because he is the oldest, or the wisest, or the most experienced, but because, according to the circumstances in which the Roman family was placed, he incarnated the old familial communism. Despotism, at least when it is not a pathological, decadent phenomenon, is nothing else than transformed communism.

In the second place, we see from what precedes how false is the theory which makes egotism the point of departure for humanity, and altruism only a recent conquest.

What gives this hypothesis authority in the eyes of certain persons is that it appears to be the logical consequence of the principles of Darwinism. In the name of the dogma of struggle for existence and natural selection, they paint for us in the sad-

dest colors this primitive humanity whose hunger and thirst, always badly satisfied, were their only passions; those sombre times
when men had no other care and no other occupation than to
quarrel with one another over their miserable nourishment. To
react against those retrospective reveries of the philosophy of the
eighteenth century and also against certain religious doctrines, to
show with some force that the paradise lost is not behind us and
that there is in our past nothing to regret, they believe we ought
to make it dreary and belittle it systematically. Nothing is less scientific than this prejudice in the opposite direction. If the hypotheses of Darwin have a moral use, it is with more reserve and
measure than in other sciences. They overlook the essential element of moral life, that is, the moderating influence that society
exercises over its members, which tempers and neutralizes the
brutal action of the struggle for existence and selection. Wherever
there are societies, there is altruism, because there is solidarity.

Thus, we find altruism from the beginning of humanity and
even in a truly intemperate form. For these privations that the
savage imposes upon himself in obedience to religious tradition,
the abnegation with which he sacrifices his life when society
demands such sacrifice, the irresistible desire of the widow of
India to follow her husband to the grave, of the Gaul not to survive the head of his clan, of the old Celt to free his companions
from useless trouble by voluntary death—is not all this altruism?
Shall we treat these practices as superstitions? What matter, so
long as they evince an aptitude for surrendering oneself? And
where do superstitions begin and end? It would be very difficult
to reply and give a scientific answer to this question. Is it not also
a superstition of ours to feel affection for the places in which we
have lived, and for the persons with whom we have had durable
relations? And is not this power of attachment the mark of a sane
moral constitution? To speak rigorously, our whole sensible life
is made up of superstitions, since it precedes and dominates judgment more than it depends upon it.

Scientifically, conduct is egotistical in the measure that it is
determined by sentiments and representations which are exclusively personal. If, then, we remember to what extent in lower

societies the conscience of the individual is wrapped in the collective conscience, we may even be led to believe that it is a thing totally different from the individual himself, that it is completely altruistic, as Condillac would say. This conclusion, however, would be exaggerated, for there is a sphere of psychic life which, however developed the collective type may be, varies from one man to another and remains peculiar with each. It is that which is formed by representations, by sentiments and tendencies which relate to the organism and to the state of the organism. It is the world of internal and external sensations and the movements which are directly linked to them. This first foundation of all individuality is inalienable and does not depend upon any social state. Thus, one must not say that altruism is born from egotism. Such a derivation would be possible only through a *creatio ex nihilo*. But, to speak rigorously, these two sides of conduct are found present from the beginning in all human consciences, for there cannot be things which do not reflect both of these aspects, the one relating to the individual alone and the other relating to the things which are not personal to him.

All that we can say is that, among savages, this inferior part of ourselves represents a more considerable fraction of total life, because this total has a smaller extent, since the higher spheres of the psychic life are less developed there. It thus has greater relative importance and, accordingly, greater sway over the will. But, on the other hand, with respect to what goes beyond this circle of physical necessities, the primitive conscience, to use a strong expression of Espinas, is completely outside of itself. Contrariwise, among the civilized, egotism is introduced in the midst of higher representations. Each of us has his opinions, his beliefs, his personal aspirations, and holds to them. It is even mingled with altruism, for it happens that we have a way of our own of being altruistic which clings to our personal character, to the texture of our spirit, and which we refuse to cast off. Of course, we must not conclude that the place of egotism has become greater throughout the whole of life, for we must take account of the fact that the whole conscience has been extended. It is none the less true that individualism has developed in absolute value by penetrating into regions which originally were closed to it.

But this individualism, the fruit of an historical development, is not at all that which Spencer described. The societies that he calls industrial do not resemble organized societies any more than military societies resemble segmental societies with a familial base. That is what we shall see in the following chapter.

7

ORGANIC SOLIDARITY AND
CONTRACTUAL SOLIDARITY

I

IT IS TRUE that in the industrial societies that Spencer speaks of, just as in organized societies, social harmony comes essentially from the division of labor.[1] It is characterized by a co-operation which is automatically produced through the pursuit by each individual of his own interests. It suffices that each individual consecrate himself to a special function in order, by the force of events, to make himself solidary with others. Is this not the distinctive sign of organized societies?

But if Spencer has justly noted what the principal cause of social solidarity in higher societies is, he has misunderstood the manner in which this cause produces its effect, and, accordingly, misunderstood the nature of the latter.

In short, for him, industrial solidarity, as he calls it, presents the two following characters:

Since it is spontaneous, it does not require any coercive force either to produce or to maintain it. Society does not have to intervene to assure the harmony which is self-established. Spencer says that each man can maintain himself through his work, can

From *The Division of Labor in Society*, translated and with an introduction by George Simpson (New York: Macmillan Co., 1933), pp. 200–229. Originally published as *De la division du travail social: Etude sur l'organisation des sociétés supérieures* (Paris: Félix Alcan, 1893); 2d ed. with a new preface entitled "Quelques remarques sur les groupements professionels," 1902.

exchange his produce for the goods of another, can lend assistance and receive payment, can enter into some association for
pursuing some enterprise, small or large, without obeying the
direction of society in its totality.[2] The sphere of social action
would thus grow narrower and narrower, for it would have no
other object than that of keeping individuals from disturbing and
harming one another. That is to say, it would have only a negative regulative force.

Under these conditions, the only remaining link between men
would be that of an absolutely free exchange. As Spencer says,
all industrial affairs take place through the medium of free exchange, and this relation becomes predominant in society in so
far as individual activity becomes dominant.[3] But the normal
form of exchange is the contract. That is why in proportion to the
decline of militarism and the ascendancy of industrialism, power
as the gateway to authority becomes of less importance and free
activity increases, and the relationship of contract becomes general. Finally, in the fully developed industrial type, this relationship becomes universal.[4]

By that, Spencer does not mean that society always rests on
an implicit or formal contract. The hypothesis of a social contract
is irreconcilable with the notion of the division of labor. The
greater the part taken by the latter, the more completely must
Rousseau's postulate be renounced. For in order for such a contract to be possible, it is necessary that, at a given moment, all
industrial wills direct themselves toward the common bases of
the social organization, and, consequently, that each particular
conscience pose the political problem for itself in all its generality.
But that would make it necessary for each individual to leave his
special sphere, so that all might equally play the same role, that
of statesman and constituents. Thus, this is the situation when
society makes a contract: if adhesion is unanimous, the content
of all consciences is identical. Then, in the measure that social
solidarity proceeds from such a cause, it has no relation with
the division of labor.

Nothing, however, less resembles the spontaneous, antomatic
solidarity which, according to Spencer, distinguishes industrial

societies, for he sees, on the contrary, in this conscious pursuit of social ends the characteristic of military societies.[5] Such a contract supposes that all individuals are able to represent in themselves the general conditions of the collective life in order to make a choice with knowledge. But Spencer understands that such a representation goes beyond the bounds of science in its actual state, and, consequently, beyond the bounds of conscience. He is so convinced of the vanity of reflection when it is applied to such matters that he wishes to take them away even from the legislator, to say nothing of submitting them to public opinion. He believes that social life, just as all life in general, can naturally organize itself only by an unconscious, spontaneous adaptation under the immediate pressure of needs, and not according to a rational plan of reflective intelligence. He does not believe that higher societies can be built according to a rigidly drawn program.

Thus, the conception of a social contract is today difficult to defend, for it has no relation to the facts. The observer does not meet it along his road, so to speak. Not only are there no societies which have such an origin, but there is none whose structure presents the least trace of a contractual organization. It is neither a fact acquired through history nor a tendency which grows out of historical development. Hence, to rejuvenate this doctrine and accredit it, it would be necessary to qualify as a contract the adhesion which each individual, as adult, gave to the society when he was born, solely by reason of which he continues to live. But then we would have to term contractual every action of man which is not determined by constraint.[6] In this light, there is no society, neither present nor past, which is not or has not been contractual, for there is none which could exist solely through pressure. We have given the reason for this above. If it has sometimes been thought that force was greater previously than it is today, that is because of the illusion which attributes to a coercive regime the small place given over to individual liberty in lower societies. In reality, social life, wherever it is normal, is spontaneous, and if it is abnormal, it cannot endure. The individual abdicates spontaneously. In fact, it is unjust to speak of abdication where there

is nothing to abdicate. If this large and somewhat warped interpretation is given to this word, no distinction can be made between
different social types, and if we understand by type only the very
defined juridical tie which the word designates, we can be sure
that no tie of this kind has ever existed between individuals and
society.

But if higher societies do not rest upon a fundamental contract which sets forth the general principles of political life, they
would have, or would be considered to have, according to Spencer,
the vast system of particular contracts which link individuals as a
unique basis. They would depend upon the group only in proportion to their dependence upon one another, and they would depend upon one another only in proportion to conventions privately
entered into and freely concluded. Social solidarity would then
be nothing else than the spontaneous accord of individual interests, an accord of which contracts are the natural expression.
The typical social relation would be the economic, stripped of all
regulation and resulting from the entirely free initiative of the
parties. In short, society would be solely the stage where individuals exchanged the products of their labor, without any action
properly social coming to regulate this exchange.

Is this the character of societies whose unity is produced by
the division of labor? If this were so, we could with justice doubt
their stability. For if interest relates men, it is never for more than
some few moments. It can create only an external link between
them. In the fact of exchange, the various agents remain outside of
each other, and when the business has been completed, each one
retires and is left entirely on his own. Consciences are only superficially in contact; they neither penetrate each other, nor do they
adhere. If we look further into the matter, we shall see that this
total harmony of interests conceals a latent or deferred conflict.
For where interest is the only ruling force each individual finds
himself in a state of war with every other since nothing comes to
mollify the egos, and any truce in this eternal antagonism would
not be of long duration. There is nothing less constant than interest. Today, it unites me to you; tomorrow, it will make me your

enemy. Such a cause can only give rise to transient relations and passing associations. We now understand how necessary it is to see if this is really the nature of organic solidarity.

In no respect, according to Spencer, does industrial society exist in a pure state. It is a partially ideal type which slowly disengages itself in the evolutionary process, but it has not yet been completely realized. Consequently, to rightly attribute to it the qualities we have just been discussing, we would have to establish systematically that societies appear in a fashion as complete as they are elevated, discounting cases of regression.

It is first affirmed that the sphere of social activity grows smaller and smaller, to the great advantage of the individual. But to prove this proposition by real instances, it is not enough to cite, as Spencer does, some cases where the individual has been effectively emancipated from collective influence. These examples, numerous as they may be, can serve only as illustrations, and are, by themselves, devoid of any demonstrative force. It is very possible that, in this respect, social action has regressed, but that, in other respects, it has been extended, and that, ultimately, we are mistaking a transformation for a disappearance. The only way of giving objective proof is not to cite some facts taken at random, but to follow historically, from its origins until recent times, the way in which social action has essentially manifested itself, and to see whether, in time, it has added or lost volume. We know that this is law. The obligations that society imposes upon its members, as inconsequential and unenduring as they may be, take on a juridical form. Consequently, the relative dimensions of this system permit us to measure with exactitude the relative extent of social action.

But it is very evident that, far from diminishing, it grows greater and greater and becomes more and more complex. The more primitive a code is, the smaller its volume. On the contrary, it is as large as it is more recent. There can be no doubt about this. To be sure, it does not result in making the sphere of individual activity smaller. We must not forget that if there is more regulation in life, there is more life in general. This is sufficient proof that social discipline has not been relaxing. One of its forms tends, it is true, to regress, as we have already seen, but others, much richer and much more complex, develop in its place. If repressive law loses ground, restitutive law, which originally did not exist at all, keeps growing. If society no longer imposes upon everybody certain uniform practices, it takes greater care to define and regulate the special relations between different social functions, and this activity is not smaller because it is different.

Spencer would reply that he had not insisted upon the diminution of every kind of control, but only of positive control. Let us admit this distinction. Whether it be positive or negative, the control is none the less social, and the principal question is to understand whether it has extended itself or contracted. Whether it be to command or to deny, to say *Do this* or *Do not do that*, if society intervenes more, we have not the right to say that individual spontaneity suffices more and more in all spheres. If the rules determining conduct have multiplied, whether they be imperative or prohibitive, it is not true that it depends more and more completely on private initiative.

But has this distinction itself any foundation? By positive control, Spencer means that which commands action, while negative control commands only abstention. As he says: A man has a piece of land; I cultivate it for him either wholly or in part, or else I impose upon him either wholly or in part the way in which he should cultivate it. This is a positive control. On the other hand, I give him neither aid nor advice about its cultivation; I simply do not molest my neighbor's crop, or trespass upon my neighbor's land, or put rubbish on his clearing. This is a negative control. The difference is very marked between ordering him to follow, as a citizen, a certain course, or suggesting means for the citizen to employ, and, on the other hand, not disturbing the course which some citizen is pursuing.[7] If such is the meaning of these terms, then positive control is not disappearing.

We know, of course, that restitutive law is growing. But, in the large majority of cases, it either points out to a citizen the course he ought to pursue, or it interests itself in the means that this citizen is employing to attain his end. It answers the two following questions for each juridical relation: (1) Under what conditions and in what form does it normally exist? (2) What are the obligations it entails? The determination of the form and the conditions is essentially positive, since it forces the individual to follow a certain procedure in order to attain his end. As for the obligations, if they only forbid, in principle, our troubling another person in the exercise of his functions, Spencer's thesis would be true, at least in part. But they consist most often in the statement of services of a positive nature.

On this point we must go into some detail.

II

It is quite true that contractual relations, which originally were rare or completely absent, multiply as social labor becomes divided. But what Spencer seems to have failed to see is that non-contractual relations develop at the same time.

First, let us examine that part of law which is improperly termed private, and which, in reality, regulates diffuse social functions, or what may be called the visceral life of the social organism.

In the first place, we know that domestic law, as simple as it was in the beginning, has become more and more complex. That is to say, that the different species of juridical relations to which family life gives rise are much more numerous than heretofore. But the obligations which result from this are of an eminently positive nature; they constitute a reciprocity of rights and duties. Moreover, they are not contractual, at least in their typical form. The conditions upon which they are dependent are related to our personal status which, in turn, depends upon birth, on our consanguineous relations, and, consequently, upon facts which are beyond volition.

Marriage and adoption, however, are sources of domestic relations, and they are contracts. But it rightly happens that the closer we get to the most elevated social types, the more also do these two juridical operations lose their properly contractual character.

Not only in lower societies, but in Rome itself until the end of the Empire, marriage remains an entirely private affair. It generally is a sale, real among primitive people, later fictive, but valid only through the consent of the parties duly attested. Neither solemn formalities of any kind nor intervention by some authority were then necessary. It is only with Christianity that marriage took on another character. The Christians early got into the habit of having their union consecrated by a priest. An act of the emperor Leo the Philosopher converted this usage into a law for the East. The Council of Trent sanctioned it likewise for the West. From then on, marriage ceased to be freely contracted, and was concluded through the intermediary of a public power, the Church, and the role that the Church played was not only that of a witness, but it was she and she alone who created the juridical tie which until then the wills of the participants sufficed to establish. We know how, later, the civil authority was substituted in this function for the religious authority, and how at the same time the part played by society and its necessary formalities was extended.[8]

The history of the contract of adoption is still more instructive.

We have already seen with what facility and on what a large scale adoption was practiced among the Indian tribes of North America. It could give rise to all the forms of kinship. If the adopted was of the same age as the adopting, they became brothers and sisters; if the adopted was already a mother, she became the mother of the one who adopted her.

Among the Arabs, before Mohammed, adoption often served to establish real families.[9] It frequently happened that several persons would mutually adopt one another. They then became brothers and sisters, and the kinship which united them was just as strong as if they had been descended from a common origin. We find the same type of adoption among the Slavs. Very often, the members of different families became brothers and sisters and formed what is called a confraternity (*probatinstvo*). These societies were contracted for freely and without formality; agreement was enough to establish them. Moreover, the tie which binds these elective brothers is even stronger than that which results from natural fraternity.[10]

Among the Germans, adoption was probably quite as easy and frequent. Very simple ceremonies were enough to establish it.[11] But in India, Greece, and Rome, it was already subordinated to determined conditions. The one adopting had to be of a certain age, could not stand in such relation to the age of the adopted that it would be impossible to be his natural father. Ultimately, this change of family became a highly complex juridical operation which necessitated the intervention of a magistrate. At the same time, the number of those who could enjoy the right of adoption became more restricted. Only the father of a family or a bachelor *sui juris* could adopt, and the first could, only if he had no legitimate children.

In our current law the restrictive conditions have been even more multiplied. The adopted must be of age, the adopting must be more than fifty years of age, and have long treated the adopted as his child. We must notice that, thus limited, it has become a very rare event. Before the appearance of the French code, the whole procedure had almost completely fallen into disuse, and today it is, in certain countries such as Holland and lower Canada, not permitted at all.

At the same time that it became more rare, adoption lost its efficacy. In the beginning, adoptive kinship was in all respects similar to natural kinship. In Rome, the similarity was still very great. It was no longer, however, a perfect identity.[12] In the sixteenth century, the adopted no longer has the right of succession if the adoptive father dies intestate.[13] The French Code has reestablished this right, but the kinship to which the adoption gives rise does not extend beyond the adopting and the adopted.

We see how insufficient the traditional explanation is, which attributes this custom of adoption among ancient societies to the need of assuring the perpetuity of the ancestral cult. The peoples who have practiced it in the greatest and freest manner, as the Indians of America, the Arabs, the Slavs, had no such cult, and, furthermore, at Rome and Athens, where domestic religion was at its height, this law is for the first time submitted to control and restrictions. If it was able to satisfy these needs, it was not established to satisfy them, and, inversely, if it tends to disappear, it is not because we have less desire to perpetuate our name and our race. It is in the structure of actual societies and in the place which the family occupies that we must seek the determining cause for this change.

Another proof of the truth of this is that it has become even more impossible to leave a family by an act of private authority than to enter into it. As the kinship-tie does not result from a contract, it cannot be broken as a contract can. Among the Iroquois, we sometimes see a part of a clan leave to go to join a neighboring clan.[14] Among the Slavs, a member of the Zadruga who is tired of the common life can separate himself from the rest of the family and become a juridical stranger to it, even as he can be excluded by it.[15] Among the Germans, a ceremony of some slight complexity permitted every Frank who so desired to completely drop off all kinship-obligations.[16] In Rome, the son could not leave the family of his own will, and by this sign we recognize a more elevated social type. But the tie that the son could not break could be broken by the father. Thus was emancipation possible. Today neither the father nor the son can alter the natural state of domestic relations. They remain as birth determines them.

In short, at the same time that domestic obligations become more numerous, they take on, as is said, a public character. Not only in early times do they not have a contractual origin, but the role which contract plays in them becomes ever smaller. On the contrary, social control over the manner in which they form, break down, and are modified, becomes greater. The reason lies in the progressive effacement of segmental organization. The family, in truth, is for a long time a veritable social segment. In origin, it confounds itself with the clan. If, later, it becomes distinguished from the clan, it is as a part of the whole. It is a product of a secondary segmentation of the clan, identical with that which has given birth to the clan itself, and when the latter has disappeared, it still keeps the same quality. But everything segmental tends to be more and more reabsorbed into the social mass. That is why the family is forced to transform itself. Instead of remaining an autonomous society alongside of the great society, it becomes more and more involved in the system of social organs. It even becomes one of the organs, charged with special functions, and, accordingly, everything that happens within it is capable of general repercussions. That is what brings it about that the regulative organs of society are forced to intervene in order to exercise a moderating influence over the functioning of the family, or even, in certain cases, a positively arousing influence.[17]

But it is not only outside of contractual relations, it is in the play of these relations themselves that social action makes itself felt. For everything in the contract is not contractual. The only engagements which deserve this name are those which have been desired by the individuals and which have no other origin except in this manifestation of free will. Inversely, every obligation which has not been mutually consented to has nothing contractual about it. But wherever a contract exists, it is submitted to regulation which is the work of society and not that of individuals, and which becomes ever more voluminous and more complicated.

It is true that the contracting parties can, in certain respects, arrange to act contrary to the dispositions of the law. But, of course, their rights in this regard are not unlimited. For example, the agreement of the parties cannot make a contract valid if it does not satisfy the conditions of validity required by law. To be sure, in the great majority of cases, a contract is no longer restricted to determined forms. Still it must not be forgotten that there are in our Codes solemn contracts. But if law no longer has the formal exigencies of yesterday, it subjects contracts to obligations of a different sort. It refuses all obligatory force to engagements contracted by an incompetent, or without object, or with illicit purpose, or made by a person who cannot sell, or transacted over an article which cannot be sold. Among the obligations which it attaches to various contracts, there are some which cannot be changed by any stipulation. Thus, a vendor cannot fail in his obligation to guarantee the purchaser against any eviction which results from something personal to the vendor (art. 1628); he cannot fail to repay the purchase-price in case of eviction, whatever its origin, provided that the buyer has not known of the danger (art. 1629), nor to set forth clearly what is being contracted for (art. 1602). Indeed, in a certain measure, he cannot be exempt from guaranteeing against hidden defects (arts. 1641 and 1643), particularly when known. If it is a question of fixtures, it is the buyer who must not profit from the situation by imposing a price too obviously below the real value of the thing (art. 1674), etc. Moreover, everything that relates to proof, the nature of the actions to which the contract gives a right, the time in which they must be begun, is absolutely independent of individual transactions.

In other cases social action does not manifest itself only by the refusal to recognize a contract formed in violation of the law, but by a positive intervention. Thus, the judge can, whatever the terms of the agreement, grant a delay to a debtor (arts. 1184, 1244, 1655, 1900), or even oblige the borrower to restore the article to the lender before the term agreed upon, if the latter has pressing need of it (art. 1189). But what shows better than anything else that contracts give rise to obligations which have not been contracted for is that they "make obligatory not only what there is expressed in them, but also all consequences which equity, usage, or the law imputes from the nature of the obligation" (art. 1135). In virtue of this principle, there must be supplied in the contract "clauses pertaining to usage, although they may not be expressed therein" (art. 1160).

But even if social action should not express itself in this way, it would not cease to be real. This possibility of derogating the law, which seems to reduce the contractual right to the role of eventual substitute for contracts properly called, is, in the very great majority of cases, purely theoretical. We can convince ourselves of this by showing what it consists in.

To be sure, when men unite in a contract, it is because, through the division of labor, either simple or complex, they need each other. But in order for them to co-operate harmoniously, it is not enough that they enter into a relationship, nor even that they feel the state of mutual dependence in which they find themselves. It is still necessary that the conditions of this co-operation be fixed for the duration of their relations. The rights and duties of each must be defined, not only in view of the situation such as it presents itself at the moment when the contract is made, but with foresight for the circumstances which may arise to modify it. Otherwise, at every instant, there would be conflicts and endless difficulties. We must not forget that, if the division of labor makes interests solidary, it does not confound them; it keeps them distinct and opposite. Even as in the internal workings of the individual organism each organ is in conflict with others while co-operating with them, each of the contractants, while needing the other, seeks to obtain what he needs at the least expense; that is to say, to acquire as many rights as possible in exchange for the smallest possible obligations.

It is necessary therefore to pre-determine the share of each, but this cannot be done according to a preconceived plan. There is nothing in the nature of things from which one can deduce what the obligations of one or the other ought to be until a certain limit is reached. Every determination of this kind can only result in compromise. It is a compromise between the rivalry of interests present and their solidarity. It is a position of equilibrium which can be found only after more or less laborious experiments. But it is quite evident that we can neither begin these experiments over again nor restore this equilibrium at fresh expense every time that we engage in some contractual relation. We lack all ability to do that. It is not at the moment when difficulties surge upon us that we must resolve them, and, moreover, we can neither foresee the variety of possible circumstances in which our contract will involve itself, nor fix in advance with the aid of simple mental calculus what will be in each case the rights and duties of each, save in matters in which we have a very definite experience. Moreover, the material conditions of life oppose themselves to the repetition of such operations. For, at each instant, and often at the most inopportune, we find ourselves contracting, either for something we have bought, or sold, somewhere we are traveling, our hiring of one's services, some acceptance of hostelry, etc. The greater part of our relations with others is of a contractual nature. If, then, it were necessary each time to begin the struggles anew, to again go through the conferences necessary to establish firmly all the conditions of agreement for the present and the future, we would be put to rout. For all these reasons, if we were linked only by the terms of our contracts, as they are agreed upon, only a precarious solidarity would result.

But contract-law is that which determines the juridical consequences of our acts that we have not determined. It expresses the normal conditions of equilibrium, as they arise from themselves or from the average. A résumé of numerous, varied experiences, what we cannot foresee individually is there provided for, what we cannot regulate is there regulated, and this regulation imposes itself upon us, although it may not be our handiwork, but that of society and tradition. It forces us to assume obligations that we have not contracted for, in the exact sense of the word, since we have not deliberated upon them, nor even, occasionally, had any knowledge about them in advance. Of course, the initial act is always contractual, but there are consequences, sometimes immediate, which run over the limits of the contract. We co-operate because we wish to, but our voluntary co-operation creates duties for us that we did not desire.

From this point of view, the law of contracts appears in an entirely different light. It is no longer simply a useful complement of individual conventions; it is their fundamental norm. Imposing itself upon us with the authority of traditional experience, it constitutes the foundation of our contractual relations. We cannot evade it, except partially and accidentally. The law confers its rights upon us and subjects us to duties deriving from such acts of our will. We can, in certain cases, abandon them or change them for others. But both are none the less the normal type of rights and duties which circumstance lays upon us, and an express act is necessary for their modification. Thus, modifications are relatively rare. In principle, the rule applies; innovations are exceptional. The law of contracts exercises over us a regulative force of the greatest importance, since it determines what we ought to do and what we can require. It is a law which can be changed only by the consent of the parties, but so long as it is not abrogated or replaced, it guards its authority, and, moreover, a legislative act can be passed only in rare cases. There is, then, only a difference of degree between the law which regulates the obligations which that contract engenders and those which fix the other duties of citizens.

Finally, besides this organized, defined pressure which law exercises, there is one which comes from custom. In the way in which we make our contracts and in which we execute them, we are held to conform to rules which, though not sanctioned either directly or indirectly by any code, are none the less imperative. There are professional obligations, purely moral, which are, however, very strict. They are particularly apparent in the so-called liberal professions, and if they are perhaps less numerous in others, there is place for demanding them, as we shall see, if such demand is not the result of a morbid condition. But if this action is more diffuse than the preceding, it is just as social. Moreover, it is necessarily as much more extended as the contractual relations are more developed, for it is diversified like contracts.

In sum, a contract is not sufficient unto itself, but is possible only thanks to a regulation of the contract which is originally social. It is implied, first, because it has for its function much less the creation of new rules than the diversification in particular cases of pre-established rules; then, because it has and can have the power to bind only under certain conditions which it is necessary to define. If, in principle, society lends it an obligatory force, it is because, in general, the accord of particular wills suffices to assure, with the preceding reservations, the harmonious coming together of diffuse social functions. But if it conflicts with social purposes, if it tends to trouble the regular operation of organs, if, as is said, it is not just, it is necessary, while depriving it of all social value, to strip it of all authority as well. The role of society is not, then, in any case, simply to see passively that contracts are carried out. It is also to determine under what conditions they are executable, and if it is necessary, to restore them to their normal form. The agreement of parties cannot render a clause just which by itself is unjust, and there are rules of justice whose violation social justice prevents, even if it has been consented to by the interested parties.

A regulation whose extent cannot be limited in advance is

thus necessary. A contract, says Spencer, has for its object assuring the worker the equivalent of the expense which his work has cost him.[18] If such is truly the role of a contract, it will never be able to fulfill it unless it is more minutely regulated than it is today, for it surely would be a miracle if it succeeded in bringing about this equivalence. In fact, it is as much the gain which exceeds the expense, as the expense which exceeds the gain, and the disproportion is often striking. But, replies a whole school, if the gains are too small, the function will be abandoned for others. If they are too high, they will be sought after and this will diminish the profits. It is forgotten that one whole part of the population cannot thus quit its task, because no other is accessible to it. The very ones who have more liberty of movement cannot replace it in an instant. Such revolutions always take long to accomplish. While waiting, unjust contracts, unsocial by definition, have been executed with the agreement of society, and when the equilibrium in this respect has been reestablished, there is no reason for not breaking it for another.

There is no need for showing that this intervention, under its different forms, is of an eminently positive nature, since it has for its purpose the determination of the way in which we ought to co-operate. It is not it, it is true, which gives the impulse to the functions concurring, but once the concourse has begun, it rules it. As soon as we have made the first step towards co-operation, we are involved in the regulative action which society exercises over us. If Spencer qualified this as negative, it is because, for him, contract consists only in exchange. But, even from this point of view, the expression he employs is not exact. No doubt, when, after having an object delivered, or profiting from a service, I refuse to furnish a suitable equivalent, I take from another what belongs to him, and we can say that society, by obliging me to keep my promise, is only preventing an injury, an indirect aggression. But if I have simply promised a service without having previously received remuneration, I am not less held to keep my engagement. In this case, however, I do not enrich myself at the expense of another; I only refuse to be useful to him. Moreover, exchange, as we have seen, is not all there is to a contract. There is also the proper harmony of functions concurring. They are not only in contact for the short time during which things pass from one hand to another; but more extensive relations necessarily result from them, in the course of which it is important that their solidarity be not troubled.

Even the biological comparisons on which Spencer willingly bases his theory of free contract are rather the refutation of it. He compares, as we have done, economic functions to the visceral life of the individual organism, and remarks that the latter does not directly depend upon the cerebro-spinal system, but upon a special system whose principal branches are the great sympathetic and the pneumo-gastric. But if from this comparison he is permitted to induce, with some probability, that economic functions are not of a kind to be placed under the immediate influence of the social brain, it does not follow that they can be freed of all regulative influences, for, if the great sympathetic is, in certain measure, independent of the brain, it dominates the movements of the visceral system just as the brain does those of the muscles. If, then, there is in society a system of the same kind, it must have an analogous action over the organs subject to it.

What corresponds to it, according to Spencer, is this exchange of information which takes place unceasingly from one place to another through supply and demand, and which, accordingly, stops or stimulates production.[19] But there is nothing here which resembles a regulatory action. To transmit a new movement is not to command movements. This function pertains to the afferent nerves, but it has nothing in common with that of the nerve-ganglia. It is the latter which exercise the domination of which we have been speaking. Interposed in the path of sensations, it is exclusively through their mediation that the latter reflect themselves in movements. Very probably, if the study were more advanced, we would see that their role, whether they are central or not, is to assure the harmonious concourse of the functions that they govern, which would at every instant be disorganized if it had to vary with each variation of the excitatory impressions. The great social sympathetic must, then, comprise, besides a system of roads for transmission, organs truly regulative which, charged to combine the intestinal acts as the cerebral ganglion combines the external acts, would have the power either to stop the excitations, or to amplify them, or to moderate them according to need.

This comparison induces us to think that the regulative action to which economic life is actually submitted is not what it should normally be. Of course, it is not nil; we have just shown that. Either it is diffuse, or else it comes directly from the State. We will with difficulty find in contemporary societies regulative centres analogous to the ganglia of the great sympathetic. Assuredly, if this doubt had no other basis than the lack of symmetry between the individual and society, it would not merit any attention. But it must not be forgotten that up until recent times these intermediary organizations existed; they were the bodies of workers. We do not have to discuss here their advantages or disadvantages. Moreover, it is difficult to be objective about such discussion, for we cannot settle questions of practical utility without regard to personal feelings. But because of this fact alone, that an institution has been necessary to societies for centuries, it appears improbable that it should all at once fall away. No doubt, societies have changed, but it is legitimate to presume *a priori* that the changes through which they have passed demand less a radical destruction of this type of organization than a transformation. In any case, we have not lived under present conditions long enough to know if this state is normal and definitive or simply accidental and morbid. Even the uneasiness which is felt during this epoch in this sphere of social life does not seem to prejudge a favorable reply. We shall find in the rest of this work other facts which confirm this presumption.[20]

III

Finally, there is administrative law. We give this name to the totality of rules which determine, first, the functions of the central organ and their relations; then, the functions of the organs which are immediately subordinate to the first, their relations with one another, their relations with the first and with the diffuse functions of society. If we again borrow biological terminology which, though metaphorical, is none the less useful, we may say that these rules determine the way in which the cerebro-spinal system of the social organism functions. This system, in current parlance, is designated by the name, State.

There is no contesting the fact that social action which is thus expressed has a positive nature. In effect, its object is to fix the manner in which these special functions must co-operate. In certain respects, it even imposes such co-operation, for these various organs can be held together only with help imperatively demanded of each citizen. But, according to Spencer, this regulative system would be regressing as the industrial type gains sway over the military type, and finally the functions of the State would be reduced solely to administering justice.

The reasons employed in support of this proposition, however, are remarkably poor; they consist almost completely of a short comparison between England and France, and between England of yesterday and today. It is from this that Spencer claims to induce his general law of historical development.[21] The standards of proof, however, are not different in sociology from those in other sciences. To prove an hypothesis is not to show that it accounts very well for certain facts considered appropriate; one must make experiments with method. It must be shown that the phenomena between which we are establishing a relation either concur universally, or cannot exist one without the other, or that they vary in the same sense and in direct relationship. But some few examples thrown together in helter-skelter fashion do not constitute proof.

These facts taken by themselves do not prove anything of the kind. All that they prove is that the place of the individual becomes greater and the governmental power becomes *less absolute*. But there is no contradiction in the fact that the sphere of individual action grows at the same time as that of the State, or that the functions which are not made immediately dependent upon the central regulative system develop at the same time as it. Moreover, a power can be at once absolute and very simple. Nothing is less complex than the despotic government of a barbarian chief. The functions he fills are rudimentary and not very numerous. That is because the directive organ of social life can absorb all these in itself, without on that account being very highly developed if social life itself is not very highly developed. This organ exerts an exceptional force upon the rest of society, because there is nothing to hold it in check or to neutralize it. But it can very well happen that it takes up more volume at the same time that other organs are formed which balance it. It suffices on this account that the total volume of the organism be increased. No doubt, the action that it exerts under these conditions is no longer of the same nature, but the points at which it exercises its power have multiplied, and if it is less violent, it still imposes itself quite as formally. Acts of disobedience to constituted authority are no longer treated as sacrilegious, nor, consequently, repressed with the same severity. But they are not tolerated any the more, and these orders are more numerous and govern very different types. But the question which is posed is that of finding out, not if the coercive power which this regulative system dispenses is more or less intense, but whether this system itself has become more or less voluminous.

Once the problem has been thus formulated, there can be no doubt as to the solution. History surely shows, in very systematic fashion, that administrative law is as much more developed as societies approach a more elevated type. On the other hand, the farther back to origins we go, the more rudimentary is this type of law. The ideal State of Spencer is really the primitive form of the State. In fact, the only functions which normally pertain to the State in English philosophy are those relating to justice and to war, in the measure at least to which war is necessary. In lower societies, the State does not effectively play any other role. To be sure, these functions are not there conceived as they are now, but they are no different because of that. The whole tyrannical intervention which Spencer notes there is only one of the ways in which judicial power is exercised. In repressing attacks against religion, etiquette, against traditions of all sorts, the State fills the same office that judges do today when they protect the lives and property of individuals. But these duties become more and more numerous and varied as we approach higher social types. The very organ of justice, which is originally very simple, more and more moves towards differentiation. Various tribunals grow up, distinct magistracies are set up, the respective role of each is determined through its relations with others. A multitude of functions which were diffuse become concentrated. The care of educating the young, of protecting the public health, of presiding over the ways of administering public aid, of administering the means of transport and communication, little by little move over into the sphere of the central organ. Accordingly, the central organ develops and, at the same time, it progressively extends a more compact system over the whole surface of the territory, a system more and more complex with ramifications which displace or assimilate pre-existing local organs. Statistical services keep it informed of everything important that goes on in the organism. The system of international relations, that is, diplomacy, takes on greater and greater proportions. As institutions, such as great credit-establishments, are formed, having a general interest because of their dimensions and proportional multiplicity of function, the State exercises a moderating influence over them. Finally, even the military system, whose regression Spencer affirms, seems to develop and centralize itself in an uninterrupted manner.

This evolution is proved by so many evidences from historical fact that we do not think it necessary to go into any further detail in proof of it. If we compare tribes devoid of all central authority with centralized tribes, and the latter to the city, the city to feudal societies, feudal societies to present societies, we follow, step by step, the principal stages of development whose general march we have just traced. It is thus contrary to all method to regard the present dimensions of the governmental organ as a symptom of social illness, due to a concourse of accidental circumstances. Everything forces us to see in it a normal phenomenon, which holds even of the structure of higher societies, since it progresses in a perfectly continuous way, as societies tend to approach this type.

We can, moreover, show, at least in the large, how this results from the very progress of the division of labor and from the transformation which effects the passage of societies from a segmental type to an organized type.

As each segment has its life peculiar to it, it forms a small society within the great, and has, consequently, its own regulative organs, just as the great society. But their vitality is necessarily proportional to the intensity of this local life. They cannot fail to weaken when it is itself weakened. But we know that this enfeeblement is produced with the progressive effacement of segmental organization. The central organ, finding less resistance before it, since the forces which held it in check have lost their energy, develops and takes unto itself these functions, similar to those which it exercises, but which can no longer be held by those who formerly held them. These local organs, instead of holding to their individuality and remaining diffuse, become confounded in the central system which grows accordingly, grows in proportion to the vastness of society and the completeness of the fusion. That is to say, it is as much more voluminous as societies are of a more elevated type.

This phenomenon is produced with mechanical necessity, and, moreover, it is useful, for it corresponds to the new state of things. In the measure that society ceases to be formed by a repetition of similar segments, the regulative system must itself cease to be formed by a repetition of segmental, autonomous organs. We do not wish to imply, however, that the State normally absorbs into itself all the regulative organs of society no matter what they are, but only those which are of the same type as its own; that is to say, those which preside over life in general. As for those which take care of special functions, such as economic functions, they are outside its sphere of influence. It can even produce among them coalescence of the same kind, but not between them and it, or at least, if they are within the power of superior authorities, they remain distinct from them. Among the vertebrates, the cerebro-spinal system is very highly developed. It has influence over the great sympathetic, but it permits this latter great autonomy.

In the second place, when society is made up of segments, whatever is produced in one of the segments has as little chance of re-echoing in the others as the segmental organization is strong. The cellular system naturally lends itself to the localization of social events and their consequents. Thus it happens that in a colony of polyps one of the individuals can be sick without the others feeling it. This is no longer true when society is made up of a system of organs. According to their mutual dependence, what strikes one strikes the others, and thus every change, even slightly significant, takes on a general interest.

This generalization is further validated by two other circumstances. The more divided labor is, the less each social organ consists of distinct parts. As large-scale industry is substituted for small, the number of different enterprises grows less. Each has more relative importance, because it represents a greater fraction of the whole. Whatever happens therein has much more extensive social repercussions. The closing of a small shop causes very little trouble, which is felt only within small compass. The failure of a great industrial company results, on the contrary, in public distress. Moreover, as the progress of the division of labor demands a very great concentration of the social mass, there is between the different parts of the same tissue, of the same organ, or the same system, a more intimate contact which makes happenings much more contagious. A movement in one part rapidly communicates itself to others. We need only look at how speedily a strike becomes general today in the same body of workers. But distress of some general scope cannot be produced without affecting the higher centres. These, being badly affected, are forced to intervene, and this intervention is more frequent as the social type is more elevated. But, on that account, it is necessary that they be organized. They must extend their ramifications in all directions in such a way as to be in relation with different regions of the organism, also in such manner as to hold in immediate dependence certain organs whose free play would, on occasion, have exceptionally grave repercussions. In short, since their functions become more numerous and complex, it is necessary for the organ which serves as their foundation to develop, just as the body of juridical rules which determine them.

To the reproach often leveled against him for contradicting

his own doctrine by admitting that the development of the higher centres has been accomplished in a sense inverse in societies and organisms, Spencer replies that the different variations of the organ are linked to corresponding variations of the function. According to him, the essential role of the cerebro-spinal system would be to regulate the relations of the individual with the outside world, to combine movements either for grasping booty or escaping the enemy.[22] As a system of attack and defense, it is naturally very voluminous among the most elevated organisms where the external relations are themselves very developed. Such is the case in military societies which live in a state of chronic hostility with their neighbors. On the contrary, among industrial peoples war is the exception; social interests are principally of an internal order; the external regulative system, no longer having the same reason for existence, necessarily regresses.

But this explanation rests on a double error.

First, every organism, whether or not it has predatory instincts, lives in an environment with which it has relations as much more numerous as it is more complex. If, then, the relations of hostility diminish in the measure that societies become more pacific, they are replaced by others. Industrial peoples have a commerce developed differently from that which lower peoples have with one another, as bellicose as they are. We are speaking, not of the commerce which is established between individuals, but of that which unites social bodies together. Each society has general interests to defend against other societies, if not through force of arms, at least through negotiations, coalitions, treaties.

Moreover, it is not true that the brain presides over only external relations. Not only can it modify the state of the organs through means wholly internal, but even when it acts externally, it exercises its action within. Even the most internal viscera cannot function without the aid of materials which come from without, and as the brain sovereignly takes care of these materials, it thus has an influence over the total organism at all times. The stomach, it is said, has nothing to do with this order, but the presence of food is enough to excite peristaltic movements. If food is present, however, the brain has willed it, and the food is there in the quantity that it has fixed and the quality it has chosen. It does not command the beatings of the heart, but it can, by appropriate treatment, retard or accelerate them. There are not many tissues which do not undergo some one of the disciplines that it imposes, and the empire that it rules is as much more extensive and profound as the animal is of a more elevated type. Its true role is presiding, not only over relations from without, but over the totality of life. Its function is as complex as life itself is rich and concentrated. The same is true of societies. The governmental organ is more or less considerable, not because the people are more or less pacific, but rather because its growth is proportional to the progress of the division of labor, societies comprising more different organs the more intimately solidary they are.

IV

The following propositions sum up the first part of our work.

Social life comes from a double source, the likeness of consciences and the division of social labor. The individual is socialized in the first case, because, not having any real individuality, he becomes, with those whom he resembles, part of the same collective type; in the second case, because, while having a physiognomy and a personal activity which distinguishes him from others, he depends upon them in the same measure that he is distinguished from them, and consequently upon the society which results from their union.

The similitude of consciences gives rise to juridical rules which, with the threat of repressive measures, impose uniform beliefs and practices upon all. The more pronounced this is, the more completely is social life confounded with religious life, and the nearer to communism are economic institutions.

The division of labor gives rise to juridical rules which determine the nature and the relations of divided functions, but whose violation calls forth only restitutive measures without any expiatory character.

Each of these bodies of juridical rules is, moreover, accompanied by a body of purely moral rules. Where penal law is very voluminous, common morality is very extensive; that is to say, there is a multitude of collective practices placed under the protection of public opinion. Where restitutive law is highly developed, there is an occupational morality for each profession. In the interior of the same group of workers, there exists an opinion, diffuse in the entire extent of this circumscribed aggregate, which, without being furnished with legal sanctions, is rendered obedience. There are usages and customs common to the same order of functionaries which no one of them can break without incurring the censure of the corporation.[23] This morality is distinguished from the preceding by differences analogous to those which separate the two corresponding types of law. It is localized in a limited region of society. Moreover, the repressive character of the sanctions attaching to it is much less accentuated. Professional misdeeds call forth reprobation much more feeble than attacks against public morality.

The rules of occupational morality and justice, however, are as imperative as the others. They force the individual to act in view of ends which are not strictly his own, to make concessions, to consent to compromises, to take into account interests higher than his own. Consequently, even where society relies most completely upon the division of labor, it does not become a jumble of juxtaposed atoms, between which it can establish only external, transient contacts. Rather the members are united by ties which extend deeper and far beyond the short moments during which the exchange is made. Each of the functions that they exercise is, in a fixed way, dependent upon others, and with them forms a solidary system. Accordingly, from the nature of the chosen task permanent duties arise. Because we fill some certain domestic or social function, we are involved in a complex of obligations from which we have no right to free ourselves. There is, above all, an organ upon which we are tending to depend more and more; this is the State. The points at which we are in contact with it multiply as do the occasions when it is entrusted with the duty of reminding us of the sentiment of common solidarity.

Thus, altruism is not destined to become, as Spencer desires, a sort of aggreeable ornament to social life, but it will forever be its fundamental basis. How can we ever really dispense with it? Men cannot live together without acknowledging, and, consequently, making mutual sacrifices, without tying themselves to one another with strong, durable bonds. Every society is a moral society. In certain respects, this character is even more pronounced in organized societies. Because the individual is not sufficient unto himself, it is from society that he receives everything necessary to him, as it is for society that he works. Thus is formed a very strong sentiment of the state of dependence in which he finds himself. He becomes accustomed to estimating it at its just value, that is to say, in regarding himself as part of a whole, the organ of an organism. Such sentiments naturally inspire not only mundane sacrifices which assure the regular development of daily social life, but even, on occasion, acts of complete self-renunciation and wholesale abnegation. On its side, society learns to regard its members no longer as things over which it has rights, but as co-operators whom it cannot neglect and towards whom it owes duties. Thus, it is wrong to oppose a society which comes from a community of beliefs to one which has a co-operative basis, according only to the first a moral character, and seeing in the latter only an economic grouping. In reality, co-operation also has its intrinsic morality. There is, however, reason to believe, as we shall see later, that in contemporary societies this morality has not yet reached the high development which would now seem necessary to it.

But it is not of the same nature as the other. The other is strong only if the individual is not. Made up of rules which are practiced by all indistinctly, it receives from this universal, uniform practice an authority which bestows something superhuman upon it, and which puts it beyond the pale of discussion. The co-operative society, on the contrary, develops in the measure that individual personality becomes stronger. As regulated as a function may be, there is a large place always left for personal initiative. A great many of the obligations thus sanctioned have their origin in a choice of the will. It is we who choose our professions, and even certain of our domestic functions. Of course, once our resolution has ceased to be internal and has been externally translated by social consequences, we are tied down. Duties are imposed upon us that we have not expressly desired. It is, however, through a voluntary act that this has taken place. Finally, because these rules of conduct relate, not to the conditions of common life, but to the different forms of professional activity, they have a more temporal character, which, while lessening their obligatory force, renders them more accessible to the action of men.

There are, then, two great currents of social life to which two types of structure, not less different, correspond.

Of these currents, that which has its origin in social similitudes first runs on alone and without a rival. At this moment, it confounds itself with the very life of society; then, little by little, it canalizes, rarefies, while the second is always growing. Indeed, the segmental structure is more and more covered over by the other, but without ever completely disappearing.

We have just established the reality of this relation of inverse variation. We shall find the causes for it in the following book.

8

DIVISION OF LABOR IN
SOCIETY: CONSEQUENCES

I

THE PRECEDING enables us to have a better understanding of the manner in which the division of labor functions in society.

From this point of view, the division of social labor is distinguished from the division of physiological labor by an essential characteristic. In the organism, each cell has its defined role, and cannot change it. In societies, tasks have never been so immutably distributed. Even where the forms of organization are most rigid, the individual can move about in the interior of the form in which he is fixed with a certain liberty. In primitive Rome, the plebeian could freely undertake all the functions not exclusively reserved to the patricians. Even in India, the careers which were allowed to each caste had sufficient generality[1] to permit some choice. In every land, if the enemy has seized the capital, that is to say, the very brain of the nation, social life is not suspended because of that, but, at the end of a relatively short time, another city is found to fulfill this complex function, although it had in no way been prepared for it.

As work is divided more, this suppleness and liberty become greater. The same individual is seen to raise himself from the

From *The Division of Labor in Society*, translated and with an introduction by George Simpson (New York: Macmillan Co., 1933), pp. 329–50. Originally published as *De la division du travail social: Etude sur l'organisation des sociétés supérieures* (Paris Félix Alcan, 1893); 2d ed. with a new preface entitled "Quelques remarques sur les groupements professionels," 1902.

most humble to the most important occupations. The principle according to which all employments are equally accessible to all citizens would not be generalized to this point if it did not receive constant applications. What is still more frequent is that a worker leaves his career for a neighboring one. When scientific activity was not specialized, the scholar, encompassing all science, could scarcely change his function, for it would have been necessary to renounce science itself. Today, it often happens that he devotes himself to different sciences, passing from chemistry to biology, from physiology to psychology, from psychology to sociology. This aptitude for successively taking very diverse forms is nowhere so discernible as in the economic world. As nothing is more variable than the tastes and needs these functions answer to, commerce and industry must be held in a perpetual state of unstable equilibrium to be able to yield to all the changes produced in the demand. Whereas formerly immobility was the almost natural state of capital, even the law forbidding too easy mobilization, today it can scarcely be followed in all its transformations, so great is the rapidity with which it is engaged in enterprise, withdrawing from one to rest elsewhere where it remains only for some moments. Thus, workers must be ready to follow it, and, consequently, to serve in different employments.

The nature of the causes upon which the division of labor in society depends explains this character. If the role of each cell is fixed in an immutable manner, it is because this is imposed by birth. It is imprisoned in a system of hereditary customs which mark its path, and which cannot be overcome. It cannot even sensibly modify them, because these customs have too profoundly affected the substance from which it is formed. Its structure predetermines its life. We have just seen that it is not the same in society. Origins do not determine the special career of an individual; his congenital constitution does not predestine him necessarily to one role alone, making him incapable for any other, but he receives from heredity only very general dispositions, consequently very supple, and able to take different forms.

It is true that he determines them himself by the use which he makes of them. As he must employ his faculties in particular functions and specialize them, he is forced to make those immediately required for his use undergo very intensive cultivation, and let the others partially atrophy. Thus, he cannot develop his brain beyond a certain point without losing a part of his muscular force, or his reproductive power; he cannot rouse his powers of analysis and reflection to a high pitch without enfeebling the energy of his will and the vivacity of his sentiments, nor make a habit of observation without losing his ability at dialectic. Moreover, by the very force of things, that faculty which he makes keen to the detriment of others is forced to assume definite forms in which it becomes imprisoned little by little. This faculty gets into the habit of certain practices, of functioning in a set way which becomes more difficult to change as it continues to endure. But, as this specialization results from purely individual efforts, it has neither the fixity nor the rigidity which a long heredity alone can produce. These practices are very supple, because they are very young. As it is the individual who engaged himself in them, he can disengage himself, and betake himself to new ones. He can call forth faculties dulled through dormancy, infuse new life into them, replace them in their original state, although, truly, this kind of resurrection is by that time very difficult.

One is tempted, at first glance, to see in these facts of the phenomena of regression either proof of a certain inferiority, or at least a transitory state of an incomplete being in process of formation. In effect, it is especially among lower animals that the different parts of the aggregate can quite easily change their functions and substitute them for others. But in so far as organization becomes perfected, it becomes more and more impossible for them to leave the role which is assigned to them. One is thus led to ask whether society may not some day arrive at a point where it will assume an arrested form, where each organ, each individual, will have a definite function and will no longer change. This was, it seems, Comte's idea;[2] it is certainly Spencer's.[3] This induction, however, is precipitate, for the phenomenon of substitution is not special to very simple beings, but is equally observable in the highest ranks of the hierarchy, and especially in the higher organs of the higher organisms. Thus, "the consecutive disturbances in the ablation of certain domains of the cerebral surface very often disappear after a lapse of time. This phenomenon can only be explained by the following supposition: other elements come in to take over the function of the suppressed elements. This implies that the substituted elements are employed at new functions. . . . An element which, during the normal relations of conduction, causes a visual sensation, becomes, thanks to a change of conditions, the cause of a tactile sensation, of a muscular sensation, or of a motor innervation. Indeed, one is almost obliged to suppose that, if the central network of nervous cords has the power to transmit phenomena of diverse natures to one and the same element, this element will be able to unite in itself a plurality of different functions."[4] Thus, the motor-nerves can become centripetal, and the sensible nerves centrifugal.[5] Finally, if a new partition of all these functions can occur when the conditions of transmission are modified, there is reason for presuming, according to Wundt, that "even in its normal state, it presents oscillations or variations which depend upon the variable development of individuals."[6]

Thus it is that a rigid specialization is not necessarily a mark of superiority. It is far from being a good thing in every circumstance; often what the organ does *not* congeal in its role is of advantage. Of course, where the environment itself is fixed, even a very great fixity is useful. This is the case, for example, with the nutritive functions of the individual organism. They are not subject to great changes in the same organic type. Consequently, there is an advantage rather than inconvenience from their assuming a definitely stationary form. That is why the polyp, whose internal and external tissue so easily replace each other, is less well armed for the struggle than more elevated animals with whom this substitution is always incomplete and almost impossible. But it is quite otherwise when the circumstances upon which the organ depends change often. Then it must itself change or perish. That is what happens with complex functions which adapt us to complex milieux. The latter, because of their very complexity, are essentially unstable. Some break in equilibrium, or some innovation, is always being produced. To remain adapted, the function must always be ready to change, to accommodate itself to new situations. But, of all existing environments, there is none more complex than the social. Thus, it is very natural that the specialization of social functions is not as definitive as that of biological functions, and, since this complexity increases with a greater division of labor, this elasticity becomes ever greater. No doubt, it is always enclosed in certain limits, but they steadily recede.

What definitely attests to this relative and ever growing flexibility is that the function is becoming more and more independent of the organ. In effect, nothing realizes a function as much as being tied to a structure that is highly defined, for, of all arrangements, there is none more stable nor more opposed to changes. Structure is not only a way of acting; it is a way of existing that necessitates a certain way of acting. It implies not only a certain manner of vibrating, special to molecules, but an arrangement of the latter which makes any other kind of vibrations almost impossible. If, then, function gains greater suppleness, it is because it is less strictly related to the form of the organ, because the tie between the two becomes looser.

We observe, in effect, that this loosening comes about in proportion to the greater complexity of societies and their functions. In lower societies, where tasks are general and simple, the different classes charged with their execution are distinguished from one another by morphological characters. In other words, each organ is anatomically distinguished from the others. As each caste, each stratum of the population, has its way of eating, dressing, etc., so these differences are accompanied by physical differences. As Spencer tells us. Fijian chiefs are very tall, strongly built, and very muscular; the people of lower class are emaciated from excessive work and poor food. In the Sandwich Islands, Spencer continues, the chiefs are large and vigorous, and their external appearance is so different from the people of lower station that one might think the latter were of a different race. We learn from Spencer that Ellis, confirming Cook, says that the Tahitian chiefs are almost without exception as far above the peasants in physical force as they are in station and wealth, and that Erskine notices an analogous difference among the natives of the Tonga Islands.[7]

In higher societies, on the contrary, these differences disappear. Many facts tend to prove that men executing different social functions are distinguished less than heretofore by the form of their bodies, by their features, and their appearance. Some are even offended because they do not have the traits of their calling. If, according to Tarde, statistics and anthropometry were used to determine the constitutive characters of various occupational types with greater precision, we would probably find that they differ less than in the past, particularly if we consider the greater differentiation of functions.

A fact which confirms this assumption is that the custom of occupational dress more and more falls into desuetude. In effect, although modes of dress have assuredly served to make functional differences clear, we cannot see in this role their only reason for existing, since they disappear as social functions become more differentiated. They must, then, correspond to differences of another nature. If, moreover, before the institution of this practice, the men of different classes had not already presented apparent somatic differences, we do see why they should have thought of distinguishing themselves in this fashion. These external signs of conventional origin must have been invented only in imitation of external signs of natural origin. Dress, to us, does not signify anything other than the occupational type which, in order to manifest itself in clothes, marks them with its imprint, and differentiates them in its own image. They are, as it were, a prolongation of it. This is particularly evident with the distinctions which play the same role as dress and certainly derive from the same causes, such as the custom of cutting the beard in a certain way, or of not having a beard at all, or of having the hair cut short or left long, etc. They are the very traits of the occupational type which, after being produced and spontaneously constituted, reproduces itself imitatively and artificially. The diversity of dress symbolizes, then, above all, morphological differences. Consequently, if differences in dress disappear, it is because morphological differences are obliterated. If the members of different occupations no longer see the need of distinguishing themselves from others by visual signs, it is because this distinction no longer corresponds to anything in reality. Functional differences, however, tend to become more numerous and more pronounced; this is because morphological types are leveling off. That certainly does not mean that all brains are indifferently apt at every function, but that their functional indifference, while remaining limited, becomes greater.

But this enfranchisement of function, far from being a mark of inferiority, only proves that it is becoming more complex. For if it is more difficult for the constitutive elements of tissues to arrange themselves in a certain way and incarnate it, and, consequently, to keep it together and imprison it, that is because it is made up of dispositions that are too subtle and delicate. It may even be asked if, beginning with a certain degree of complexity, it does not definitely escape them, if it does not end by breaking away from the organ in such a way that it is impossible for the latter to reabsorb it completely. That, in fact, it is independent of the form of substratum is a truth long ago established by naturalists. When it is general and simple, however, it cannot long remain in this state of liberty because the organ easily assimilates it, and, at the same time, shackles it. But there is no reason for supposing that this power of assimilation is indefinite. Everything points, on the contrary, to the fact that, from a certain moment, the disproportion between the simplicity of the molecular arrangements and the complexity of functional arrangements becomes ever greater. The link between the second and the first loosens. Of course, it does not follow that function can exist without any organ, nor even that it can ever lack all relation with it. But the relation does become less immediate.

Progress would then result in more and more detaching, without ever separating, however, function from the organ, life from matter; consequently, in spiritualizing it, in making it more supple, more unrestrained, more complex. It is because spiritualism believes that the character of higher forms of existence is such that it always refuses to consider the psychic life a simple consequence of the molecular constitution of the brain. In fact, we know that the functional indifference of different regions of the encephalos, if not absolute, is nevertheless great. Hence, cerebral functions are the last to assume an immutable form. They remain plastic longer than the others, and defend their plasticity the more complex they are. Thus, their evolution is prolonged much later with the learned man than with the uncultivated. If, then, social functions present this same character in still more telling fashion, it is not in accordance with an exception without precedent, but because they correspond to a still more elevated stage in the development of nature.

II

In determining the principal cause of the progress of the division of labor, we have at the same time determined the essential factor of what is called civilization.

Civilization is itself the necessary consequence of the changes which are produced in the volume and in the density of societies. If science, art, and economic activity develop, it is in accordance with a necessity which is imposed upon men. It is because there is, for them, no other way of living in the new conditions in which they have been placed. From the time that the number of individuals among whom social relations are established begins to increase, they can maintain themselves only by greater specialization, harder work, and intensification of their faculties. From this general stimulation, there inevitably results a much higher degree of culture. From this point of view, civilization appears, not as an end which moves people by its attraction for them, not as a good foreseen and desired in advance, of which they seek to assure themselves the largest possible part, but as the effect of a cause, as the necessary resultant of a given state. It is not the pole towards which historic development is moving and to which men seek to get nearer in order to be happier or better, for neither happiness nor morality necessarily increases with the intensity of life. They move because they must move, and what determines the speed of this march is the more or less strong pressure which they exercise upon one another, according to their number.

This does not mean that civilization has no use, but that it is not the services that it renders that make it progress. It develops because it cannot fail to develop. Once effectuated, this development is found to be generally useful, or, at least, it is utilized. It responds to needs formed at the same time because they depend upon the same causes. But this is an adjustment after the fact. Yet, we must notice that the good it renders in this direction is not a positive enrichment, a growth in our stock of happiness, but only repairs the losses that it has itself caused. It is because this superactivity of general life fatigues and weakens our nervous system that it needs reparations proportionate to its expenditures, that is to say, more varied and complex satisfactions. In that, we see even better how false it is to make civilization the function of the division of labor; it is only a consequence of it. It can explain neither the existence nor the progress of the division of labor, since it has, of itself, no intrinsic or absolute value, but, on the contrary, has a reason for existing only in so far as the division of labor is itself found necessary.

We shall not be astonished by the importance attached to the numerical factor if we notice the very capital role it plays in the history of organisms. In effect, what defines a living being is the double property it has of nourishing itself and reproducing itself, and reproduction is itself only a consequence of nourishment. Therefore, the intensity of organic life is proportional, all things being equal, to the activity of nourishment, that is, to the number of elements that the organism is capable of incorporating. Hence, what has not only made possible, but even necessitated the appearance of complex organisms is that, under certain conditions, the more simple organisms remain grouped together in a way to form more voluminous aggregates. As the constitutive parts of the animal are more numerous, their relations are no longer the same, the conditions of social life are changed, and it is these changes which, in turn, determine both the division of labor, polymorphism, and the concentration of vital forces and their greater energy. The growth of organic substance is, then, the fact which dominates all zoological development. It is not surprising that social development is submitted to the same law.

Moreover, without recourse to arguments by analogy, it is easy to explain the fundamental role of this factor. All social life is made up of a system of facts which come from positive and durable relations established between a plurality of individuals. It is, thus, as much more intense as the reactions exchanged between the component units are themselves more frequent and more energetic. But, upon what does this frequency and this energy depend? Upon the nature of the elements present, upon their more or less great vitality? But we shall see in this very chapter that individuals are much more a product of common life than they are determinants of it. If from each of them we take away everything due to social action, the residue that we obtain, besides being picayune, is not capable of presenting much variety. Without the diversity of social conditions upon which they depend, the differences which separate them would be inexplicable. It is not, then, in the unequal aptitudes of men that we must seek the cause for the unequal development of societies. Will it be in the unequal duration of these relations? But time, by itself, produces nothing. It is only necessary in bringing latent energies to light. There remains no other variable factor than the number of individuals in relation and their material and moral proximity, that is to say, the volume and density of society. The more numerous they are and the more they act upon one another, the more they react with force and rapidity; consequently, the more intense social life becomes. But it is this intensification which constitutes civilization.[8]

But, while being an effect of necessary causes, civilization can become an end, an object of desire, in short, an ideal. Indeed, at each moment of a society's history, there is a certain intensity of the collective life which is normal, given the number and distribution of the social units. Assuredly, if everything happens normally, this state will be realized of itself, but we cannot bring it to pass that things will happen normally. If health is in nature, so is sickness. Health is, indeed, in societies as in individual organisms, only an ideal type which is nowhere entirely realized. Each healthy individual has more or less numerous traits of it, but there is none that unites them all. Thus, it is an end worthy of pursuit to seek to bring society to this degree of perfection.

Moreover, the direction to follow in order to attain this end can be laid out. If, instead of letting causes engender their effects by chance and according to the energy in them, thought intervenes to direct the course, it can spare men many painful efforts. The development of the individual reproduces that of the species in abridged fashion; he does not pass through all the stages that it passed through; there are some he omits and others he passes through more quickly because the experiences of the race help him to accelerate them. But thought can produce analogous results, for it is equally a utilization of anterior experience, with a view to facilitating future experience. By thought, moreover, one must not understand exclusively scientific knowledge of means and ends. Sociology, in its present state, is hardly in a position to lead us efficaciously to the solution of these practical problems. But beyond these clear representations in the milieu in which the scholar moves, there are obscure ones to which tendencies are linked. For need to stimulate the will, it is not necessary that it be clarified by science. Obscure gropings are enough to teach men that there is something lacking, to awaken their aspirations and at the same time make them feel in what direction they ought to bend their efforts.

Hence, a mechanistic concept of society does not preclude ideals, and it is wrong to reproach it with reducing man to the status of an inactive witness of his own history. What is an ideal, really, if not an anticipated representation of a desired result whose realization is possible only thanks to this very anticipation? Because things happen in accordance with laws, it does not follow that we have nothing to do. We shall perhaps find such an objective mean, because, in sum, it is only a question of living in a state of health. But this is to forget that, for the cultivated man, health consists in regularly satisfying his most elevated needs as well as others, for the first are no less firmly rooted in his nature than the second. It is true that such an ideal is near, that the horizons it opens before us have nothing unlimited about them. In any event, it cannot consist in exalting the forces of society beyond measure, but only in developing them to the limit marked by the definite state of the social milieu. All excess is bad as well as all insufficiency. But what other ideal can we propose? To seek to realize a civilization superior to that demanded by the nature of surrounding conditions is to desire to turn illness loose in the very society of which we are part, for it is not possible to increase collective activity beyond the degree determined by the state of the social organism without compromising health. In fact, in every epoch there is a certain refinement of civilization whose sickly character is attested by the uneasiness and restlessness which accompanies it. But there is never anything desirable about sickness.

But if the ideal is always definite, it is never definitive. Since progress is a consequence of changes in the social milieu, there is no reason for supposing that it must ever end. For it to have a limit, it would be necessary for the milieu to become stationary at some given moment. But such an hypothesis is contrary to the most legitimate inductions. As long as there are distinct societies, the number of social units will necessarily be variable in each of them. Even supposing that the number of births ever becomes constant, there will always be movements of population from one country to another, through violent conquests or slow and unobtrusive infiltrations. Indeed, it is impossible for the strongest peoples not to tend to incorporate the feeblest, as the most dense overflow into the least dense. That is a mechanical law of social equilibrium not less necessary than that which governs the equilibrium of liquids. For it to be otherwise, it would be necessary for all human societies to have the same vital energy and the same density. What is irrepresentable would only be so because of the diversity of habitats.

It is true that this source of variations would be exhausted if all humanity formed one and the same society. But, besides our not knowing whether such an ideal is realizable, in order for progress to cease it would still be necessary for the relations between social units in the interior of this gigantic society to be themselves recalcitrant to all change. It would be necessary for them always to remain distributed in the same way, for not only the total aggregate but also each of the elementary aggregates of which it would be formed, to keep the same dimensions. But such a uniformity is impossible, solely because these partial groups do not all have the same extent nor the same vitality. Population cannot be concentrated in the same way at all points; it is inevitable that the greatest centres, those where life is most intense, exercise an attraction for the others proportionate to their importance. The migrations which are thus produced result in further concentrating social units in certain regions, and, consequently, in determining new advances there which irradiate little by little from the homes in which they were born into the rest of the country. Moreover, these changes call for others, without it being possible to say where the repercussions stop. In fact, far from societies approaching a stationary position in proportion to their development, they become, on the contrary, more mobile and more plastic.

If, nevertheless, Spencer could claim that social evolution has a limit which cannot be passed,[9] that is because, according to him, progress has no other reason for existing than to adapt the individual to the cosmic environment which surrounds him. For this thinker, perfection consists in the growth of individual life, that is, in a more complete correspondence between the organism and its physical conditions. As for society, it is one of the means by which this correspondence is established rather than the object of a special correspondence. Because the individual is not alone in the world, but is surrounded by rivals who dispute over the means of existence, he has every interest in establishing between himself and those like him relations such that they will be of use to him rather than harm him. Thus society was born, and all social progress consists in ameliorating these relations in such a way as to make them more completely produce the effect in view of which they were established. Thus, in spite of the biological analogies upon which he lays stress Spencer does not see a reality *sui generis* in society, which exists by itself and by virtue of specific and necessary causes, and which, consequently, confound themselves with man's own nature, and to which he is held to adapt himself in order to live, just as to his physical environment—but he sees it as an arrangement instituted by individuals to extend individual life in length and breadth.[10] It consists entirely in co-operation, whether positive or negative, and both have no other object than the adapting of the individual to his physical environment. Of course, society is in this sense a secondary condition of this adaptation; it can, in accordance with the way in which it is organized, lead man to, or keep him from, a state of perfect equilibrium, but it is not itself a contributory factor in the determination of the nature of this equilibrium. Moreover, as the cosmic environment is relatively constant, as changes in it are infinitely few and far between, the development whose object is to put us in harmony with it is necessarily limited. It is inevitable that a moment will arrive when there will no longer be any external relations to which some internal relations do not correspond. Then, social progress cannot fail to halt, since it will have arrived at the goal for which it was headed and which was its reason for existing. It will have been achieved.

But, under these conditions, the very progress of the individual becomes inexplicable.

In short, why should he aim for this more perfect correspondence with the physical environment? In order to be happier? We have already disposed of this point. We cannot say of a correspondence that it is more complete than another simply because it is more complex. Indeed, we speak of an organism being in equilibrium when it responds in an appropriate manner, not to all external forces, but only to those which make an impression upon it. If there are some which do not affect it, it is as if they did not exist, and, accordingly, it does not have to adapt itself to them. Whatever may be their material proximity, they are outside its circle of adaptation because it is outside the sphere of their action. If, then, the subject is of a simple, homogeneous constitution, there will be only a small number of external circumstances which will naturally arouse it, and consequently it will respond to these stimuli, that is, realize a state of irreproachable equilibrium with very little effort. If, on the contrary, it is very complex, the conditions of adaptation will be more numerous and more complicated, but the adaptation itself will not be more complete on that account. Because many stimuli which received no response from the nervous system of men who came before us act upon us, we are forced, in order to adjust ourselves, to a more considerable development. But the product of this development, that is, the adjustment which results from it, is not more perfect in one case than in the other. It is only different because the organisms which are adjusted are themselves different. The savage whose epidermis does not feel the variations in temperature very much is as well adapted as the civilized man who protects himself with clothes.

If, then, man does not depend upon a variable milieu, we do not see what reason he would have had for varying. Hence, society is itself, not the secondary condition, but the determining factor in progress. It is a reality which is no more our work than the external world, and to which, consequently, we must submit in order to exist. It is because it changes that we must change. For progress to halt, it would be necessary at some moment for the social milieu to come to a stationary position, and we have just shown that such an hypothesis is contrary to all the precepts of science.

Thus, not only does a mechanistic theory of progress not deprive us of an ideal, but it permits us to believe that we shall never lack for one. Precisely because the ideal depends upon the essentially mobile social milieu, it ceaselessly changes. There is no reason for fearing that the world will ever fail us, that our activity will come to an end and that our horizon will be closed. But, although we never pursue any but definite, limited ends, there is, and there will always be, between the extreme points at which we arrive and the end towards which we are tending, a free field open to our efforts.

III

With societies, individuals are transformed in accordance with the changes produced in the number of social units and their relations.

First, they are made more and more free of the yoke of the organism. An animal is almost completely under the influence of his physical environment; its biological constitution predetermines its existence. Man, on the contrary, is dependent upon social causes. Of course, animals also form societies, but, as they are very restricted, collective life is very simple. They are also stationary because the equilibrium of such small societies is necessarily stable. For these two reasons, it easily fixes itself in the organism. It not only has its roots in the organism, but it is entirely enveloped in it to such a point that it loses its own characteristics. It functions through a system of instincts, of reflexes which are not essentially distinct from those which assure the functioning of organic life. They present, it is true, the particular characteristic of adapting the individual to the social environment, not to the physical environment, and are caused by occurrences of the common life. They are not of different nature, however, from those which, in certain cases, determine without any previous education the necessary movements in locomotion. It is quite otherwise with man, because the societies he forms are much vaster. Even the smallest we know of are more extensive than the majority of animal societies. Being more complex, they also change more, and these two causes together see to it that social life with man is not congealed in a biological form. Even where it is most simple, it clings to its specificity. There are always beliefs and practices common to men which are not inscribed in their tissues. But this character is more manifest as the social mass and density grow. The more people there are in association, and the more they react upon one another, the more also does the product of these reactions pass beyond the bounds of the organism. Man thus finds himself placed under the sway of causes *sui generis* whose relative part in the constitution of human nature becomes ever more considerable.

Moreover, the influence of this factor increases not only in relative value, but also in absolute value. The same cause which increases the importance of the collective environment weakens the organic environment in such a manner as to make it accessible to the action of social causes and to subordinate it to them. Because there are more individuals living together, common life is richer and more varied, but for this variety to be possible, the organic type must be less definite to be able to diversify itself. We have seen, in effect, that the tendencies and aptitudes transmitted by heredity became ever more general and more indeterminate, more refractory consequently, to assuming the form of instincts. Thus, a phenomenon is produced which is exacly the inverse of that which we observe at the beginning of evolution. With animals, the organism assimilates social facts to it, and, stripping them of their special nature, transforms them into biological facts. Social life is materialized. In man, on the contrary, and particularly in higher societies, social causes substitute themselves for organic causes. The organism is spiritualized.

The individual is transformed in accordance with this change in dependence. Since this activity which calls forth the special action of social causes cannot be fixed in the organism, a new life, also *sui generis*, is superimposed upon that of the body. Freer, more complex, more independent of the organs which support it, its distinguishing characteristics become ever more apparent as it progresses and becomes solid. From this description we can recognize the essential traits of psychic life. To be sure, it would be exaggerating to say that psychic life begins only with societies, but certainly it becomes extensive only as societies develop. That is why, as has often been remarked, the progress of conscience is in inverse ratio to that of instinct. Whatever may be said of them, it is not the first which breaks up the second. Instinct, the product of the accumulated experience of generations, has a much greater resistive force to dissolution simply because it becomes conscious. Truly, conscience only invades the ground which instinct has ceased to occupy, or where instinct cannot be established. Conscience does not make instinct recede; it only fills the space instinct leaves free. Moreover, if instinct regresses rather than extends as general life extends, the greater importance of the social factor is the cause of this. Hence, the great difference which separates man from animals, that is, the greater development of his psychic life, comes from his greater sociability. To understand why psychic functions have been carried, from the very beginnings of the human species, to a degree of perfection unknown among animal species, one would first have to know why it is that men, instead of living in solitude or in small bands, were led to form more extensive societies. To put it in terms of the classical definition, if man is a reasonable animal, that is because he is a sociable animal, or at least infinitely more sociable than other animals.[11]

This is not all. In so far as societies do not reach certain dimensions nor a certain degree of concentration, the only psychic life which may be truly developed is that which is common to all the members of the group, which is found identical in each. But, as societies become more vast and, particularly, more condensed, a psychic life of a new sort appears. Individual diversities, at first lost and confused amidst the mass of social likenesses, become disengaged, become conspicuous, and multiply. A multitude of things which used to remain outside consciences because they did not affect the collective being become objects of representations. Whereas individuals used to act only by involving one another, except in cases where their conduct was determined by physical needs, each of them becomes a source of spontaneous activity. Particular personalities become constituted, take conscience of themselves. Moreover, this growth of psychic life in the individual does not obliterate the psychic life of society, but only transforms it. It becomes freer, more extensive, and as it has, after all, no other bases than individual consciences, these extend, become complex, and thus become flexible.

Hence, the cause which called forth the differences separating man from animals is also that which has forced him to elevate himself above himself. The ever growing distance between the savage and the civilized man has no other source. If the faculty of ideation is slowly disengaged from the confused feeling of its origin, if man has learned to formulate concepts and laws, if his spirit has embraced more and more extensive portions of space and time, if, not content with clinging to the past, he has trespassed upon the future, if his emotions and his tendencies, at first simple and not very numerous, have multiplied and diversified, that is because the social milieu has changed without interruption. In effect, unless these transformations were born from nothing, they can have had for causes only the corresponding transformations of surrounding milieux. But, man depends only upon three sorts of milieux: the organism, the external world, society. If one leaves aside the accidental variations due to combinations of heredity—and their role in human progress is certainly not very considerable—the organism is not automatically modified; it is necessary that it be impelled by some external cause. As for the physical world, since the beginning of history it has remained sensibly the same, at least if one does not take account of novelties which are of social origin.[12] Consequently, there is only society which has changed enough to be able to explain the parallel changes in individual nature.

It is not, then, audacious to affirm that, from now on, whatever progress is made in psycho-physiology will never represent more than a fraction of psychology, since the major part of psychic phenomena does not come from organic causes. This is what spiritualist philosophers have learned, and the great service that they have rendered science has been to combat the doctrines which reduce psychic life merely to an efflorescence of physical life. They have very justly felt that the first, in its highest manifestations, is much too free and complex to be merely a prolongation of the second. Because it is partly independent of the organism, however, it does not follow that it depends upon no natural cause, and that it must be put outside nature. But all these facts whose explanation we cannot find in the constitution of tissues derive from properties of the social milieu. This hypothesis assumes, at least, very great probability from what has preceded. But the social realm is not less natural than the organic realm. Consequently, because there is a vast region of conscience whose genesis is unintelligible through psycho-physiology alone, we must not conclude that it has been formed of itself and that it is, accordingly, refractory to scientific investigation, but only that it derives from some other positive science which can be called socio-psychology. The phenomena which would constitute its matter are, in effect, of a mixed nature. They have the same essential characters as other psychic facts, but they arise from social causes.

It is not necessary, then, with Spencer, to present social life as a simple resultant of individual natures, since, on the contrary, it is rather the latter which come from the former. Social facts are not the simple development of psychic facts, but the second are in large part only the prolongation of the first in the interior of consciences. This proposition is very important, for the contrary point of view exposes the sociologist, at every moment, to mistaking the cause for the effect, and conversely. For example, if, as often happens, we see in the organization of the family the logically necessary expression of human sentiments inherent in every conscience, we are reversing the true order of facts. On the contrary, it is the social organization of the relations of kinship which has determined the respective sentiments of parents and children. They would have been completely different if the social structure had been different, and the proof of this is, in effect, that paternal love is unknown in a great many societies.[13] One could cite many other examples of the same error.[14] Of course, it is a self-evident truth that there is nothing in social life which is not in individual consciences. Everything that is found in the latter, however, comes from society. The major part of our states of conscience would not have been produced among isolated beings and would have been produced quite otherwise among beings grouped in some other manner. They come, then, not from the psychological nature of man in general, but from the manner in which men once associated mutually affect one another, according as they are more or less numerous, more or less close. Products of group life, it is the nature of the group which alone can explain them. Of course, they would not be possible if individual constitutions did not lend themselves to such action, but individual constitutions are only remote conditions, not determinate causes. Spencer in one place[15] compares the work of the sociologist to the calculation of a mathematician who, from the form of a certain number of balls, deduces the manner in which they must be combined in order to keep them in equilibrium. The comparison is inexact and does not apply to social facts. Here, instead, it is rather the form of all which determines that of the parts. Society does not find the bases on which it rests fully laid out in consciences; it puts them there itself.[16]

9

DIVISION OF LABOR IN
SOCIETY: CONCLUSION

I

We are now in a position to solve the practical problem that we posed for ourselves at the beginning of this work.

If there is one rule of conduct which is incontestable, it is that which orders us to realize in ourselves the essential traits of the collective type. Among lower peoples, this reaches its greatest rigor. There, one's first duty is to resemble everybody else, not to have anything personal about one's beliefs or actions. In more advanced societies, required likenesses are less numerous; the absences of some likenesses, however, is still a sign of moral failure. Of course, crime falls into fewer different categories; but today, as heretofore, if a criminal is the object of reprobation, it is because he is unlike us. Likewise, in lesser degree, acts simply immoral and prohibited as such are those which evince dissemblances less profound but nevertheless considered serious. Is this not the case with the rule which common morality expresses when it orders a man to be a man in every sense of the word, which is to say, to have all the ideas and sentiments which go to make up a human conscience? No doubt, if this formula is taken literally,

From *The Division of Labor in Society*, translated and with an introduction by George Simpson (New York: Macmillan Co., 1933), pp. 396–409. Originally published as *De la division du travail social: Etude sur l'organisation des sociétés supérieures* (Paris: Félix Alcan, 1893); 2d ed. with a new preface entitled "Quelques remarques sur les groupements professionels," 1902.

the man prescribed would be man in general and not one of some particular social species. But, in reality, this human conscience that we must integrally realize is nothing else than the collective conscience of the group of which we are a part. For what can it be composed of, if not the ideas and sentiments to which we are most attached? Where can we find the traits of our model, if not within us and around us? If we believe that this collective ideal is that of all humanity, that is because it has become so abstract and general that it appears fitting for all men indiscriminately. But, really, every people makes for itself some particular conception of this type which pertains to its personal temperament. Each represents it in its own image. Even the moralist who thinks he can, through thought, overcome the influence of transient ideas, cannot do so, for he is impregnated with them, and no matter what he does, he finds these precepts in the body of his deductions. That is why each nation has its own school of moral philosophy conforming to its character.

On the other hand, we have shown that this rule had as its function the prevention of all agitation of the common conscience, and, consequently, of social solidarity, and that it could accomplish this role only by having a moral character. It is impossible for offenses against the most fundamental collective sentiments to be tolerated without the disintegration of society, and it is necessary to combat them with the aid of the particularly energetic reaction which attaches to moral rules.

But the contrary rule, which orders us to specialize, has exactly the same function. It also is necessary for the cohesion of societies, at least at a certain period in their evolution. Of course, its solidarity is different from the preceding, but though it is different, it is no less indispensable. Higher societies can maintain themselves in equilbrium only if labor is divided; the attraction of like for like less and less suffices to produce this result. If, then, the moral character of the first of these rules is necessary to the playing of its role, it is no less necessary to the second. They both correspond to the same social need, but satisfy the need differently, because the conditions of existence in the societies themselves differ. Consequently, without speculating concerning the first principle of ethics, we can induce the moral value of one from the moral value of the other. If, from certain points of view, there is a real antagonism between them, that is not because they serve different ends. On the contrary, it is because they lead to the same end, but through opposed means. Accordingly, there is no necessity for choosing between them once for all nor of condemning one in the name of the other. What is necessary is to give each, at each moment in history, the place that is fitting to it.

Perhaps we can even generalize further in this matter.

The requirements of our subject have obliged us to classify moral rules and to review the principal types. We are thus in a better position than we were in the beginning to see, or at least to conjecture, not only upon the external sign, but also upon the internal character which is common to all of them and which can serve to define them. We have put them into two groups: rules with repressive sanctions, which may be diffuse or organized, and rules with restitutive sanctions. We have seen that the first of these express the conditions of the solidarity, *sui generis,* which comes from resemblances, and to which we have given the name mechanical; the second, the conditions of negative solidarity[1] and organic solidarity. We can thus say that, in general, the characteristic of moral rules is that they enunciate the fundamental conditions of social solidarity. Law and morality are the totality of ties which bind each of us to society, which make a unitary, coherent aggregate of the mass of individuals. Everything which is a source of solidarity is moral, everything which forces man to take account of other men is moral, everything which forces him to regulate his conduct through something other than the striving of his ego is moral, and morality is as solid as these ties are numerous and strong. We can see how inexact it is to define it, as is often done, through liberty. It rather consists in a state of dependence. Far from serving to emancipate the individual, or disengaging him from the environment which surrounds him, it has, on the contrary, the function of making him an integral part of a whole, and, consequently, of depriving him of some liberty of movement. We sometimes, it is true, come across people not without nobility who find the idea of such dependence intolerable. But that is because they do not perceive the source from which their own morality flows, since these sources are very deep. Conscience is a bad judge of what goes on in the depths of a person, because it does not penetrate to them.

Society is not, then, as has often been thought, a stranger to the moral world, or something which has only secondary repercussions upon it. It is, on the contrary, the necessary condition of its existence. It is not a simple juxtaposition of individuals who bring an intrinsic morality with them, but rather man is a moral being only because he lives in society, since morality consists in being solidary with a group and varying with this solidarity. Let all social life disappear, and moral life will disappear with it, since it would no longer have any objective. The state of nature of the philosophers of the eighteenth century, if not immoral, is, at least, *amoral.* Rousseau himself recognized this. Through this, however, we do not come upon the formula which expresses morality as a function of social interest. To be sure, society cannot exist if its parts are not solidary, but solidarity is only one of its conditions of existence. There are many others which are no less necessary and which are not moral. Moreover, it can happen that, in the system of ties which make up morality, there are some which are not useful in themselves or which have power without any relation to their degree of utility. The idea of utility does not enter as an essential element in our definition.

As for what is called individual morality, if we understand by that a totality of duties of which the individual would, at the same time, be subject and object, and which would link him only to himself, and which would, consequently, exist even if he were solitary—that is an abstrict conception which has no relation to reality. Morality, in all its forms, is never met with except in society. It never varies except in relation to social conditions. To ask what it would be if societies did not exist is thus to depart from facts and enter the domain of gratuitous hypotheses and unverifiable flights of the imagination. The duties of the individual towards himself are, in reality, duties towards society. They correspond to certain collective sentiments which he cannot offend, whether the offended and the offender are one and the same person, or whether they are distinct. Today, for example, there is in all healthy consciences a very lively sense of respect for human dignity, to which we are supposed to conform as much in our relations with ourselves as in our relations with others, and this constitutes the essential quality of what is called individual morality. Every act which contravenes this is censured, even when the agent and the sufferer are the same person. That is why, according to the Kantian formula, we ought to respect human personality wherever we find it, which is to say, in ourselves as in those like us. The sentiment of which it is the object is not less offended in one case than in the other.

But not only does the division of labor present the character by whch we have defined morality; it more and more tends to become the essential condition of social solidarity. As we advance in the evolutionary scale, the ties which bind the individual to his family, to his native soil, to traditions which the past has given to him, to collective group usages, become loose. More mobile, he changes his environment more easily, leaves his people to go elsewhere to live a more autonomous existence, to a greater extent forms his own ideas and sentiments. Of course, the whole common conscience does not, on this account, pass out of existence. At least there will always remain this cult of personality, of individual dignity of which we have just been speaking, and which, today, is the rallying-point of so many people. But how little a thing it is when one contemplates the ever increasing extent of social life, and, consequently, of individual consciences! For, as they become more voluminous, as intelligence becomes richer, activity more varied, in order for morality to remain constant, that is to say, in order for the individual to remain attached to the group with a force equal to that of yesterday, the ties which bind him to it must become stronger and more numerous. If, then, he formed no others than those which come from resemblances, the effacement of the segmental type would be accompanied by a systematic debasement of morality. Man would no longer be sufficiently obligated; he would no longer feel about and above him this salutary pressure of society which moderates his egoism and makes him a moral being. This is what gives moral value to the division of labor. Through it, the individual becomes cognizant of his dependence upon society; from it come the forces which keep him in check and restrain him. In short, since the division of labor becomes the chief source of social solidarity, it becomes, at the same time, the foundation of the moral order.

We can then say that, in higher societies, our duty is not to spread our activity over a large surface, but to concentrate and specialize it. We must contract our horizon, choose a definite task and immerse ourselves in it completely, instead of trying to make ourselves a sort of creative masterpiece, quite complete, which contains its worth in itself and not in the services that it renders. Finally, this specialization ought to be pushed as far as the elevation of the social type, without assigning any other limit to it.[2] No doubt, we ought so to work as to realize in ourselves the collective type as it exists. There are common sentiments, common ideas, without which, as has been said, one is not a man. The rule which orders us to specialize remains limited by the contrary rule. Our conclusion is not that it is good to press specialization as far as possible, but as far as necessary. As for the part that is to be played by these two opposing necessities, that is determined by experience and cannot be calculated *a priori*. It is enough for us to have shown that the second is not of a different nature from the first, but that it also is moral, and that, moreover, this duty becomes ever more important and pressing, because the general qualities which are in question suffice less and less to socialize the individual.

It is not without reason that public sentiment reproves an ever more pronounced tendency on the part of dilettantes and even others to be taken up with an exclusively general culture and refuse to take any part in occupational organization. That is because they are not sufficiently attached to society, or, if one wishes, society is not sufficiently attached to them, and they escape it. Precisely because they feel its effect neither with vivacity nor with the continuity that is necessary, they have no cognizance of all the obligations their positions as social beings demand of them. The general ideal to which they are attached being, for the reasons we have spoken of, formal and shifting, it cannot take them out of themselves. We do not cling to very much when we have no very determined objective, and, consequently, we cannot very well elevate ourselves beyond a more or less refined egotism. On the contrary, he who gives himself over to a definite task is, at every moment, struck by the sentiment of common solidarity in the thousand duties of occupational morality.[3]

II

But does not the division of labor by making each of us an incomplete being bring on a diminution of individual personality? That is a reproach which has often been levelled at it.

Let us first of all remark that it is difficult to see why it would be more in keeping with the logic of human nature to develop superficially rather than profoundly. Why would a more extensive activity, but more dispersed, be superior to a more concentrated, but circumscribed, activity? Why would there be more dignity in being complete and mediocre, rather than in living a more specialized, but more intense life, particularly if it is thus possible for us to find what we have lost in this specialization, through our association with other beings who have what we lack and who complete us? We take off from the principle that man ought to realize his nature as man, to accomplish his *oikeion ergon*, as Aristotle said. But this nature does not remain constant throughout history; it is modified with societies. Among lower peoples, the proper duty of man is to resemble his companions, to realize in himself all the traits of the collective type which are then confounded, much more than today, with the human type. But, in more advanced societies, his nature is, in large part, to be an organ of society, and his proper duty, consequently, is to play his role as an organ.

Moreover, far from being trammelled by the progress of specialization, individual personality develops with the division of labor.

To be a person is to be an autonomous source of action. Man acquires this quality only in so far as there is something in him which is his alone and which individualizes him, as he is something more than a simple incarnation of the generic type of his race and his group. It will be said that he is endowed with free will and that is enough to establish his personality. But although there may be some of this liberty in him, an object of so many discussions, it is not this metaphysical, impersonal, invariable attribute which can serve as the unique basis for concrete personality, which is empirical and variable with individuals. That could not be constituted by the wholly abstract power of choice between two opposites, but it is still necessary for this faculty to be exercised towards ends and aims which are proper to the agent. In other words, the very materials of conscience must have a personal character. But we have seen in the second book of this work that this result is progressively produced as the division of labor progresses. The effacement of the segmental type, at the same time that it necessitates a very great specialization, partially lifts the individual conscience from the organic environment which supports it, as from the social environment which envelops it, and, accordingly, because of this double emancipation, the individual becomes more of an independent factor in his own conduct. The division of labor itself contributes to this enfranchisement, for individual natures, while specializing, become more complex, and by that are in part freed from collective action and hereditary influences which can only enforce themselves upon simple, general things.

It is, accordingly, a real illusion which makes us believe that personality was so much more complete when the division of labor had penetrated less. No doubt, in looking from without at the diversity of occupations which the individual then embraces, it may seem that he is developing in a very free and complete manner. But, in reality, this activity which he manifests is not really his. It is society, it is the race acting in and through him; he is only the intermediary through which they realize themselves. His liberty is only apparent and his personality borrowed. Because the life of these societies is, in certain respects, less regular, we imagine that original talents have more opportunity for free play, that it is easier for each one to pursue his own tastes, that a very large place is left to free fantasy. But this is to forget that personal sentiments are then very rare. If the motives which govern conduct do not appear as periodically as they do today, they do not leave off being collective, and, consequently, impersonal, and it is the same with the actions that they inspire. Moreover, we have shown above how activity becomes richer and more intense as it becomes more specialized.

Thus, the progress of individual personality and that of the division of labor depend upon one and the same cause. It is thus impossible to desire one without desiring the other. But no one today contests the obligatory character of the rule which orders us to be more and more of a person.

One last consideration will make us see to what extent the division of labor is linked with our whole moral life.

Men have long dreamt of finally realizing in fact the ideal of human fraternity. People pray for a state where war will no longer be the law of international relations, where relations between societies will be pacifically regulated, as those between individuals already are, where all men will collaborate in the same work and live the same life. Although these aspirations are in part neutralized by those which have as their object the particular society of which we are a part, they have not left off being active and are even gaining in force. But they can be satisfied only if all men form one society, subject to the same laws. For, just as private conflicts can be regulated only by the action of the society in which the individuals live, so intersocial conflicts can be regulated only by a society which comprises in its scope all others. The only power which can serve to moderate individual egotism is the power of the group; the only power which can serve to moderate the egotism of groups is that of some other group which embraces them.

Truly, when the problem has been posed in these terms, we must recognize that this ideal is not on the verge of being integrally realized, for there are too many intellectual and moral diversities between different social types existing together on the earth to admit of fraternalization in the same society. But what is possible is that societies of the same type may come together, and it is, indeed, in this direction that evolution appears to move.

We have already seen that among European peoples there is a tendency to form, by spontaneous movement, a European society which has, at present, some idea of itself and the beginning of organization. If the formation of a single human society is forever impossible, a fact which has not been proved,[4] at least the formation of continually larger societies brings us vaguely near the goal. These facts, moreover, in no wise contradict the definition of morality that we have given, for if we cling to humanity and if we ought to cling to it, it is because it is a society which is in process of realizing itself in this way, and with which we are solidary.[5]

But we know that greater societies cannot be formed except through the development of the division of labor, for not only could they not maintain themselves in equilibrium without a greater specialization of functions, but even the increase in the number of those competing would suffice to produce this result mechanically; and that, so much the more, since the growth of volume is generally accompanied by a growth in density. We can then formulate the following proposition: the ideal of human fraternity can be realized only in proportion to the progress of the division of labor. We must choose: either to renounce our dream, if we refuse further to circumscribe our activity, or else to push forward its accomplishment under the condition we have just set forth.

III

But if the division of labor produces solidarity, it is not only because it makes each individual an *exchangist*, as the economists say;[6] it is because it creates among men an entire system of rights and duties which link them together in a durable way. Just as social similitudes give rise to a law and a morality which protect them, so the division of labor gives rise to rules which assure pacific and regular concourse of divided functions. If economists have believed that it would bring forth an abiding solidarity, in some manner of its own making, and if, accordingly, they have held that human societies could and would resolve

themselves into purely economic associations, that is because
they believed that it affected only individual, temporary interests.
Consequently, to estimate the interests in conflict and the way
in which they ought to equilibrate, that is to say, to determine
the conditions under which exchange ought to take place, is solely
a matter of individual competence; and, since these interests are
in a perpetual state of becoming, there is no place for any permanent regulation. But such a conception is, in all ways, inadequate
for the facts. The division of labor does not present individuals
to one another, but social functions. And society is interested in
the play of the latter; in so far as they regularly concur, or do
not concur, it will be healthy or ill. Its existence thus depends
upon them, and the more they are divided the greater its dependence. That is why it cannot leave them in a state of indetermina-
tion. In addition to this, they are determined by themselves. Thus
are formed those rules whose number grows as labor is divided,
and whose absence makes organic solidarity either impossible
or imperfect.

But it is not enough that there be rules; they must be just,
and for that it is necessary for the external conditions of competition to be equal. If, moreover, we remember that the collective
conscience is becoming more and more a cult of the individual, we
shall see that what characterizes the morality of organized societies, compared to that of segmental societies, is that there is something more human, therefore more rational, about them. It does
not direct our activities to ends which do not immediately concern us; it does not make us servants of ideal powers of a nature
other than our own, which follow their directions without occupying themselves with the interests of men. It only asks that we be
thoughtful of our fellows and that we be just, that we fulfill our
duty, that we work at the function we can best execute, and receive the just reward for our services. The rules which constitute
it do not have a constraining force which snuffs out free thought;
but, because they are rather made for us and, in a certain sense,
by us, we are free. We wish to understand them; we do not fear
to change them. We must, however, guard against finding such
an ideal inadequate on the pretext that it is too earthly and too

much to our liking. An ideal is not more elevated because more transcendent, but because it leads up to vaster perspectives. What is important is not that it tower high above us, until it becomes a stranger to our lives, but that it open to our activity a large enough field. This is far from being on the verge of realization. We know only too well what a laborious work it is to erect this society where each individual will have the place he merits, will be rewarded as he deserves, where everybody, accordingly, will spontaneously work for the good of all and of each. Indeed, a moral code is not above another because it commands in a drier and more authoritarian manner, or because it is more sheltered from reflection. Of course, it must attach us to something besides ourselves but it is not necessary for it to chain us to it with impregnable bonds.

It has been said[7] with justice that morality—and by that must be understood, not only moral doctrines, but customs—is going through a real crisis. What precedes can help us to understand the nature and causes of this sick condition. Profound changes have been produced in the structure of our societies in a very short time; they have been freed from the segmental type with a rapidity and in proportions such as have never before been seen in history. Accordingly, the morality which corresponds to this social type has regressed, but without another developing quickly enough to fill the ground that the first left vacant in our consciences. Our faith has been troubled; tradition has lost its sway; individual judgment has been freed from collective judgment. But, on the other hand, the functions which have been disrupted in the course of the upheaval have not had the time to adjust themselves to one another; the new life which has emerged so suddenly has not been able to be completely organized, and above all, it has not been organized in a way to satisfy the need for justice which has grown more ardent in our hearts. If this be so, the remedy for the evil is not to seek to resuscitate traditions and practices which, no longer responding to present conditions of society, can only live an artificial, false existence. What we must do to relieve this anomy is to discover the means for making the organs which are still wasting themselves in discordant movements harmoniously concur by introducing into their relations more justice by more and more extenuating the external inequalities which are the source of the evil. Our illness is not, then, as has often been believed, of an intellectual sort; it has more profound causes. We shall not suffer because we no longer know on what theoretical notion to base the morality we have been practicing, but because, in certain of its parts, this morality is irremediably shattered, and that which is necessary to us is only in process of formation. Our anxiety does not arise because the criticism of scholars has broken down the traditional explanation we used to give to our duties; consequently, it is not a new philosophical system which will relieve the situation. Because certain of our duties are no longer founded in the reality of things, a breakdown has resulted which will be repaired only in so far as a new discipline is established and consolidated. In short, our first duty is to make a moral code for ourselves. Such a work cannot be improvised in the silence of the study; it can arise only through itself, little by little, under the pressure of internal causes which make it necessary. But the service that thought can and must render is in fixing the goal that we must attain. That is what we have tried to do.

IV. The Learning of Morality

THE DUALISM OF HUMAN NATURE

AND ITS SOCIAL CONDITIONS

ALTHOUGH SOCIOLOGY IS DEFINED as the science of societies, it cannot, in reality, deal with the human groups that are the immediate object of its investigation without eventually touching on the individual who is the basic element of which these groups are composed. For society can exist only if it penetrates the consciousness of individuals and fashions it in "its image and resemblance." We can say, therefore, with assurance and without being excessively dogmatic, that a great number of our mental states, including some of the most important ones, are of social origin. In this case, then, it is the whole that, in a large measure, produces the part; consequently, it is impossible to attempt to explain the whole without explaining the part—without explaining, at least, the part as a result of the whole. The supreme product of collective activity is that ensemble of intellectual and moral goods that we call civilization; it is for this reason that Auguste Comte referred to sociology as the science of civilization. However, it is civilization that has made man what he is; it is what distinguishes him from the animal: man is man only because he is civilized. To look for the causes and conditions upon which civilization depends is, therefore, to seek out also the causes

Reprinted from "The Dualism of Human Nature and Its Social Conditions," translated by Charles Blend, in *Emile Durkheim, 1858–1917*, edited by Kurt H. Wolff (Columbus: Ohio State University Press, 1960), pp. 325–40; reprinted as *Essays on Sociology and Philosophy* (New York: Harper and Row, 1964). Originally published as "Le dualisme de la nature humaine et ses conditions sociales," *Scientia* 15 (1914): 206–21.

and conditions of what is most specifically human in man. And so sociology, which draws on psychology and could not do without it, brings to it, in a just return, a contribution that equals and surpasses in importance the services that it receives from it. It is only by historical analysis that we can discover what makes up man, since it is only in the course of history that he is formed.

The work that we recently published, *The Elementary Forms of the Religious Life*,[1] offers an example of this general truth. In attempting to study religious phenomena from the sociological point of view, we came to envisage a way of explaining scientifically one of the most characteristic peculiarities of our nature. Since the critics who have discussed the book up to the present have not—to our great surprise—perceived the principle upon which this explanation rests, it seemed to us that a brief outline of it would be of some interest to the readers of *Scientia*.

The peculiarity referred to is the constitutional duality of human nature. In every age, man has been intensely aware of this duality. He has, in fact, everywhere conceived of himself as being formed of two radically heterogeneous beings: the body and the soul. Even when the soul is represented in a material form, its substance is not thought of as being of the same nature as the body. It is said that it is more ethereal, more subtle, more plastic, that it does not affect the senses as do the other objects to which they react, that it is not subject to the same laws as these objects, and so on. And not only are these two beings substantially different, they are in a large measure independent of each other, and are often even in conflict. For centuries it was believed that after this life the soul could escape from the body and lead an autonomous existence far from it. This independence was made manifest at the time of death when the body dissolved and disappeared and the soul survived and continued to follow, under new conditions and for varying lengths of time, the path of its own destiny. It can even be said that although the body and the soul are closely associated, they do not belong to the same world. The body is an integral part of the material universe, as it is made known to us by sensory experience; the abode of the soul is elsewhere, and the soul tends ceaselessly to return to it. This abode is the world of the sacred. Therefore, the soul is invested with a dignity that has always been denied the body, which is considered essentially profane, and it inspires those feelings that are everywhere reserved for that which is divine. It is made of the same substance as are the sacred beings: it differs from them only in degree.

A belief that is as universal and permanent as this cannot be purely illusory. There must be something in man that gives rise to this feeling that his nature is dual, a feeling that men in all known civilizations have experienced. Psychological analysis has, in fact, confirmed the existence of this duality: it finds it at the very heart of our inner life.

Our intelligence, like our activity, presents two very different forms: on the one hand, are sensations[2] and sensory tendencies; on the other, conceptual thought and moral activity. Each of these two parts of ourselves represents a separate pole of our being, and these two poles are not only distinct from one another but are opposed to one another. Our sensory appetites are necessarily egoistic: they have our individuality and it alone as their object. When we satisfy our hunger, our thirst, and so on, without bringing any other tendency into play, it is ourselves, and ourselves alone, that we satisfy.[3] [Conceptual thought] and moral activity are, on the contrary, distinguished by the fact that the rules of conduct to which they conform can be universalized. Therefore, by definition, they pursue impersonal ends. Morality begins with disinterest, with attachment to something other than ourselves.[4] A sensation of color or sound is closely dependent on my individual organism, and I cannot detach the sensation from my organism. In addition, it is impossible for me to make my awareness pass over into someone else. I can, of course, invite another person to face the same object and expose himself to its effect, but the perception that he will have of it will be his own work and will be proper to him, as mine is proper to me. Concepts, on the contrary, are always common to a plurality of men. They are constituted by means of words, and neither the vocabulary nor the grammar of a language is the work or product of one particular person. They are rather the result of a collective elaboration, and they express the anonymous collectivity that employs them. The ideas of *man* or *animal* are not personal and are not restricted to me; I share them, to a large degree, with all the men who belong to the same social group that I do. Because they are held in common, concepts are the supreme instrument of all intellectual exchange. By means of them minds communicate. Doubtless, when one thinks through the concepts that he receives from the community, he individualizes them and marks them with his personal imprint, but there is nothing personal that is not susceptible to this type of individualization.[5]

These two aspects of our psychic life are, therefore, opposed to each other as are the personal and the impersonal. There is in us a being that represents everything in relation to itself and from its own point of view; in everything that it does, this being has no other object but itself. There is another being in us, however, which knows things *sub specie aeternitis,* as if it were participating in some thought other than its own, and which, in its acts, tends to accomplish ends that surpass its own. The old formula *homo duplex* is therefore verified by the facts. Far from being simple, our inner life has something that is like a double center of gravity. On the one hand is our individuality—and, more particularly, our body in which it is based;[6] on the other is everything in us that expresses something other than ourselves.

Not only are these two groups of states of consciousness different in their origins and their properties, but there is a true antagonism between them. They mutually contradict and deny each other. We cannot pursue moral ends without causing a split within ourselves, without offending the instincts and the penchants that are the most deeply rooted in our bodies. There is no moral act that does not imply a sacrifice, for, as Kant has shown, the law of duty cannot be obeyed without humiliating our individual, or, as he calls it, our "empirical" sensitivity. We can accept this sacrifice without resistance and even with enthusiasm, but even when it is accomplished in a surge of joy, the sacrifice is no less real. The pain that the ascetic seeks is pain nonetheless, and this antinomy is so deep and so radical that it can never be completely resolved. How can we belong entirely to ourselves, and entirely to others at one and the same time? The ego cannot be something completely other than itself, for, if it were, it would vanish—this is what happens in ecstasy. In order to think, we must be, we must have an individuality. On the other hand, however, the ego cannot be entirely and exclusively itself, for, if it were, it would be emptied of all content. If we must be in order to think, then we must have something to think about. To what would consciousness be reduced if it expressed nothing but the body and its states? We cannot live without representing to ourselves the world around us and the objects of every sort which fill it. And because we represent it to ourselves, it enters into us and becomes part of us. Consequently, we value the world and are attached to it just as we are to ourselves. Something else in us besides ourselves stimulates us to act. It is an error to believe that it is easy to live as egoists. Absolute egoism, like absolute altruism, is an ideal limit which can never be attained in reality. Both are states that we can approach indefinitely without ever realizing them completely.

It is no different in the sphere of our knowledge. We understand only when we think in concepts. But sensory reality is not made to enter the framework of our concepts spontaneously and by itself. It resists, and, in order to make it conform, we have to do some violence to it, we have to submit it to all sorts of laborious operations that alter it so that the mind can assimilate it. However, we never completely succeed in triumphing over its resistance. Our concepts never succeed in mastering our sensations and in translating them completely into intelligible terms. They take on a conceptual form only by losing that which is most concrete in them, that which causes them to speak to our sensory being and to involve it in action; and, in so doing, they become something fixed and dead. Therefore, we cannot understand things without partially renouncing a feeling for their life, and we cannot feel that life without renouncing the understanding of it. Doubtless, we sometimes dream of a science that would adequately express all of reality; but this is an ideal that we can only approach ceaselessly, not one that is possible for us to attain.

This inner contradiction is one of the characteristics of our nature. According to Pascal's formula, man is both "angel and beast" and not exclusively one or the other. The result is that we are never completely in accord with ourselves for we cannot follow one of our two natures without causing the other to suffer. Our joys can never be pure; there is always some pain mixed with them; for we cannot simultaneously satisfy the two beings that are within us. It is this disagreement, this perpetual division against ourselves, that produces both our grandeur and our misery: our misery because we are thus condemned to live in suffering; and our grandeur because it is this division that distinguishes us from all other beings. The animal proceeds to his pleasure in a single and exclusive movement; man alone is normally obliged to make a place for suffering in his life.

Thus the traditional antithesis of the body and soul is not a vain mythological concept that is without foundation in reality. It is true that we are double, that we are the realization of an antinomy. In connection with this truth, however, a question arises that philosophy and even positive psychology cannot avoid: Where do this duality and this antinomy come from? How is it that each of us is, to quote another of Pascal's phrases, a "monster of contradictions" that can never completely satisfy itself? And, certainly, if this odd condition is one of the distinctive traits of humanity, the science of man must try to account for it.

The proposed solutions to this problem are neither numerous nor varied. Two doctrines that occupy an important place in the history of thought held that the difficulty could be removed by denying it; that is, by calling the duality of man an illusion. These doctrines are empirical monism and idealistic monism.

According to the first of these doctrines, concepts are only more or less elaborate sensations. They consist entirely of groups of similar images, groups that have a kind of individuality because each of the images that comprise the group is identified by the same word; however, outside of these images and sensations of which they are the extension, concepts have no reality at all. In the same way, this doctrine holds, moral activity is only another aspect of self-interested activity: the man who obeys the call of duty is merely pursuing his own self-interest as he understands it. When our nature is seen in this way, the problem of its duality disappears: man is one, and if there are serious strains within him, it is because he is not acting in conformity with his nature. If properly interpreted, a concept cannot be contrary to the sensation to which it owes its existence; and the moral act cannot be in conflict with the egoistic act, because, fundamentally, it derives from utilitarian motives.

Unfortunately, however, the facts that posed the question in the first place still exist. It is still true that at all times man has been disquieted and malcontent. He has always felt that he is pulled apart, divided against himself; and the beliefs and practices to which, in all societies and all civilizations, he has always attached the greatest value, have as their object not to suppress these inevitable divisions but to attenuate their consequences, to give them meaning and purpose, to make them more bearable, and at the very least, to console man for their existence. We cannot admit that this universal and chronic state of malaise is the product of a simple aberration, that man has been the creator of his own suffering, and that he has stupidly persisted in it, although his nature truly predisposed him to live harmoniously. Experience should have corrected such a deplorable error long ago. At the very least, it should be able to explain the origin of this inconceivable blindness. Moreover, the serious objections to the hypothesis of empirical monism are well known. It has never been able to explain how the inferior can become the superior; or how individual sensation, which is obscure and confused, can become the clear and distinct impersonal concept; or how self-interest can be transformed into disinterest.

It is no different with the absolute idealist. For him, too, reality is one; but for him it is made up entirely of concepts, while for the empiricist it is made up entirely of sensations. According to the idealist, an absolute intelligence seeing things as they are would find that the world is a system of definite ideas connected with each other in relationships that are equally definite. To the idealist, sensations are nothing by themselves; they are only concepts that are not clear and are intermixed. They assume the particular aspect in which they are revealed to us in experience only because we do not know how to distinguish their elements. If we knew how, there would be no fundamental opposition between the world and ourselves or between the different parts of ourselves. The opposition that we think we perceive is due to a simple error in perspective that needs only to be corrected. However, if this were true, we should be able to establish that this error diminishes to the degree that the domain of conceptual thought is extended and we learn to think less by sensation and more in concepts; to the degree, that is, that science develops and becomes a more important factor in our mental life. But, unfortunately, history is far from confirming these optimistic hopes. It seems that, on the contrary, human malaise continues to increase. The great religions of modern man are those which insist the most on the existence of the contradictions in the midst of which we struggle. These continue to depict us as tormented and suffering, while only the crude cults of inferior societies breathe forth and inspire a joyful confidence.[7] For what religions express is the experience through which humanity has lived, and it would be very surprising if our nature became unified and harmonious when we feel that our discords are increasing. Moreover, even if we assume that these discords are only superficial and apparent, it is still necessary to take this appearance into consideration. If the sensations are nothing outside of concepts, it is still necessary to determine why it is that the latter do not appear to us as they really are, but seem to us mixed and confused. What is it that has imposed on them a lack of distinctness that is contrary to their nature? Idealism faces considerable difficulty in trying to solve these problems, and its failure to do so gives rise to objections that are precisely the opposite of those that have so often and so legitimately been made against empiricism. The latter has never explained how the inferior can become the superior—that is, how a sensation can be raised to the dignity of a concept while remaining unchanged; and the former faces equal difficulty in explaining how the superior can become the inferior, how the concept can wither and degenerate in such a way as to become sensation. This degeneration cannot be spontaneous; it must be determined by some contradictory principle. However, there is no place for a principle of this kind in a doctrine that is essentially monistic.

If we reject the theories which eliminate the problem rather than solve it, the only remaining ones that are valid and merit examination are those which limit themselves to affirming the fact that must be explained, but which do not account for it.

First of all, there is the ontological explanation for which Plato gave the formula. Man is double because two worlds meet in him: that of non-intelligent and amoral matter, on the one hand, and that of ideas, the spirit, and the good, on the other. Because these two worlds are naturally opposed, they struggle within us; and, because we are part of both, we are necessarily in conflict with ourselves. But if this answer—completely metaphysical as it is—has the merit of affirming the fact that must be interpreted without trying to weaken it, it does confine itself, nevertheless, to distinguishing the two aspects of human nature and does not account for them. To say that we are double because there are two contrary forces in us is to repeat the problem in different terms; it does not resolve it. It is still necessary to explain their opposition. Doubtless, one can admit that because of the excellence that is attributed to it the world of ideas and of good contains within itself the reason for its existence; but how does it happen that outside of it there is a principle of evil, of darkness, of non-being? And what is the function of this principle?

We understand even less how these two worlds which are wholly opposite, and which, consequently, should repulse and exclude each other, tend, nevertheless, to unite and interpenetrate in such a way as to produce the mixed and contradictory being that is man; for it seems that their antagonism should keep them apart and make their union impossible. To borrow the language of Plato, the Idea, which is perfect by definition, possesses the plenitude of being, and is, therefore, sufficient in itself, and needs only itself in order to exist. Why, then, should it lower itself toward matter when contact with it can only alter its nature and make it sink below its former level? But, on the other hand, why should matter aspire to the contrary principle—a principle that it denies—and permit itself to be penetrated by it? And, finally, it is man that is the theatre par excellence of the struggle that we have described, a struggle that is not found in other beings; according to the hypothesis, however, man is not the only place where the two worlds ought to meet.

The theory that is most widely accepted at present offers an even less satisfactory explanation of human dualism: it does not base it on two metaphysical principles that are the basis of all reality, but on the existence of two antithetical faculties within us. We possess both a faculty for thinking as individuals and a faculty for thinking in universal and impersonal terms. The first is called sensitivity, and the second reason. Our activity can, therefore, manifest two completely opposed characters depending on whether it is based on sensory or on rational motives. Kant more than anyone else has insisted on this contrast between reason and sensitivity, between rational activity and sensory activity. But even if this classification is perfectly legitimate, it offers no solution to the problem that occupies us here; for the important thing to determine from our consideration of the fact that we have aptitudes for living both a personal and an impersonal life, is not what name it is proper to give to these contrary aptitudes, but how it is that in spite of their opposition, they exist in a single and identical being. How is it that we can participate concurrently in these two existences? How is it that we are made up of two halves that appear to belong to two different beings? Merely to give a name to each being does nothing toward answering the fundamental question.

If we have too often been satisfied with this purely verbal answer, it is because we have generally thought of man's mental nature as a sort of ultimate given which need not be accounted for. Thus we tend to believe that all has been said and done when we attach such and such a fact, whose causes we are seeking, to a human faculty. But why should the human spirit, which is—to put it briefly—only a system of phenomena that are comparable in all ways to other observable phenomena, be outside and above explanation? We know that our organism is the product of a genesis; why should it be otherwise with our psychic constitution? And if there is anything in us that urgently requires explanation, it is precisely this strange antithesis which is involved in this constitution.

The statement made previously that human dualism has always expressed itself in religious form is sufficient to suggest that the answer to our question must be sought in a quite different direction. As we have said, the soul has everywhere been considered something sacred; it has been viewed as a bit of divinity which lives only a brief terrestrial life and tends, as if by itself, to return to its place of origin. Thus the soul is opposed to the body, which is regarded as profane; and everything in our mental life that is related to the body—the sensations and the sensory appetites—has this same character. For this reason, we think that sensations are inferior forms of our activity, and we attribute a higher dignity to reason and moral activity which are the faculties by which, so we are told, we communicate with God. Even the man who is most free of professed belief makes a distinction of this kind, attributing an unequal value to our varying psychic functions, and giving to each, according to its relative value, a place in a hierarchy, in which those that are most closely related to the body are at the bottom. Furthermore, as we have shown,[8] there is no morality that is not infused with religiosity. Even to the secular mind, duty, the moral imperative, is something august and sacred; and reason, the indispensable ally of moral activity, naturally inspires similar feelings. The duality of our nature is thus only a particular case of that division of things into the sacred and the profane that is the foundation of all religions, and it must be explained on the basis of the same principles.

It is precisely this explanation that we attempted in the previously cited work, *The Elementary Forms of the Religious Life*, where we tried to show that sacred things are simply collective ideals that have fixed themselves on material objects.[9] The ideas and sentiments that are elaborated by a collectivity, whatever it may be, are invested by reason of their origin with an ascendancy and an authority that cause the particular individuals who think them and believe in them to represent them in the form of moral forces that dominate and sustain them. When these ideals move our wills, we feel that we are being led, directed, and carried along by singular energies that, manifested, do not come from us but are imposed on us from the outside. Our feelings toward them are respect and reverent fear, as well as gratitude for the comfort that we receive from them; for they cannot communicate themselves to us without increasing our vitality. And the particular virtues that we attribute to these ideals are not due to any mysterious action of an external agency; they are simply the effects of that singularly creative and fertile psychic operation—which is scientifically analyzable—by which a plurality of individual consciousnesses enter into communion and are fused into a common consciousness.

From another point of view, however, collective representations originate only when they are embodied in material objects, things, or beings of every sort—figures, movements, sounds, words, and so on—that symbolize and delineate them in some outward appearance. For it is only by expressing their feelings, by translating them into signs, by symbolizing them externally, that the individual consciousnesses, which are, by nature, closed to each other, can feel that they are communicating and are in unison.[10] The things that embody the collective representations arouse the same feelings as do the mental states that they represent and, in a manner of speaking, materialize. They, too, are respected, feared, and sought after as helping powers. Consequently, they are not placed on the same plane as the vulgar things that interest only our physical individualities, but are set apart from them. Therefore, we assign them a completely different place in the complex of reality and separate them; and it is this radical separation that constitutes the essence of their sacred character.[11] This system of conceptions is not purely imaginary and hallucinatory, for the moral forces that these things awaken in us are quite real—as real as the ideas that words recall to us after they have served to form the ideas. This is the dynamogenic influence that religions have always exercised on men.

However, these ideals, these products of group life, cannot originate—let alone persist—unless they penetrate the individual consciousness where they are organized in a lasting fashion. Once the group has dissolved and the social communion has done its work, the individuals carry away within themselves these great religious, moral, and intellectual conceptions that societies draw from their very hearts during their periods of greatest creativity. Doubtless, once the creativity has ceased and each individual has again taken up his private existence, removing himself from the source of his inspiration, the vitality of these conceptions is not maintained at the same intensity. It is not extinguished, however; for the action of the group does not cease altogether: it perpetually gives back to the great ideals a little of the strength that the egoistic passions and daily personal preoccupations tend to take away from them. This replenishment is the function of public festivals, cere- monies, and rites of all kinds.

In mingling with our individual lives in this way, however, these various ideals are themselves individualized. Because they are in a close relation with our other representations, they har- monize with them, and with our temperaments, characters, habits, and so on. Each of us puts his own mark on them; and this accounts for the fact that each person has his own particular way of think- ing about the beliefs of his church, the rules of common morality, and the fundamental notions that serve as the framework of con- ceptual thought. But even while they are being individualized— and thus becoming elements of our personalities—collective ideals preserve their characteristic property: the prestige with which they are clothed. Although they are our own, they speak in us with a tone and an accent that are entirely different from those of our other states of consciousness. They command us; they im- pose respect on us; we do not feel ourselves to be on an even foot- ing with them. We realize that they represent something within us that is superior to us.

It is not without reason, therefore, that man feels himself to be double: he actually is double. There are in him two classes of states of consciousness that differ from each other in origin and nature, and in the ends toward which they aim. One class merely expresses our organisms and the objects to which they are most directly related. Strictly individual, the states of conscious- ness of this class connect us only with ourselves, and we can no more detach them from us than we can detach ourselves from our bodies. The states of consciousness of the other class, on the contrary, come to us from society; they transfer society into us and connect us with something that surpasses us. Being collective, they are impersonal; they turn us toward ends that we hold in common with other men; it is through them and them alone that we can communicate with others. It is, therefore, quite true that we are made up of two parts, and are like two beings, which, although they are closely associated, are composed of very different elements and orient us in opposite directions.

In brief, this duality corresponds to the double existence that we lead concurrently: the one purely individual and rooted in our organisms, the other social and nothing but an extension of society. The origin of the antagonism that we have described is evident from the very nature of the elements involved in it. The conflicts of which we have given examples are between the sensations and the sensory appetites, on the one hand, and the intellectual and moral life, on the other; and it is evident that passions and egoistic tendencies derive from our individual constitutions, while our rational activity—whether theoretical or practical—is dependent on social causes. We have often had occasion to prove that the rules of morality are norms that have been elaborated by society;[12] the obligatory character with which they are marked is nothing but the authority of society, communicating itself to everything that comes from it. In the book that is the occasion of the present study but which we can only mention here, we have tried to demonstrate that concepts, the material of all logical thought, were originally collective representations. The impersonality that characterizes them is proof that they are the product of an anonymous and impersonal action.[13] We have even found a basis for conjecturing that the fundamental and lofty concepts that we call categories are formed on the model of social phenomena.[14]

The painful character of the dualism of human nature is explained by this hypothesis. There is no doubt that if society were only the natural and spontaneous development of the individual, these two parts of ourselves would harmonize and adjust to each other without clashing and without friction: the first part, since it is only the extension and, in a way, the complement of the second, would encounter no resistance from the latter. In fact, however, society has its own nature, and, consequently, its requirements are quite different from those of our nature as individuals: the interests of the whole are not necessarily those of the part. Therefore, society cannot be formed or maintained without our being required to make perpetual and costly sacrifices. Because society surpasses us, it obliges us to surpass ourselves; and to surpass itself, a being must, to some degree, depart from its nature—a departure that does not take place without causing more or less painful tensions. We know that only the action of society arouses us to give our attention voluntarily. Attention presupposes effort: to be attentive we must suspend the spontaneous course of our representations and prevent our consciousness from pursuing the dispersive movement that is its natural course. We must, in a word, do violence to certain of our strongest inclinations. Therefore, since the role of the social being in our single selves will grow ever more important as history moves ahead, it is wholly improbable that there will ever be an era in which man is required to resist himself to a lesser degree, an era in which he can live a life that is easier and less full of tension. To the contrary, all evidence compels us to expect our effort in the struggle between the two beings within us to increase with the growth of civilization.

V. Social Creativity

ORIGIN OF THE IDEA
OF THE TOTEMIC PRINCIPLE
OR MANA

THE PROPOSITION established in the preceding chapter determines the terms in which the problem of the origins of totemism
should be posed. Since totemism is everywhere dominated by the
idea of a quasi-divine principle, imminent in certain categories
of men and things and thought of under the form of an animal
or vegetable, the explanation of this religion is essentially the explanation of this belief; to arrive at this, we must seek to learn
how men have been led to construct this idea and out of what
materials they have constructed it.

I

IT IS OBVIOUSLY not out of the sensations which the things
serving as totems are able to arouse in the mind; we have shown
that these things are frequently insignificant. The lizard, the cater-
pillar, the rat, the ant, the frog, the turkey, the bream-fish, the
plum-tree, the cockatoo, etc., to cite only those names which appear frequently in the lists of Australian totems, are not of a nature to produce upon men these great and strong impressions
which in a way resemble religious emotions and which impress

From *The Elementary Forms of the Religious Life: A Study in Religious
Sociology*, translated by Joseph Ward Swain (London: Allen and Unwin;
New York: Macmillan Co., 1915; New York: Free Press, 1947, 1965), pp.
205–23. Originally published as *Les formes élémentaires de la vie religieuse:
Le système totémique en Australie*, Travaux de l'année sociologique (Paris:
Félix Alcan, 1912).

a sacred character upon the objects they create. It is true that this is not the case with the stars and the great atmospheric phenomena, which have, on the contrary, all that is necessary to strike the imagination forcibly; but as a matter of fact, these serve only very exceptionally as totems. It is even probable that they were very slow in taking this office. So it is not the intrinsic nature of the thing whose name the clan bears that marked it out to become the object of a cult. Also, if the sentiments which it inspired were really the determining cause of the totemic rites and beliefs, it would be the pre-eminently sacred thing; the animals or plants employed as totems would play an eminent part in the religious life. But we know that the centre of the cult is actually elsewhere. It is the figurative representations of this plant or animal and the totemic emblems and symbols of every sort, which have the greatest sanctity; so it is in them that is found the source of that religious nature, of which the real objects represented by these emblems receive only a reflection.

Thus the totem is before all a symbol, a material expression of something else.[1] But of what?

From the analysis to which we have been giving our attention, it is evident that it expresses and symbolizes two different sorts of things. In the first place, it is the outward and visible form of what we have called the totemic principle or god. But it is also the symbol of the determined society called the clan. It is its flag; it is the sign by which each clan distinguishes itself from the others, the visible mark of its personality, a mark borne by everything which is a part of the clan under any title whatsoever, men, beasts or things. So if it is at once the symbol of the god and of the society, is that not because the god and the society are only one? How could the emblem of the group have been able to become the figure of this quasi-divinity, if the group and the divinity were two distinct realities? The god of the clan, the totemic principle, can therefore be nothing else than the clan itself, personified and represented to the imagination under the visible form of the animal or vegetable which serves as totem.

But how has this apotheosis been possible, and how did it happen to take place in this fashion?

II

In a general way, it is unquestionable that a society has all that is necessary to arouse the sensation of the divine in minds, merely by the power that it has over them; for to its members it is what a god is to his worshippers. In fact, a god is, first of all, a being whom men think of as superior to themselves, and upon whom they feel that they depend. Whether it be a conscious personality, such as Zeus or Jahveh, or merely abstract forces such as those in play in totemism, the worshipper, in the one case as in the other, believes himself held to certain manners of acting which are imposed upon him by the nature of the sacred principle with which he feels that he is in communion. Now society also gives us the sensation of a perpetual dependence. Since it has a nature which is peculiar to itself and different from our individual nature, it pursues ends which are likewise special to it; but, as it cannot attain them except through our intermediacy, it imperiously demands our aid. It requires that, forgetful of our own interests, we make ourselves its servitors, and it submits us to every sort of inconvenience, privation and sacrifice, without which social life would be impossible. It is because of this that at every instant we are obliged to submit ourselves to rules of conduct and of thought which we have neither made nor desired, and which are sometimes even contrary to our most fundamental inclinations and instincts.

Even if society were unable to obtain these concessions and sacrifices from us except by a material constraint, it might awaken in us only the idea of a physical force to which we must give way of necessity, instead of that of a moral power such as religions adore. But as a matter of fact, the empire which it holds over consciences is due much less to the physical supremacy of which it has the privilege than to the moral authority with which it is invested. If we yield to its orders, it is not merely because it is strong enough to triumph over our resistance; it is primarily because it is the object of a venerable respect.

We say that an object, whether individual or collective, inspires respect when the representation expressing it in the mind is gifted with such a force that it automatically causes or inhibits actions, *without regard for any consideration relative to their useful or injurious effects*. When we obey somebody because of the moral authority which we recognize in him, we follow out his opinions, not because they seem wise, but because a certain sort of physical energy is imminent in the idea that we form of this person, which conquers our will and inclines it in the indicated direction. Respect is the emotion which we experience when we feel this interior and wholly spiritual pressure operating upon us. Then we are not determined by the advantages or inconveniences of the attitude which is prescribed or recommended to us; it is by the way in which we represent to ourselves the person recommending or prescribing it. This is why commands generally take a short, peremptory form leaving no place for hesitation; it is because, in so far as it is a command and goes by its own force, it excludes all idea of deliberation or calculation; it gets its efficacy from the intensity of the mental state in which it is placed. It is this intensity which creates what is called a moral ascendancy.

Now the ways of action to which society is strongly enough attached to impose them upon its members, are, by that very fact, marked with a distinctive sign provocative of respect. Since they are elaborated in common, the vigour with which they have been thought of by each particular mind is retained in all the other minds, and reciprocally. The representations which express them within each of us have an intensity which no purely private states of consciousness could ever attain; for they have the strength of the innumerable individual representations which have served to form each of them. It is society who speaks through the mouths of those who affirm them in our presence; it is society whom we hear in hearing them; and the voice of all has an accent which that of one alone could never have.[2] The very violence with which society reacts, by way of blame or material suppression, against every attempted dissidence, contributes to strengthening its empire by manifesting the common conviction through this burst of ardour.[3] In a word, when something is the object of such a state of opinion, the representation which each individual has of it gains a power of action from its origins and the conditions in which it was born, which even those feel who do not submit themselves to it. It tends to repel the representations which contradict it, and it keeps them at a distance; on the other hand, it commands those acts which will realize it, and it does so, not by a material coercion or by the perspective of something of this sort, but by the simple radiation of the mental energy which it contains. It has an efficacy coming solely from its psychical properties, and it is by just this sign that moral authority is recognized. So opinion, primarily a social thing, is a source of authority, and it might even be asked whether all authority is not the daughter of opinion.[4] It may be objected that science is often the antagonist of opinion, whose errors it combats and rectifies. But it cannot succeed in this task if it does not have sufficient authority, and it can obtain this authority only from opinion itself. If a people did not have faith in science, all the scientific demonstrations in the world would be without any influence whatsoever over their minds. Even to-day, if science happened to resist a very strong current of public opinion, it would risk losing its credit there.[5]

Since it is in spiritual ways that social pressure exercises itself, it could not fail to give men the idea that outside themselves there exist one or several powers, both moral and, at the same time, efficacious, upon which they depend. They must think of these powers, at least in part, as outside themselves, for these address them in a tone of command and sometimes even order them to do violence to their most natural inclinations. It is undoubtedly true that if they were able to see that these influences which they feel emanate from society, then the mythological system of interpretations would never be born. But social action follows ways that are too circuitous and obscure, and employs psychical mechanisms that are too complex to allow the ordinary observer to see whence it comes. As long as scientific analysis does not come to teach it to them, men know well that they are acted upon, but they do not know by whom. So they must invent by themselves the idea of these powers with which they feel themselves in connection, and from that, we are able to catch a glimpse of the way by which they were led to represent them under forms that are really foreign to their nature and to transfigure them by thought.

But a god is not merely an authority upon whom we depend; it is a force upon which our strength relies. The man who has obeyed his god and who, for this reason, believes the god is with him, approaches the world with confidence and with the feeling of an increased energy. Likewise, social action does not confine itself to demanding sacrifices, privations and efforts from us. For the collective force is not entirely outside of us; it does not act upon us wholly from without; but rather, since society cannot exist except in and through individual consciousnesses,[6] this force must also penetrate us and organize itself within us; it thus becomes an integral part of our being and by that very fact this is elevated and magnified.

There are occasions when this strengthening and vivifying action of society is especially apparent. In the midst of an assembly animated by a common passion, we become susceptible of acts and sentiments of which we are incapable when reduced to our own forces; and when the assembly is dissolved and when, finding ourselves alone again, we fall back to our ordinary level, we are then able to measure the height to which we have been raised above ourselves. History abounds in examples of this sort. It is enough to think of the night of the Fourth of August, 1789, when an assembly was suddenly led to an act of sacrifice and abnegation which each of its members had refused the day before, and at which they were all surprised the day after.[7] This is why all parties, political, economic or confessional, are careful to have periodical reunions where their members may revivify their common faith by manifesting it in common. To strengthen those sentiments which, if left to themselves, would soon weaken, it is sufficient to bring those who hold them together and to put them into closer and more active relations with one another. This is the explanation of the particular attitude of a man speaking to a crowd, at least if he has succeeded in entering into communion with it. His language has a grandiloquence that would be ridiculous in ordinary circumstances; his gestures show a certain domination;

his very thought is impatient of all rules, and easily falls into all sorts of excesses. It is because he feels within him an abnormal over-supply of force which overflows and tries to burst out from him; sometimes he even has the feeling that he is dominated by a moral force which is greater than he and of which he is only the interpreter. It is by this trait that we are able to recognize what has often been called the demon of oratorical inspiration. Now this exceptional increase of force is something very real; it comes to him from the very group which he addresses. The sentiments provoked by his words come back to him, but enlarged and amplified, and to this degree they strengthen his own sentiment. The passionate energies he arouses re-echo within him and quicken his vital tone. It is no longer a simple individual who speaks; it is a group incarnate and personified.

Beside these passing and intermittent states, there are other more durable ones, where this strengthening influence of society makes itself felt with greater consequences and frequently even with greater brilliancy. There are periods in history when, under the influence of some great collective shock, social interactions have become much more frequent and active. Men look for each other and assemble together more than ever. That general effervescence results which is characteristic of revolutionary or creative epochs. Now this greater activity results in a general stimulation of individual forces. Men see more and differently now than in normal times. Changes are not merely of shades and degrees; men become different. The passions moving them are of such an intensity that they cannot be satisfied except by violent and unrestrained actions, actions of superhuman heroism or of bloody barbarism. This is what explains the Crusades,[8] for example, or many of the scenes, either sublime or savage, of the French Revolution.[9] Under the influence of the general exaltation, we see the most mediocre and inoffensive bourgeois become either a hero or a butcher.[10] And so clearly are all these mental processes the ones that are also at the root of religion that the individuals themselves have often pictured the pressure before which they thus gave way in a distinctly religious form. The Crusaders believed that they felt God present in the midst of them, enjoining them to go to the conquest of the Holy Land; Joan of Arc believed that she obeyed celestial voices.[11]

But it is not only in exceptional circumstances that this stimulating action of society makes itself felt; there is not, so to speak, a moment in our lives when some current of energy does not come to us from without. The man who has done his duty finds, in the manifestations of every sort expressing the sympathy, esteem or affection which his fellows have for him, a feeling of comfort, of which he does not ordinarily take account, but which sustains him, none the less. The sentiments which society has for him raise the sentiments which he has for himself. Because he is in moral harmony with his comrades, he has more confidence, courage and boldness in action, just like the believer who thinks that he feels the regard of his god turned graciously towards him. It thus produces, as it were, a perpetual sustenance for our moral nature. Since this varies with a multitude of external circumstances, as our relations with the groups about us are more or less active and as these groups themselves vary, we cannot fail to feel that this moral support depends upon an external cause; but we do not perceive where this cause is nor what it is. So we ordinarily think of it under the form of a moral power which, though immanent in us, represents within us something not ourselves: this is the moral conscience, of which, by the way, men have never made even a slightly distinct representation except by the aid of religious symbols.

In addition to these free forces which are constantly coming to renew our own, there are others which are fixed in the methods and traditions which we employ. We speak a language that we did not make; we use instruments that we did not invent; we invoke rights that we did not found; a treasury of knowledge is transmitted to each generation that it did not gather itself, etc. It is to society that we owe these varied benefits of civilization, and if we do not ordinarily see the source from which we get them, we at least know that they are not our own work. Now it is these things that give man his own place among things; a man is a man only because he is civilized. So he could not escape the feeling that outside of him there are active causes from which he gets the characteristic attributes of his nature and which, as benevolent powers, assist him, protect him and assure him of a privileged fate. And of course he must attribute to these powers a dignity corresponding to the great value of the good things he attributes to them.[12]

Thus the environment in which we live seems to us to be peopled with forces that are at once imperious and helpful, august and gracious, and with which we have relations. Since they exercise over us a pressure of which we are conscious, we are forced to localize them outside ourselves, just as we do for the objective causes of our sensations. But the sentiments which they inspire in us differ in nature from those which we have for simple visible objects. As long as these latter are reduced to their empirical characteristics as shown in ordinary experience, and as long as the religious imagination has not metamorphosed them, we entertain for them no feeling which resembles respect, and they contain within them nothing that is able to raise us outside ourselves. Therefore, the representations which express them appear to us to be very different from those aroused in us by collective influences. The two form two distinct and separate mental states in our consciousness, just as do the two forms of life to which they correspond. Consequently, we get the impression that we are in relations with two distinct sorts of reality and that a sharply drawn line of demarcation separates them from each other: on the one hand is the world of profane things, on the other, that of sacred things.

Also, in the present day just as much as in the past, we see society constantly creating sacred things out of ordinary ones. If it happens to fall in love with a man and if it thinks it has found in him the principal aspirations that move it, as well as the means of satisfying them, this man will be raised above the others and, as it were, deified. Opinion will invest him with a majesty exactly analogous to that protecting the gods. This is what has happened to so many sovereigns in whom their age had faith: if they were not made gods, they were at least regarded as direct representatives of the deity. And the fact that it is society alone which is the author of these varieties of apotheosis, is evident since it frequently chances to consecrate men thus who have no right to it from their own merit. The simple deference inspired by men invested with high social functions is not different in nature from religious respect. It is expressed by the same movements: a man keeps at a distance from a high personage; he approaches him only with precautions; in conversing with him, he uses other gestures and language than those used with ordinary mortals. The sentiment felt on these occasions is so closely related to the religious sentiment that many peoples have confounded the two. In order to explain the consideration accorded to princes, nobles and political chiefs, a sacred character has been attributed to them. In Melanesia and Polynesia, for example, it is said that an influential man has *mana*, and that his influence is due to this *mana*.[13] However, it is evident that his situation is due solely to the importance attributed to him by public opinion. Thus the moral power conferred by opinion and that with which sacred beings are invested are at bottom of a single origin and made up of the same elements. That is why a single word is able to designate the two.

In addition to men, society also consecrates things, especially ideas. If a belief is unanimously shared by a people, then, for the reason which we pointed out above, it is forbidden to touch it, that is to say, to deny it or to contest it. Now the prohibition of criticism is an interdiction like the others and proves the presence of something sacred. Even to-day, howsoever great may be the liberty which we accord to others, a man who should totally deny progress or ridicule the human ideal to which modern societies are attached, would produce the effect of a sacrilege. There is at least one principle which those the most devoted to the free examination of everything tend to place above discussion and to regard as untouchable, that is to say, as sacred: this is the very principle of free examination.

This aptitude of society for setting itself up as a god or for creating gods was never more apparent than during the first years of the French Revolution. At this time, in fact, under the influence of the general enthusiasm, things purely laical by nature were transformed by public opinion into sacred things: these were the Fatherland, Liberty, Reason.[14] A religion tended to become established which had its dogmas,[15] symbols,[16] altars[17] and feasts.[18] It was to these spontaneous aspirations that the cult of Reason and the Supreme Being attempted to give a sort of official satisfaction. It is true that this religious renovation had only an ephemeral duration. But that was because the patriotic enthusiasm which at first transported the masses soon relaxed.[19] The cause being gone, the effect could not remain. But this experiment, though short-lived, keeps all its sociological interest. It remains true that in one determined case we have seen society and its essential ideas become, directly and with no transfiguration of any sort, the object of a veritable cult.

All these facts allow us to catch glimpses of how the clan was able to awaken within its members the idea that outside of them there exist forces which dominate them and at the same time sustain them, that is to say in fine, religious forces: it is because there is no society with which the primitive is more directly and closely connected. The bonds uniting him to the tribe are much more lax and more feebly felt. Although this is not at all strange or foreign to him, it is with the people of his own clan that he has the greatest number of things in common; it is the action of this group that he feels the most directly; so it is this also which, in preference to all others, should express itself in religious symbols.

But this first explanation has been too general, for it is applicable to every sort of society indifferently, and consequently to every sort of religion. Let us attempt to determine exactly what form this collective action takes in the clan and how it arouses the sensation of sacredness there. For there is no place where it is more easily observable or more apparent in its results.

III

The life of the Australian societies passes alternately through two distinct phases.[20] Sometimes the population is broken up into little groups who wander about independently of one another, in their various occupations; each family lives by itself, hunting and fishing, and in a word, trying to procure its indispensable food by all the means in its power. Sometimes, on the contrary, the population concentrates and gathers at determined points for a length of time varying from several days to several months.

This concentration takes place when a clan or a part of the tribe[21] is summoned to the gathering, and on this occasion they celebrate a religious ceremony, or else hold what is called a corrobbori[22] in the usual ethnological language.

These two phases are contrasted with each other in the sharpest way. In the first, economic activity is the preponderating one, and it is generally of a very mediocre intensity. Gathering the grains or herbs that are necessary for food, or hunting and fishing are not occupations to awaken very lively passions.[23] The dispersed condition in which the society finds itself results in making its life uniform, languishing and dull.[24] But when a corrobbori takes place, everything changes. Since the emotional and passional faculties of the primitive are only imperfectly placed under the control of his reason and will, he easily loses control of himself. Any event of some importance puts him quite outside himself. Does he receive good news? There are at once transports of enthusiasm. In the contrary conditions, he is to be seen running here and there like a madman, giving himself up to all sorts of immoderate movements, crying, shrieking, rolling in the dust, throwing it in every direction, biting himself, brandishing his arms in a furious manner, etc.[25] The very fact of the concentration acts as an exceptionally powerful stimulant. When they are once come together, a sort of electricity is formed by their collecting which quickly transports them to an extraordinary degree of exaltation. Every sentiment expressed finds a place without resistance in all the minds, which are very open to outside impressions; each re-echoes the others, and is re-echoed by the others. The initial impulse thus proceeds, growing as it goes, as an avalanche grows in its advance. And as such active passions so free from all control could not fail to burst out, on every side one sees nothing but violent gestures, cries, veritable howls, and deafening noises of every sort, which aid in intensifying still more the state of mind which they manifest. And since a collective sentiment cannot express itself collectively except on the condition of observing a certain order permitting co-operation and movements in unison, these gestures and cries naturally tend to become rhythmic and regular; hence come songs and dances. But in taking a more regular form, they lose nothing of their natural violence; a regulated tumult remains tumult. The human voice is not sufficient for the task; it is reinforced by means of artificial processes: boomerangs are beaten against each other; bull-roarers are whirled. It is probable that these instruments, the use of which is so general in the Australian religious ceremonies, are used primarily to express in a more adequate fashion the agitation felt. But while they express it, they also strengthen it. This effervescence often reaches such a point that it causes unheard-of actions. The passions released are of such an impetuosity that they can be restrained by nothing. They are so far removed from their ordinary conditions of life, and they are so thoroughly conscious of it, that they feel that they must set themselves outside of and above their ordinary morals. The sexes unite contrarily to the rules governing sexual relations. Men exchange wives with each other. Sometimes even incestuous unions, which in normal times are thought abominable and are severely punished, are now contracted openly and with impunity.[26] If we add to all this that the ceremonies generally take place at night in a darkness pierced here and there by the light of fires, we can easily imagine what effect such scenes ought to produce on the minds of those who participate. They produce such a violent super-excitation of the whole physical and mental life that it cannot be supported very long: the actor taking the principal part finally falls exhausted on the ground.[27]

To illustrate and make specific this necessarily schematic picture, let us describe certain scenes taken from Spencer and Gillen.

One of the most important religious ceremonies among the Warramunga is the one concerning the snake Wollunqua. It consists in a series of ceremonies lasting through several days. On the fourth day comes the following scene.

According to the ceremonial used among the Warramunga, representatives of the two phratries take part, one as officiants, the other as preparers and assistants. Only the members of the Uluuru phratry are qualified to celebrate the rite, but the members of the Kingilli phratry must decorate the actors, make ready the place and the instruments, and play the part of an audience. In this capacity, they are charged with making a sort of mound in advance out of wet sand, upon which a design is marked with red down which represents the snake Wollunqua. The real ceremony only commenced after nightfall. Towards ten or eleven o'clock, the Uluuru and Kingilli men arrived on the ground, sat down on the mound and commenced to sing. Everyone was evidently very excited. A little later in the evening, the Uluuru brought up their wives and gave them over to the Kingilli,[28] who had intercourse with them. Then the recently initiated young men were brought in and the whole ceremony was explained to them in detail, and until three o'clock in the morning singing went on without a pause. Then followed a scene of the wildest excitement. While fires were lighted on all sides, making the whiteness of the gum-trees stand out sharply against the surrounding darkness, the Uluuru knelt down one behind another beside the mound, then rising from the ground they went around it, with a movement in unison, their two hands resting upon their thighs, then a little farther on they knelt down again, and so on. At the same time they swayed their bodies, now to the right and now to the left, while uttering at each movement a piercing cry, a veritable yell, "*Yrrsh! Yrrsh! Yrrsh!*" In the meantime the Kingilli, in a state of great excitement, clanged their boomerangs and their chief was even more agitated than his companions. When the procession of the Uluuru had twice gone around the mound, quitting the kneeling position, they sat down and commenced to sing again; at moments the singing died away, then suddenly took up again. When day commenced to dawn, all leaped to their feet; the fires that had gone out were relighted and the Uluuru, urged on by the Kingilli, attacked the mound furiously with boomerangs, lances and clubs; in a few minutes it was torn to pieces. The fires died away and profound silence reigned again.[29]

A still more violent scene at which these same observers assisted was in connection with the fire ceremonies among the Warramunga.

Commencing at nightfall, all sorts of processions, dances and songs had taken place by torchlight; the general effervescence was constantly increasing. At a given moment, twelve assistants each took a great lighted torch in their hands, and one of them holding his like a bayonet, charged into a group of natives. Blows were warded off with clubs and spears. A general mêlée followed. The men leaped and pranced about, uttering savage yells all the time; the burning torches continually came crashing down on the heads and bodies of the men, scattering lighted sparks in every direction. "The smoke, the blazing torches, the showers of sparks falling in all directions and the masses of dancing, yelling men," say Spencer and Gillen, "formed altogether a genuinely wild and savage scene of which it is impossible to convey any adequate idea in words."[30]

One can readily conceive how, when arrived at this state of exaltation, a man does not recognize himself any longer. Feeling himself dominated and carried away by some sort of an external power which makes him think and act differently than in normal times, he naturally has the impression of being himself no longer. It seems to him that he has become a new being: the decorations he puts on and the masks that cover his face figure materially in this interior transformation, and to a still greater extent, they aid in determining its nature. And as at the same time all his companions feel themselves transformed in the same way and express this sentiment by their cries, their gestures and their general attitude, everything is just as though he really were transported into a special world, entirely different from the one where he ordinarily lives, and into an environment filled with exceptionally intense forces that take hold of him and metamorphose him. How could such experiences as these, especially when they are repeated every day for weeks, fail to leave in him the conviction that there really exist two heterogeneous and mutually incomparable worlds? One is that where his daily life drags wearily along; but he cannot penetrate into the other without at once entering into relations with extraordinary powers that excite him to the point of frenzy. The first is the profane world, the second, that of sacred things.

So it is in the midst of these effervescent social environments and out of this effervescence itself that the religious idea seems to be born. The theory that this is really its origin is confirmed by the fact that in Australia the really religious activity is almost entirely confined to the moments when these assemblies are held. To be sure, there is no people among whom the great solemnities of the cult are not more or less periodic; but in the more advanced societies, there is not, so to speak, a day when some prayer or offering is not addressed to the gods and some ritual act is not performed. But in Australia, on the contrary, apart from the celebrations of the clan and tribe, the time is nearly all filled with lay and profane occupations. Of course there are prohibitions that should be and are preserved even during these periods of temporal activity; it is never permissible to kill or eat freely of the totemic animal, at least in those parts where the interdiction has retained its original vigour; but almost no positive rites are then celebrated, and there are no ceremonies of any importance. These take place only in the midst of assembled groups. The religious life of the Australian passes through successive phases of complete lull and of superexcitation, and social life oscillates in the same rhythm. This puts clearly into evidence the bond uniting them to one another, but among the peoples called civilized, the relative continuity of the two blurs their relations. It might even be asked whether the violence of this contrast was not necessary to disengage the feeling of sacredness in its first form. By concentrating itself almost entirely in certain determined moments, the collective life has been able to attain its greatest intensity and efficacy, and consequently to give men a more active sentiment of the double existence they lead and of the double nature in which they participate.

But this explanation is still incomplete. We have shown how the clan, by the manner in which it acts upon its members, awakens within them the idea of external forces which dominate them and exalt them; but we must still demand how it happens that these forces are thought of under the form of totems, that is to say, in the shape of an animal or plant.

It is because this animal or plant has given its name to the clan and serves it as emblem. In fact, it is a well-known law that the sentiments aroused in us by something spontaneously attach themselves to the symbol which represents them. For us, black is a sign of mourning; it also suggests sad impressions and ideas. This transference of sentiments comes simply from the fact that the idea of a thing and the idea of its symbol are closely united in our minds; the result is that the emotions provoked by the one extend contagiously to the other. But this contagion, which takes place in every case to a certain degree, is much more complete and more marked when the symbol is something simple, definite and easily representable, while the thing itself, owing to its dimensions, the number of its parts and the complexity of their arrangement, is difficult to hold in the mind. For we are unable to consider an abstract entity, which we can represent only laboriously and confusedly, the source of the strong sentiments which we feel. We cannot explain them to ourselves except by connecting them to some concrete object of whose reality we are vividly aware. Then if the thing itself does not fulfill this condition, it cannot serve as the accepted basis of the sentiments felt, even though it may be what really aroused them. Then some sign takes its place; it is to this that we connect the emotions it excites. It is this which is loved, feared, respected; it is to this that we are grateful; it is for this that we sacrifice ourselves. The soldier who dies for his flag, dies for his country; but as a matter of fact, in his own consciousness, it is the flag that has the first place. It sometimes happens that this even directly determines action. Whether one isolated standard remains in the hands of the enemy or not does not determine the fate of the country, yet the soldier allows himself to be killed to regain it. He loses sight of the fact that the flag is only a sign, and that it has no value in itself, but only brings to mind the reality that it represents; it is treated as if it were this reality itself.

Now the totem is the flag of the clan. It is therefore natural that the impressions aroused by the clan in individual minds—impressions of dependence and of increased vitality—should fix themselves to the idea of the totem rather than that of the clan: for the clan is too complex a reality to be represented clearly in all its complex unity by such rudimentary intelligences. More than that, the primitive does not even see that these impressions come to him from the group. He does not know that the coming together of a number of men associated in the same life results in disengaging new energies, which transform each of them. All that he knows is that he is raised above himself and that he sees a different life from the one he ordinarily leads. However, he must connect these sensations to some external object as their cause. Now what does he see about him? On every side those things which appeal to his senses and strike his imagination are the numerous images of the totem. They are the waninga and the nurtunja, which are symbols of the sacred being. They are churinga and bull-roarers, upon which are generally carved combinations of lines having the same significance. They are the decorations covering the different parts of his body, which are totemic marks. How could this image, repeated everywhere and in all sorts of forms, fail to stand out with exceptional relief in his mind? Placed thus in the centre of the scene, it becomes representative. The sentiments experienced fix themselves upon it, for it is the only concrete object upon which they can fix themselves. It continues to bring them to mind and to evoke them even after the assembly has dissolved, for it survives the assembly, being carved upon the instruments of the cult, upon the sides of rocks, upon bucklers, etc. By it, the emotions experienced are perpetually sustained and revived. Everything happens just as if they inspired them directly. It is still more natural to attribute them to it for, since they are common to the group, they can be associated only with something that is equally common to all. Now the totemic emblem is the only thing satisfying this condition. By definition, it is common to all. During the ceremony, it is the centre of all regards. While generations change, it remains the same; it is the permanent element of the social life. So it is from it that those mysterious forces seem to emanate with which men feel that they are related, and thus they have been led to represent these forces under the form of the animate or inanimate being whose name the clan bears.

When this point is once established, we are in a position to understand all that is essential in the totemic beliefs.

Since religious force is nothing other than the collective and anonymous force of the clan, and since this can be represented in the mind only in the form of the totem, the totemic emblem is like the visible body of the god. Therefore, it is from it that those kindly or dreadful actions seem to emanate, which the cult seeks to provoke or prevent; consequently, it is to it that the cult is addressed. This is the explanation of why it holds the first place in the series of sacred things.

But the clan, like every other sort of society, can live only in and through the individual consciousnesses that compose it. So if religious force, in so far as it is conceived as incorporated in the totemic emblem, appears to be outside of the individuals and to be endowed with a sort of transcendence over them, it, like the clan of which it is the symbol, can be realized only in and through them; in this sense, it is immanent in them and they necessarily represent it as such. They feel it present and active within them, for it is this which raises them to a superior life. This is why men have believed that they contain within them a principle comparable to the one residing in the totem, and consequently, why they have attributed a sacred character to themselves, but one less marked than that of the emblem. It is because the emblem is the pre-eminent source of the religious life; the man participates in it only indirectly, as he is well aware; he takes into account the fact that the force that transports him into the world of sacred things is not inherent in him, but comes to him from the outside.

But for still another reason, the animals or vegetables of the totemic species should have the same character, and even to a higher degree. If the totemic principle is nothing else than the clan, it is the clan thought of under the material form of the totemic emblem; now this form is also that of the concrete beings whose name the clan bears. Owing to this resemblance, they could not fail to evoke sentiments analogous to those aroused by the emblem itself. Since the latter is the object of a religious respect, they too should inspire respect of the same sort and appear to be sacred. Having external forms so nearly identical, it would be impossible for the native not to attribute to them forces of the same nature. It is therefore forbidden to kill or eat the totemic animal, since its flesh is believed to have the positive virtues resulting from the rites; it is because it resembles the emblem of the clan, that is to say, it is in its own image. And since the animal naturally resembles the emblem more than the man does, it is placed on a superior rank in the hierarchy of sacred things. Between these two beings there is undoubtedly a close relationship, for they both partake of the same essence: both incarnate something of the totemic principle. However, since the principle itself is conceived under an animal form, the animal seems to incarnate it more fully than the man. Therefore, if men consider it and treat it as a brother, it is at least as an elder brother.[31]

But even if the totemic principle has its preferred seat in a determined species of animal or vegetable, it cannot remain localized there. A sacred character is to a high degree contagious; it therefore spreads out from the totemic being to everything that is closely or remotely connected with it. The religious sentiments inspired by the animal are communicated to the substances upon which it is nourished and which serve to make or remake its flesh and blood, to the things that resemble it, and to the different beings with which it has constant relations. Thus, little by little, sub-totems are attached to the totems and from the cosmological systems expressed by the primitive classifications. At last, the whole world is divided up among the totemic principles of each tribe.

We are now able to explain the origin of the ambiguity of religious forces as they appear in history, and how they are physical as well as human, moral as well as material. They are moral powers because they are made up entirely of the impressions this moral being, the group, arouses in those other moral beings, its individual members; they do not translate the manner in which physical things affect our senses, but the way in which the collective consciousness acts upon individual consciousnesses. Their authority is only one form of the moral ascendancy of society over its members. But, on the other hand, since they are conceived of under material forms, they could not fail to be regarded as closely related to material things.[32] Therefore they dominate the two worlds. Their residence is in men, but at the same time they are the vital principles of things. They animate minds and discipline them, but it is also they who make plants grow and animals reproduce. It is this double nature which has enabled religion to be like the womb from which come all the leading germs of human civilization. Since it has been made to embrace all of reality, the physical world as well as the moral one, the forces that move bodies as well as those that move minds have been conceived in a religious form. That is how the most diverse methods and practices, both those that make possible the continuation of the moral life (law, morals, beaux-arts) and those serving the material life (the natural, technical and practical sciences), are either directly or indirectly derived from religion.[33]

ELEMENTARY FORMS

OF RELIGIOUS LIFE

AT THE BEGINNING of this work we announced that the religion whose study we were taking up contained within it the most characteristic elements of the religious life. The exactness of this proposition may now be verified. Howsoever simple the system which we have studied may be, we have found within it all the great ideas and the principal ritual attitudes which are at the basis of even the most advanced religions: the division of things into sacred and profane, the notions of the soul, of spirits, of mythical personalities, and of a national and even international divinity, a negative cult with ascetic practices which are its exaggerated form, rites of oblation and communion, imitative rites, commemorative rites and expiatory rites; nothing essential is lacking. We are thus in a position to hope that the results at which we have arrived are not peculiar to totemism alone, but can aid us in an understanding of what religion in general is.

It may be objected that one single religion, whatever its field of extension may be, is too narrow a base for such an induction. We have not dreamed for a moment of ignoring the fact that an extended verification may add to the authority of a theory, but it is equally true that when a law has been proven by one well-made

From *The Elementary Forms of the Religious Life: A Study in Religious Sociology*, translated by Joseph Ward Swain (London: Allen and Unwin; New York: Macmillan Co., 1915; New York: Free Press, 1947, 1965), pp. 415–47. Originally published as *Les formes élémentaires de la vie religieuse: Le système totémique en Australie,* Travaux de l'année sociologique (Paris: Félix Alcan, 1912).

experiment, this proof is valid universally. If in one single case a scientist succeeded in finding out the secret of the life of even the most protoplasmic creature that can be imagined, the truths thus obtained would be applicable to all living beings, even the most advanced. Then if, in our studies of these very humble societies, we have really succeeded in discovering some of the elements out of which the most fundamental religious notions are made up, there is no reason for not extending the most general results of our researches to other religions. In fact, it is inconceivable that the same effect may be due now to one cause, now to another, according to the circumstances, unless the two causes are at bottom only one. A single idea cannot express one reality here and another one there, unless the duality is only apparent. If among certain peoples the ideas of sacredness, the soul and God are to be explained sociologically, it should be presumed scientifically that, in principle, the same explanation is valid for all the peoples among whom these same ideas are found with the same essential characteristics. Therefore, supposing that we have not been deceived, certain at least of our conclusions can be legitimately generalized. The moment has come to disengage these. And an induction of this sort, having at its foundation a clearly defined experiment, is less adventurous than many summary generalizations which, while attempting to reach the essence of religion at once, without resting upon the careful analysis of any religion in particular, greatly risk losing themselves in space.

I

The theorists who have undertaken to explain religion in rational terms have generally seen in it before all else a system of ideas, corresponding to some determined object. This object has been conceived in a multitude of ways: nature, the infinite, the unknowable, the ideal, etc.; but these differences matter but little. In any case, it was the conceptions and beliefs which were considered as the essential elements of religion. As for the rites, from this point of view they appear to be only an external translation, contingent and material, of these internal states which alone pass as having any intrinsic value. This conception is so commonly held that generally the disputes of which religion is the theme turn about the question whether it can conciliate itself with science or not, that is to say, whether or not there is a place beside our scientific knowledge for another form of thought which would be specifically religious.

But the believers, the men who lead the religious life and have a direct sensation of what it really is, object to this way of regarding it, saying that it does not correspond to their daily experience. In fact, they feel that the real function of religion is not to make us think, to enrich our knowledge, nor to add to the conceptions which we owe to science others of another origin and another character, but rather, it is to make us act, to aid us to live. The believer who has communicated with his god is not merely a man who sees new truths of which the unbeliever is ignorant; he is a man who is *stronger*. He feels within him more force, either to endure the trials of existence, or to conquer them. It is as though he were raised above the miseries of the world, because he is raised above his condition as a mere man; he believes that he is saved from evil, under whatever form he may conceive this evil. The first article in every creed is the belief in salvation by faith. But it is hard to see how a mere idea could have this efficacy. An idea is in reality only a part of ourselves; then how could it confer upon us powers superior to those which we have of our own nature? Howsoever rich it might be in affective virtues, it could add nothing to our natural vitality; for it could only release the motive powers which are within us, neither creating them nor increasing them. From the mere fact that we consider an object worthy of being loved and sought after, it does not follow that we feel ourselves stronger afterwards; it is also necessary that this object set free energies superior to these which we ordinarily have at our command and also that we have some means of making these enter into us and unite themselves to our interior lives. Now for that, it is not enough that we think of them; it is also indispensable that we place ourselves within their sphere of action, and that we set ourselves where we may best feel their influence; in a word, it is necessary that we act, and that we repeat the acts thus necessary every time we feel the need of renewing their effects. From this point of view, it is readily seen how that group of regularly repeated acts which form the cult get their importance. In fact, whoever has really practised a religion knows very well that it is the cult which gives rise to these impressions of joy, of interior peace, of serenity, of enthusiasm which are, for the believer, an experimental proof of his beliefs. The cult is not simply a system of signs by which the faith is outwardly translated; it is a collection of the means by which this is created and recreated periodically. Whether it consists in material acts or mental operations, it is always this which is efficacious.

Our entire study rests upon this postulate that the unanimous sentiment of the believers of all times cannot be purely illusory. Together with a recent apologist of the faith[1] we admit that these religious beliefs rest upon a specific experience whose demonstrative value is, in one sense, not one bit inferior to that of scientific experiments, though different from them. We, too, think that "a tree is known by its fruits,"[2] and that fertility is the best proof of what the roots are worth. But from the fact that a "religious experience," if we choose to call it this, does exist and that it has a certain foundation—and, by the way, is there any experience which has none?—it does not follow that the reality which is its foundation conforms objectively to the idea which believers have of it. The very fact that the fashion in which it has been conceived has varied infinitely in different times is enough to prove that none of these conceptions express it adequately. If a scientist states it as an axiom that the sensations of heat and light which we feel correspond to some objective cause, he does not conclude that this is what it appears to the senses to be. Likewise, even if the impressions which the faithful feel are not imaginary, still they are in no way privileged intuitions; there is no reason for believing that they inform us better upon the nature of their object than do ordinary sensations upon the nature of bodies and their properties. In order to discover what this object consists of, we must submit them to an examination and elaboration analogous to that which has substituted for the sensuous idea of the world another which is scientific and conceptual.

This is precisely what we have tried to do, and we have seen that this reality, which mythologies have represented under so many different forms, but which is the universal and eternal objective cause of these sensations *sui generis* out of which religious experience is made, is society. We have shown what moral forces it develops and how it awakens this sentiment of a refuge, of a shield and of a guardian support which attaches the believer to his cult. It is that which raises him outside himself; it is even that which made him. For that which makes a man is the totality of the intellectual property which constitutes civilization, and civilization is the work of society. Thus is explained the preponderating rôle of the cult in all religions, whichever they may be. This is because society cannot make its influence felt unless it is in action, and it is not in action unless the individuals who compose it are assembled together and act in common. It is by common action that it takes consciousness of itself and realizes its position; it is before all else an active co-operation. The collective ideas and sentiments are even possible only owing to these exterior movements which symbolize them, as we have established. Then it is action which dominates the religious life, because of the mere fact that it is society which is its source.

In addition to all the reasons which have been given to justify this conception, a final one may be added here, which is the result of our whole work. As we have progressed, we have established the fact that the fundamental categories of thought, and consequently of science, are of religious origin. We have seen that the same is true for magic and consequently for the different processes which have issued from it. On the other hand, it has long been known that up until a relatively advanced moment of evolution, moral and legal rules have been indistinguishable from ritual prescriptions. In summing up, then, it may be said that nearly all the great social institutions have been born in religion.[3] Now in order that these principal aspects of the collective life may have commenced by being only varied aspects of the religious life, it is obviously necessary that the religious life be the eminent form and, as it were, the concentrated expression of the whole collective life. If religion has given birth to all that is essential in society, it is because the idea of society is the soul of religion.

Religious forces are therefore human forces, moral forces. It is true that since collective sentiments can become conscious of themselves only by fixing themselves upon external objects, they have not been able to take form without adopting some of their characteristics from other things: they have thus acquired a sort of physical nature; in this way they have come to mix themselves with the life of the material world, and then have considered themselves capable of explaining what passes there. But when they are considered only from this point of view and in this rôle, only their most superficial aspect is seen. In reality, the essential elements of which these collective sentiments are made have been borrowed by the understanding. It ordinarily seems that they should have a human character only when they are conceived under human forms;[4] but even the most impersonal and the most anonymous are nothing else than objectified sentiments.

It is only by regarding religion from this angle that it is possible to see its real significance. If we stick closely to appearances, rites often give the effect of purely manual operations: they are anointings, washings, meals. To consecrate something, it is put in contact with a source of religious energy, just as to-day a body is put in contact with a source of heat or electricity to warm or electrize it; the two processes employed are not essentially different. Thus understood, religious technique seems to be a sort of mystic mechanics. But these material manoeuvres are only the external envelope under which the mental operations are hidden. Finally, there is no question of exercising a physical constraint upon blind and, incidentally, imaginary forces, but rather of reaching individual consciousnesses, of giving them a direction and of disciplining them. It is sometimes said that inferior religions are materialistic. Such an expression is inexact. All religions, even the crudest, are in a sense spiritualistic: for the powers they put in play are before all spiritual, and also their principal object is to act upon the moral life. Thus it is seen that whatever has been done in the name of religion cannot have been done in vain: for it is necessarily the society that did it, and it is humanity that has reaped the fruits.

But, it is said, what society is it that has thus made the basis of religion? Is it the real society, such as it is and acts before our very eyes, with the legal and moral organization which it has laboriously fashioned during the course of history? This is full of defects and imperfections. In it, evil goes beside the good, injustice often reigns supreme, and truth is often obscured by error. How could anything so crudely organized inspire the sentiments of love, the ardent enthusiasm and the spirit of abnegation which all religions claim of their followers? These perfect beings which are gods could not have taken their traits from so mediocre, and sometimes even so base a reality.

But, on the other hand, does someone think of a perfect society, where justice and truth would be sovereign, and from which evil in all its forms would be banished for ever? No one would deny that this is in close relation with the religious sentiment; for, they would say, it is towards the realization of this that all religions strive. But that society is not an empirical fact, definite and observable; it is a fancy, a dream with which men have lightened their sufferings, but in which they have never really lived. It is merely an idea which comes to express our more or less obscure aspirations towards the good, the beautiful and the ideal. Now these aspirations have their roots in us; they come from the very depths of our being; then there is nothing outside of us which can account for them. Moreover, they are already religious in themselves; thus it would seem that the ideal society presupposes religion, far from being able to explain it.[5]

But, in the first place, things are arbitrarily simplified when religion is seen only on its idealistic side: in its way, it is realistic. There is no physical or moral ugliness, there are no vices or evils which do not have a special divinity. There are gods of theft and trickery, of lust and war, of sickness and of death. Christianity itself, howsoever high the idea which it has made of the divinity may be, has been obliged to give the spirit of evil a place in its mythology. Satan is an essential piece of the Christian system; even if he is an impure being, he is not a profane one. The anti-god is a god, inferior and subordinated, it is true, but nevertheless endowed with extended powers; he is even the object of rites, at least of negative ones. Thus religion, far from ignoring the real society and making abstraction of it, is in its image; it reflects all its aspects, even the most vulgar and the most repulsive. All is to be found there, and if in the majority of cases we see the good victorious over evil, life over death, the powers of light over the powers of darkness, it is because reality is not otherwise. If the relation between these two contrary forces were reversed, life would be impossible; but, as a matter of fact, it maintains itself and even tends to develop.

But if, in the midst of these mythologies and theologies we see reality clearly appearing, it is none the less true that it is found there only in an enlarged, transformed and idealized form. In this respect, the most primitive religions do not differ from the most recent and the most refined. For example, we have seen how the Arunta place at the beginning of time a mythical society whose organization exactly reproduces that which still exists to-day; it includes the same clans and phratries, it is under the same matrimonial rules and it practises the same rites. But the personages who compose it are ideal beings, gifted with powers and virtues to which common mortals cannot pretend. Their nature is not only higher, but it is different, since it is at once animal and human. The evil powers there undergo a similar metamorphosis: evil itself is, as it were, made sublime and idealized. The question now raises itself of whence this idealization comes.

Some reply that men have a natural faculty for idealizing, that is to say, of substituting for the real world another different one, to which they transport themselves by thought. But that is merely changing the terms of the problem; it is not resolving it or even advancing it. This systematic idealization is an essential characteristic of religions. Explaining them by an innate power of idealization is simply replacing one word by another which is the equivalent of the first; it is as if they said that men have made religions because they have a religious nature. Animals know only one world, the one which they perceive by experience, internal as well as external. Men alone have the faculty of conceiving the ideal, of adding something to the real. Now where does this singular privilege come from? Before making it an initial fact or a mysterious virtue which escapes science, we must be sure that it does not depend upon empirically determinable conditions.

The explanation of religion which we have proposed has precisely this advantage, that it gives an answer to this question. For our definition of the sacred is that it is something added to and above the real: now the ideal answers to this same definition; we cannot explain one without explaining the other. In fact, we have seen that if collective life awakens religious thought on reaching a certain degree of intensity, it is because it brings about a state of effervescence which changes the conditions of psychic activity. Vital energies are over-excited, passions more active, sensations stronger; there are even some which are produced only at this moment. A man does not recognize himself; he feels himself transformed and consequently he transforms the environment which surrounds him. In order to account for the very particular impressions which he receives, he attributes to the things with which he is in most direct contact properties which they have not, exceptional powers and virtues which the objects of every-day experience do not possess. In a word, above the real world where his profane life passes he has placed another which, in one sense, does not exist except in thought, but to which he attributes a higher sort of dignity than to the first. Thus, from a double point of view it is an ideal world.

The formation of the ideal world is therefore not an irreducible fact which escapes science; it depends upon conditions which observation can touch; it is a natural product of social life. For a society to become conscious of itself and maintain at the necessary degree of intensity the sentiments which it thus attains, it must assemble and concentrate itself. Now this concentration brings about an exaltation of the mental life which takes form in a group of ideal conceptions where is portrayed the new life thus awakened; they correspond to this new set of psychical forces which is added to those which we have at our disposition for the daily tasks of existence. A society can neither create itself nor recreate itself without at the same time creating an ideal. This creation is not a sort of work of supererogation for it, by which it would complete itself, being already formed; it is the act by which it is periodically made and remade. Therefore when some oppose the ideal society to the real society, like two antagonists which would lead us in opposite directions, they materialize and oppose abstractions. The ideal society is not outside of the real society; it is a part of it. Far from being divided between them as between two poles which mutually repel each other, we cannot hold to one without holding to the other. For a society is not made up merely of the mass of individuals who compose it, the ground which they occupy, the things which they use and the movements which they perform, but above all is the idea which it forms of itself. It is undoubtedly true that it hesitates over the manner in which it ought to conceive itself; it feels itself drawn in divergent directions. But these conflicts which break forth are not between the ideal and reality, but between two different ideals, that of yesterday and that of to-day, that which has the authority of tradition and that which has the hope of the future. There is surely a place for investigating whence these ideals evolve; but whatever solution may be given to this problem, it still remains that all passes in the world of the ideal.

Thus the collective ideal which religion expresses is far from being due to a vague innate power of the individual, but it is rather at the school of collective life that the individual has learned to idealize. It is in assimilating the ideals elaborated by society that he has become capable of conceiving the ideal. It is society which, by leading him within its sphere of action, has made him acquire the need of raising himself above the world of experience and has at the same time furnished him with the means of conceiving another. For society has constructed this new world in constructing itself, since it is society which this expresses. Thus both with the individual and in the group, the faculty of idealizing has nothing mysterious about it. It is not a sort of luxury which a man could get along without, but a condition of his very existence. He could not be a social being, that is to say, he could not be a man, if he had not acquired it. It is true that in incarnating themselves in individuals, collective ideals tend to individualize themselves. Each understands them after his own fashion and marks them with his own stamp; he suppresses certain elements and adds others. Thus the personal ideal disengages itself from the social ideal in proportion as the individual personality develops itself and becomes an autonomous source of action. But if we wish to understand this aptitude, so singular in appearance, of living outside of reality, it is enough to connect it with the social conditions upon which it depends.

Therefore it is necessary to avoid seeing in this theory of religion a simple restatement of historical materialism: that would be misunderstanding our thought to an extreme degree. In showing that religion is something essentially social, we do not mean to say that it confines itself to translating into another language the material forms of society and its immediate vital necessities. It is true that we take it as evident that social life depends upon its material foundation and bears its mark, just as the mental life of an individual depends upon his nervous system and in fact his whole organism. But collective consciousness is something more than a mere epiphenomenon of its morphological basis, just as individual consciousness is something more than a simple efflorescence of the nervous system. In order that the former may appear, a synthesis *sui generis* of particular consciousnesses is required. Now this synthesis has the effect of disengaging a whole world of sentiments, ideas and images which, once born, obey laws all their own. They attract each other, repel each other, unite, divide themselves, and multiply, though these combinations are not commanded and necessitated by the condition of the underlying reality. The life thus brought into being even enjoys so great an independence that it sometimes indulges in manifestations with no purpose or utility of any sort, for the mere pleasure of affirming itself. We have shown that this is often precisely the case with ritual activity and mythological thought.[6]

But if religion is the product of social causes, how can we explain the individual cult and the universalistic character of certain religions? If it is born *in foro externo*, how has it been able to pass into the inner conscience of the individual and penetrate there ever more and more profoundly? If it is the work of definite and individualized societies, how has it been able to detach itself from them, even to the point of being conceived as something common to all humanity?

In the course of our studies, we have met with the germs of individual religion and of religious cosmopolitanism, and we have seen how they were formed; thus we possess the more general elements of the reply which is to be given to this double question.

We have shown how the religious force which animates the clan particularizes itself, by incarnating itself in particular consciousness. Thus secondary sacred beings are formed; each individual has his own, made in his own image, associated to his own intimate life, bound up with his own destiny; it is the soul, the individual totem, the protecting ancestor, etc. These beings are the object of rites which the individual can celebrate by himself, outside of any group; this is the first form of the individual cult. To be sure, it is only a very rudimentary cult; but since the personality of the individual is still only slightly marked, and but little value is attributed to it, the cult which expresses it could hardly be expected to be very highly developed as yet. But as individuals have differentiated themselves more and more and the value of an individual has increased, the corresponding cult has taken a relatively greater place in the totality of the religious life and at the same time it is more fully closed to outside influences.

Thus the existence of individual cults implies nothing which contradicts or embarrasses the sociological interpretation of religion; for the religious forces to which it addresses itself are only the individualized forms of collective forces. Therefore, even when religion seems to be entirely within the individual conscience, it is still in society that it finds the living source from which it is nourished. We are now able to appreciate the value of the radical individualism which would make religion something purely individual: it misunderstands the fundamental conditions of the religious life. If up to the present it has remained in the stage of theoretical aspirations which have never been realized, it is because it is unrealizable. A philosophy may well be elaborated in the silence of the interior imagination, but not so a faith. For before all else, a faith is warmth, life, enthusiasm, the exaltation of the whole mental life, the raising of the individual above himself. Now how could he add to the energies which he possesses without going outside himself? How could he surpass himself merely by his own forces? The only source of life at which we can morally reanimate ourselves is that formed by the society of our fellow beings; the only moral forces with which we can sustain and increase our own are those which we get from others. Let us even admit that there really are beings more or less analogous to those which the mythologies represent. In order that they may exercise over souls the useful direction which is their reason for existence, it is necessary that men believe in them. Now these beliefs are active only when they are partaken by many. A man cannot retain them any length of time by a purely personal effort; it is not thus that they are born or that they are acquired; it is even doubtful if they can be kept under these conditions. In fact, a man who has a veritable faith feels an invincible need of spreading it: therefore he leaves his isolation, approaches others and seeks to convince them, and it is the ardour of the convictions which he arouses that strengthens his own. It would quickly weaken if it remained alone.

It is the same with religious universalism as with this individualism. Far from being an exclusive attribute of certain very great religions, we have found it, not at the base, it is true, but at the summit of the Australian system. Bunjil, Daramulun or Baiame are not simple tribal gods; each of them is recognized by a number of different tribes. In a sense, their cult is international. This conception is therefore very near to that found in the most recent theologies. So certain writers have felt it their duty to deny its authenticity, howsoever incontestable this may be.

And we have been able to show how this has been formed.

Neighbouring tribes of a similar civilization cannot fail to be in constant relations with each other. All sorts of circumstances give an occasion for it: besides commerce, which is still rudimentary, there are marriages; these international marriages are very common in Australia. In the course of these meetings, men naturally become conscious of the moral relationship which united them. They have the same social organization, the same division into phratries, clans and matrimonial classes; they practise the same rites of initiation, or wholly similar ones. Mutual loans and treaties result in reinforcing these spontaneous resemblances. The gods to which these manifestly identical institutions were attached could hardly have remained distinct in their minds. Everything tended to bring them together and consequently, even supposing that each tribe elaborated the notion independently, they must necessarily have tended to confound themselves with each other. Also, it is probable that it was in inter-tribal assemblies that they were first conceived. For they are chiefly the gods of initiation, and in the initiation ceremonies, the different tribes are usually represented. So if sacred beings are formed which are connected with no geographically determined society, that is not because they have an extra-social origin. It is because there are other groups above these geographically determined ones, whose contours are less clearly marked: they have no fixed frontiers, but include all sorts of more or less neighbouring and related tribes. The particular social life thus created tends to spread itself over an area with no definite limits. Naturally the mythological personages who correspond to it have the same character; their sphere of influence is not limited; they go beyond the particular tribes and their territory. They are the great international gods.

Now there is nothing in this situation which is peculiar to Australian societies. There is no people and no state which is not a part of another society, more or less unlimited, which embraces all the peoples and all the States with which the first comes in contact, either directly or indirectly; there is no national life which is not dominated by a collective life of an international nature. In proportion as we advance in history, these international groups acquire a greater importance and extent. Thus we see how, in certain cases, this universalistic tendency has been able to develop itself to the point of affecting not only the higher ideas of the religious system, but even the principles upon which it rests.

II

Thus there is something eternal in religion which is destined to survive all the particular symbols in which religious hought has successively enveloped itself. There can be no society which does not feel the need of upholding and reaffirming at regular intervals the collective sentiments and the collective ideas which make its unity and its personality. Now this moral remaking cannot be achieved except by the means of reunions, assemblies and meetings where the individuals, being closely united to one another, reaffirm in common their common sentiments; hence come ceremonies which do not differ from regular religious ceremonies, either in their object, the results which they produce, or the processes employed to attain these results. What essential difference is there between an assembly of Christians celebrating the principal dates of the life of Christ, or of Jews remembering the exodus from Egypt or the promulgation of the decalogue, and a reunion of citizens commemorating the promulgation of a new moral or legal system or some great event in the national life?

If we find a little difficulty to-day in imagining what these feasts and ceremonies of the future could consist in, it is because we are going through a stage of transition and moral mediocrity. The great things of the past which filled our fathers with enthusiasm do not excite the same ardour in us, either because they have come into common usage to such an extent that we are unconscious of them, or else because they no longer answer to our actual aspirations; but as yet there is nothing to replace them. We can no longer impassionate ourselves for the principles in the name of which Christianity recommended to masters that they treat their slaves humanely, and, on the other hand, the idea which it has formed of human equality and fraternity seems to us to-day to leave too large a place for unjust inequalities. Its pity for the outcast seems to us too Platonic; we desire another which would be more practicable; but as yet we cannot clearly see what it should be nor how it could be realized in facts. In a word, the old gods are growing old or already dead, and others are not yet born. This is what rendered vain the attempt of Comte with the old historic souvenirs artificially revived: it is life itself, and not a dead past which can produce a living cult. But this state of incertitude and confused agitation cannot last for ever. A day will come when our societies will know again those hours of creative effervescence, in the course of which new ideas arise and new formulæ are found which serve for a while as a guide to humanity; and when these hours shall have been passed through once, men will spontaneously feel the need of reliving them from time to time in thought, that is to say, of keeping alive their memory by means of celebrations which regularly reproduce their fruits. We have already seen how the French Revolution established a whole cycle of holidays to keep the principles with which it was inspired in a state of perpetual youth. If this institution quickly fell away, it was because the revolutionary faith lasted but a moment, and deceptions and discouragements rapidly succeeded the first moments of enthusiasm. But though the work may have miscarried, it enables us to imagine what might have happened in other conditions; and everything leads us to believe that it will be taken up again sooner or later. There are no gospels which are immortal, but neither is there any reason for believing that humanity is incapable of inventing new ones. As to the question of what symbols this new faith will express itself with, whether they will resemble those of the past or not, and whether or not they will be more adequate for the reality which they seek to translate, that is something which surpasses the human faculty of foresight and which does not appertain to the principal question.

But feasts and rites, in a word, the cult, are not the whole religion. This is not merely a system of practices, but also a system of ideas whose object is to explain the world; we have seen that even the humblest have their cosmology. Whatever connection there may be between these two elements of the religious life, they are still quite different. The one is turned towards action, which it demands and regulates; the other is turned towards thought, which it enriches and organizes. Then they do not depend upon the same conditions, and consequently it may be asked if the second answers to necessities as universal and as permanent as the first.

When specific characteristics are attributed to religious thought, and when it is believed that its function is to express, by means peculiar to itself, an aspect of reality which evades ordinary knowledge as well as science, one naturally refuses to ad-

mit that religion can ever abandon its speculative role. But our analysis of the facts does not seem to have shown this specific quality of
religion. The religion which we have just studied is one of those
whose symbols are the most disconcerting for the reason. There
all appears mysterious. These beings which belong to the most
heterogeneous groups at the same time, who multiply without ceasing to be one, who divide without diminishing, all seem, at first
view, to belong to an entirely different world from the one where
we live; some have even gone so far as to say that the mind which
constructed them ignored the laws of logic completely. Perhaps the
contrast between reason and faith has never been more thorough.
Then if there has ever been a moment in history when their hetero-
geneousness should have stood out clearly, it is here. But contrary to all appearances, as we have pointed out, the realities to
which religious speculation is then applied are the same as those
which later serve as the subject of reflection for philosophers: they
are nature, man, society. The mystery which appears to surround
them is wholly superficial and disappears before a more painstak-
ing observation: it is enough merely to set aside the veil with
which mythological imagination has covered them for them to appear such as they really are. Religion sets itself to translate these
realities into an intelligible language which does not differ in nature from that employed by science; the attempt is made by both
to connect things with each other, to establish internal relations
between them, to classify them and to systematize them. We have
even seen that the essential ideas of scientific logic are of religious
origin. It is true that in order to utilize them, science gives them
a new elaboration; it purges them of all accidental elements; in
a general way, it brings a spirit of criticism into all its doings,
which religion ignores; it surrounds itself with precautions to
"escape precipitation and bias," and to hold aside the passions,
prejudices and all subjective influences. But these perfectionings
of method are not enough to differentiate it from religion. In this
regard, both pursue the same end; scientific thought is only a more
perfect form of religious thought. Thus it seems natural that the
second should progressively retire before the first, as this becomes
better fitted to perform the task.

And there is no doubt that this regression has taken place in the course of history. Having left religion, science tends to substitute itself for this latter in all that which concerns the cognitive and intellectual functions. Christianity has already definitely consecrated this substitution in the order of material things. Seeing in matter that which is profane before all else, it readily left the knowledge of this to another discipline, *tradidit mundum hominum disputationi*, "He gave the world over to the disputes of men"; it is thus that the natural sciences have been able to establish themselves and make their authority recognized without very great difficulty. But it could not give up the world of souls so easily; for it is before all over souls that the god of the Christians aspires to reign. That is why the idea of submitting the psychic life to science produced the effect of a sort of profanation for a long time; even to-day it is repugnant to many minds. However, experimental and comparative psychology is founded and to-day we must reckon with it. But the world of the religious and moral life is still forbidden. The great majority of men continue to believe that here there is an order of things which the mind cannot penetrate except by very special ways. Hence comes the active resistance which is met with every time that someone tries to treat religious and moral phenomena scientifically. But in spite of these oppositions, these attempts are constantly repeated and this persistence even allows us to foresee that this final barrier will finally give way and that science will establish herself as mistress even in this reserved region.

That is what the conflict between science and religion really amounts to. It is said that science denies religion in principle. But religion exists; it is a system of given facts; in a word, it is a reality. How could science deny this reality? Also, in so far as religion is action, and in so far as it is a means of making men live, science could not take its place, for even if this expresses life, it does not create it; it may well seek to explain the faith, but by that very act it presupposes it. Thus there is no conflict except upon one limited point. Of the two functions which religion originally fulfilled, there is one, and only one, which tends to escape it more and more: that is its speculative function. That which science refuses to grant to religion is not its right to exist, but its right to dogmatize upon the nature of things and the special competence which it claims for itself for knowing man and the world. As a matter of fact, it does not know itself. It does not even know what it is made of, nor to what need it answers. It is itself a subject for science, so far is it from being able to make the law for science! And from another point of view, since there is no proper subject for religious speculation outside that reality to which scientific reflection is applied, it is evident that this former cannot play the same role in the future that it has played in the past.

However, it seems destined to transform itself rather than to disappear.

We have said that there is something eternal in religion: it is the cult and the faith. Men cannot celebrate ceremonies for which they see no reason, nor can they accept a faith which they in no way understand. To spread itself or merely to maintain itself, it must be justified, that is to say, a theory must be made of it. A theory of this sort must undoubtedly be founded upon the different sciences, from the moment when these exist; first of all, upon the social sciences, for religious faith has its origin in society; then upon psychology, for society is a synthesis of human consciousnesses; and finally upon the sciences of nature, for man and society are a part of the universe and can be abstracted from it only artificially. But howsoever important these facts taken from the constituted sciences may be, they are not enough; for faith is before all else an impetus to action, while science, no matter how far it may be pushed, always remains at a distance from this. Science is fragmentary and incomplete; it advances but slowly and is never finished; but life cannot wait. The theories which are destined to make men live and act are therefore obliged to pass science and complete it prematurely. They are possible only when the practical exigencies and the vital necessities which we feel without distinctly conceiving them push thought in advance, beyond that which science permits us to affirm. Thus religions, even the most rational and laicized, cannot and never will be able to dispense with a particular form of speculation which, though having the same subjects as science itself, cannot be really scientific:

the obscure intuitions of sensation and sentiment too often take the place of logical reasons. On one side, this speculation resembles that which we meet with in the religions of the past; but on another, it is different. While claiming and exercising the right of going beyond science, it must commence by knowing this and by inspiring itself with it. Ever since the authority of science was established, it must be reckoned with; one can go farther than it under the pressure of necessity, but he must take his direction from it. He can affirm nothing that it denies, deny nothing that it affirms, and establish nothing that is not directly or indirectly founded upon principles taken from it. From now on, the faith no longer exercises the same hegemony as formerly over the system of ideas that we may continue to call religion. A rival power rises up before it which, being born of it, ever after submits it to its criticism and control. And everything makes us foresee that this control will constantly become more extended and efficient, while no limit can be assigned to its future influence.

III

But if the fundamental notions of science are of a religious origin, how has religion been able to bring them forth? At first sight, one does not see what relations there can be between religion and logic. Or, since the reality which religious thought expresses is society, the question can be stated in the following terms, which make the entire difficulty appear even better: what has been able to make social life so important a source for the logical life? It seems as though nothing could have predestined it to this role, for it certainly was not to satisfy their speculative needs that men associated themselves together.

Perhaps we shall be found over bold in attempting so complex a question here. To treat it as it should be treated, the sociological conditions of knowledge should be known much better than they actually are; we are only beginning to catch glimpses of some of them. However, the question is so grave, and so directly implied in all that has preceded, that we must make an effort not to leave it without an answer. Perhaps it is not impossible, even at present, to state some general principles which may at least aid in the solution.

Logical thought is made up of concepts. Seeking how society can have played a role in the genesis of logical thought thus reduces itself to seeking how it can have taken a part in the formation of concepts.

If, as is ordinarily the case, we see in the concept only a general idea, the problem appears insoluble. By his own power, the individual can compare his conceptions and images, disengage that which they have in common, and thus, in a word, generalize. Then it is hard to see why this generalization should be possible only in and through society. But, in the first place, it is inadmissible that logical thought is characterized only by the greater extension of the conceptions of which it is made up. If particular ideas have nothing logical about them, why should it be different with general ones? The general exists only in the particular; it is the particular simplified and impoverished. Then the first could have no virtues or privileges which the second has not. Inversely, if conceptual thought can be applied to the class, species or variety, howsoever restricted these may be, why can it not be extended to the individual, that is to say, to the limit towards which the conception tends, proportionately as its extension diminishes? As a matter of fact, there are many concepts which have only individuals as their object. In every sort of religion, gods are individualities distinct from each other; however, they are conceived, not perceived. Each people represents its historic or legendary heroes in fashions which vary with the time. Finally, every one of us forms an idea of the individuals with whom he comes in contract, of their character, of their appearance, their distinctive traits and their moral and physical temperaments: these notions, too, are real concepts. It is true that in general they are formed crudely enough; but even among scientific concepts, are there a great many that are perfectly adequate for their object? In this direction, there are only differences of degree between them.

Therefore the concept must be defined by other characteristics. It is opposed to sensual representations of every order—sensations, perceptions or images—by the following properties.

Sensual representations are in a perpetual flux; they come after each other like the waves of a river, and even during the time that they last, they do not remain the same thing. Each of them is an integral part of the precise instant when it takes place. We are never sure of again finding a perception such as we experienced it the first time; for if the thing perceived has not changed, it is we who are no longer the same. On the contrary, the concept is, as it were, outside of time and change; it is in the depths below all this agitation; it might be said that it is in a different portion of the mind, which is serener and calmer. It does not move of itself, by an internal and spontaneous evolution, but, on the contrary, it resists change. It is a manner of thinking that, at every moment of time, is fixed and crystallized.[7] In so far as it is what it ought to be, it is immutable. If it changes, it is not because it is its nature to do so, but because we have discovered some imperfection in it; it is because it had to be rectified. The system of concepts with which we think in everyday life is that expressed by the vocabulary of our mother tongue; for every word translates a concept. Now language is something fixed; it changes but very slowly, and consequently it is the same with the conceptual system which it expresses. The scholar finds himself in the same situation in regard to the special terminology employed by the science to which he has consecrated himself, and hence in regard to the special scheme of concepts to which this terminology corresponds. It is true that he can make innovations, but these are always a sort of violence done to the established ways of thinking.

And at the same time that it is relatively immutable, the concept is universal, or at least capable of becoming so. A concept is not my concept; I hold it in common with other men, or, in any case, can communicate it to them. It is impossible for me to make a sensation pass from my consciousness into that of another; it holds closely to my organism and personality and cannot be detached from them. All that I can do is to invite others to place themselves before the same object as myself and to leave themselves to its action. On the other hand, conversation and all intellectual communication between men is an exchange of concepts. The concept is an essentially impersonal representation; it is through it that human intelligences communicate.[8]

The nature of the concept, thus defined, bespeaks its origin. If it is common to all, it is the work of the community. Since it bears the mark of no particular mind, it is clear that it was elaborated by a unique intelligence, where all others meet each other, and after a fashion, come to nourish themselves. If it has more stability than sensations or images, it is because the collective representations are more stable than the individual ones; for while an individual is conscious even of the slight changes which take place in his environment, only events of a greater gravity can succeed in affecting the mental status of a society. Every time that we are in the presence of a *type*[9] of thought or action which is imposed uniformly upon particular wills or intelligences, this pressure exercised over the individual betrays the intervention of the group. Also, as we have already said, the concepts with which we ordinarily think are those of our vocabulary. Now it is unquestionable that language, and consequently the system of concepts which it translates, is the product of a collective elaboration. What it expresses is the manner in which society as a whole represents the facts of experience. The ideas which correspond to the diverse elements of language are thus collective representations.

Even their contents bear witness to the same fact. In fact, there are scarcely any words among those which we usually employ whose meaning does not pass, to a greater or less extent, the limits of our personal experience. Very frequently a term expresses things which we have never perceived or experiences which we have never had or of which we have never been the witnesses. Even when we know some of the objects which it concerns, it is only as particular examples that they serve to illustrate the idea which they would never have been able to form by themselves. Thus there is a great deal of knowledge condensed in the word which I never collected, and which is not individual; it even surpasses me to such an extent that I cannot even completely appropriate all its results. Which of us knows all the words of the language he speaks and the entire signification of each?

This remark enables us to determine the sense in which we mean to say that concepts are collective representations. If they belong to a whole social group, it is not because they represent the average of the corresponding individual representations; for in that case they would be poorer than the latter in intellectual content, while as a matter of fact, they contain much that surpasses the knowledge of the average individual. They are not abstractions which have a reality only in particular consciousnesses, but they are as concrete representations as an individual could form of his own personal environment: they correspond to the way in which this very special being, society, considers the things of its own proper experience. If, as a matter of fact, the concepts are nearly always general ideas, and if they express categories and classes rather than particular objects, it is because the unique and variable characteristics of things interest society but rarely; because of its very extent, it can scarcely be affected by more than their general and permanent qualities. Therefore it is to this aspect of affairs that it gives its attention: it is a part of its nature to see things in large and under the aspect which they ordinarily have. But this generality is not necessary for them, and, in any case, even when these representations have the generic character which they ordinarily have, they are the work of society and are enriched by its experience.

That is what makes conceptual thought so valuable for us. If concepts were only general ideas, they would not enrich knowledge a great deal, for, as we have already pointed out, the general contains nothing more than the particular. But if before all else they are collective representations, they add to that which we can learn by our own personal experience all that wisdom and science which the group has accumulated in the course of centuries. Thinking by concepts is not merely seeing reality on its most general side, but it is projecting a light upon the sensation which illuminates it, penetrates it and transforms it. Conceiving something is both learning its essential elements better and also locating it in its place; for each civilization has its organized system of concepts which characterizes it. Before this scheme of ideas, the individual is in the same situation as the *nous* of Plato before the world of Ideas. He must assimilate them to himself, for he must have them to hold intercourse with others; but the assimilation is always imperfect. Each of us sees them after his own fashion. There are some which escape us completely and remain outside of our circle of vision; there are others of which we perceive certain aspects only. There are even a great many which we pervert in holding, for as they are collective by nature, they cannot become individualized without being retouched, modified, and consequently falsified. Hence comes the great trouble we have in understanding each other, and the fact that we even lie to each other without wishing: it is because we all use the same words without giving them the same meaning.

We are now able to see what the part of society in the genesis of logical thought is. This is possible only from the moment when, above the fugitive conceptions which they owe to sensuous experience, men have succeeded in conceiving a whole world of stable ideas, the common ground of all intelligences. In fact, logical thinking is always impersonal thinking, and is also thought *sub species aeternitatis*—as though for all time. Impersonality and stability are the two characteristics of truth. Now logical life evidently presupposes that men know, at least confusedly, that there is such a thing as truth, distinct from sensuous appearances. But how have they been able to arrive at this conception? We generally talk as though it should have spontaneously presented itself to them from the moment they opened their eyes upon the world. However, there is nothing in immediate experience which could suggest it; everything even contradicts it. Thus the child and the animal have no suspicion of it. History shows that it has taken centuries for it to disengage and establish itself. In our Western world, it was with the great thinkers of Greece that it first became clearly conscious of itself and of the consequences which it implies; when the discovery was made, it caused an amazement which Plato has translated into magnificent language. But if it is only at this epoch that the idea is expressed in philosophic formulae, it was necessarily pre-existent in the stage of an obscure sentiment. Philosophers have sought to elucidate this sentiment, but they have not succeeded. In order that they might reflect upon it and analyse it, it was necessary that it be given them, and that they seek to know whence it came, that is to say, in what experience it was founded. This is in collective experience. It is under the form of collective thought that impersonal thought is for the first time revealed to humanity; we cannot see by what other way this revelation could have been made. From the mere fact that society exists, there is also, outside of the individual sensations and images, a whole system of representations which enjoy marvellous properties. By means of them, men understand each other and intelligences grasp each other. They have within them a sort of force of moral ascendancy, in virtue of which they impose themselves upon individual minds. Hence the individual at least obscurely takes account of the fact that above his private ideas, there is a world of absolute ideas according to which he must shape his own; he catches a glimpse of a whole intellectual kingdom in which he participates, but which is greater than he. This is the first intuition of the realm of truth. From the moment when he first becomes conscious of these higher ideas, he sets himself to scrutinizing their nature; he asks whence these pre-eminent representations hold their prerogatives and, in so far as he believes that he has discovered their causes, he undertakes to put these causes into action for himself, in order that he may draw from them by his own force the effects which they produce; that is to say, he attributes to himself the right of making concepts. Thus the faculty of conception has individualized itself. But to understand its origins and function, it must be attached to the social conditions upon which it depends.

It may be objected that we show the concept in one of its aspects only, and that its unique role is not the assuring of a harmony among minds, but also, and to a greater extent, their harmony with the nature of things. It seems as though it had a reason for existence only on condition of being true, that is to say, objective, and as though its impersonality were only a consequence of its objectivity. It is in regard to things, thought of as adequately as possible, that minds ought to communicate. Nor do we deny that the evolution of concepts has been partially in this direction. The concept which was first held as true because it was collective tends to be no longer collective except on condition of being held as true: we demand its credentials of it before according it our confidence. But we must not lose sight of the fact that even to-day the great majority of the concepts which we use are not methodically constituted; we get them from language, that is to say, from common experience, without submitting them to any criticism. The scientifically elaborated and criticized concepts are always in the very slight minority. Also, between them and those which draw all their authority from the fact that they are collective, there are only differences of degree. A collective representation presents guarantees of objectivity by the fact that it is collective: for it is not without sufficient reason that it has been able to generalize and maintain itself with persistence. If it were out of accord with the nature of things, it would never have been able to acquire an extended and prolonged empire over intellects. At bottom, the confidence inspired by scientific concepts is due to the fact that they can be methodically controlled. But a collective representation is necessarily submitted to a control that is repeated indefinitely; the men who accept it verify it by their own experience. Therefore, it could not be wholly inadequate for its subject. It is true that it may express this by means of imperfect symbols; but scientific symbols themselves are never more than approximative. It is precisely this principle which is at the basis of the method which we follow in the study of religious phenomena: we take it as an axiom that religious beliefs, howsoever strange their appearance may be at times, contain a truth which must be discovered.[10]

On the other hand, it is not at all true that concepts, even when constructed according to the rules of science, get their authority uniquely from their objective value. It is not enough that they be true to be believed. If they are not in harmony with the other beliefs and opinions, or, in a word, with the mass of the other collective representations, they will be denied; minds will be closed to them; consequently it will be as though they did not exist. To-day it is generally sufficient that they bear the stamp of science to receive a sort of privileged credit, because we have faith in science. But this faith does not differ essentially from religious faith. In the last resort, the value which we attribute to science depends upon the idea which we collectively form of its nature and role in life; that is as much as to say that it expresses a state of public opinion.

In all social life, in fact, science rests upon opinion. It is undoubtedly true that this opinion can be taken as the object of a study and a science made of it; this is what sociology principally consists in. But the science of opinion does not make opinions; it can only observe them and make them more conscious of themselves. It is true that by this means it can lead them to change, but science continues to be dependent upon opinion at the very moment when it seems to be making its laws; for, as we have already shown, it is from opinion that it holds the force necessary to act upon opinion.

Saying that concepts express the manner in which society represents things is also saying that conceptual thought is coeval with humanity itself. We refuse to see in it the product of a more or less retarded culture. A man who did not think with concepts would not be a man, for he would not be a social being. If reduced to having only individual perceptions, he would be indistinguishable from the beasts. If it has been possible to sustain the contrary thesis, it is because concepts have been defined by characteristics which are not essential to them. They have been identified with general ideas[11] and with clearly limited and circumscribed general ideas.[12] In these conditions it has possibly seemed as though the inferior societies had no concepts properly called; for they have only rudimentary processes of generalization and the ideas which they use are not generally very well defined. But the greater part of our concepts are equally indetermined; we force ourselves to define them only in discussions or when doing careful work. We have also seen that conceiving is not generalizing. Thinking conceptually is not simply isolating and grouping together the common characteristics of a certain number of objects; it is relating the variable to the permanent, the individual to the social. And since logical thought commences with the concept, it follows that it has always existed; there is no period in history when men have lived in a chronic confusion and contradiction. To be sure, we cannot insist too much upon the different characteristics which logic presents at different periods in history; it develops like the societies themselves. But howsoever real these differences may be, they should not cause us to neglect the similarities, which are no less essential.

IV

We are now in a position to take up a final question which has already been raised in our introduction and which has been taken as understood in the remainder of this work. We have seen that at least some of the categories are social things. The question is where they got this character.

Undoubtedly it will be easily understood that since they are themselves concepts, they are the work of the group. It can even be said that there are no other concepts which present to an equal degree the signs by which a collective representation is recognized. In fact, their stability and impersonality are such that they have often passed as being absolutely universal and immutable. Also, as they express the fundamental conditions for an agreement between minds, it seems evident that they have been elaborated by society.

But the problem concerning them is more complex, for they are social in another sense and, as it were in the second degree. They not only come from society, but the things which they express are of a social nature. Not only is it society which has founded them, but their contents are the different aspects of the social being: the category of class was at first indistinct from the concept of the human group; it is the rhythm of social life which is at the basis of the category of time; the territory occupied by the society furnished the material for the category of space; it is the collective force which was the prototype of the concept of efficient force, an essential element in the category of causality. However, the categories are not made to be applied only to the social realm; they reach out to all reality. Then how is it that they have taken from society the models upon which they have been constructed?

It is because they are the pre-eminent concepts, which have a preponderating part in our knowledge. In fact, the function of the categories is to dominate and envelop all the other concepts: they are permanent moulds for the mental life. Now for them to embrace such an object, they must be founded upon a reality of equal amplitude.

Undoubtedly the relations which they express exist in an implicit way in individual consciousnesses. The individual lives in time, and, as we have said, he has a certain sense of temporal orientation. He is situated at a determined point in space, and it has even been held, and sustained with good reasons, that all sensations have something special about them.[13] He has a feeling of resemblances; similar representations are brought together and the new representation formed by their union has a sort of generic character. We also have the sensation of a certain regularity in the order of the succession of phenomena; even an animal is not incapable of this. However, all these relations are strictly personal for the individual who recognizes them, and consequently the notion of them which he may have can in no case go beyond his own narrow horizon. The generic images which are formed in my consciousness by the fusion of similar images represent only the objects which I have perceived directly; there is nothing there which could give me the idea of a class, that is to say, of a mould including the *whole* group of all possible objects which satisfy the same condition. Also, it would be necessary to have the idea of group in the first place, and the mere observations of our interior life could never awaken that in us. But, above all, there is no individual experience, howsoever extended and prolonged it may be, which could give a suspicion of the existence of a whole class which would embrace every single being, and to which other classes are only co-ordinated or subordinated species. This idea of *all*, which is at the basis of the classifications which we have just cited, could not have come from the individual himself, who is only a part in relation to the whole and who never attains more than an infinitesimal fraction of reality. And yet there is perhaps no other category of greater importance; for as the role of the categories is to envelop all the other concepts, the category *par excellence* would seem to be this very concept of *totality*. The theorists of knowledge ordinarily postulate it as if it came of itself, while it really surpasses the contents of each individual consciousness taken alone to an infinite degree.

For the same reasons, the space which I know by my senses, of which I am the centre and where everything is disposed in relation to me, could not be space in general, which contains all extensions and where these are co-ordinated by personal guide-lines which are common to everybody. In the same way, the concrete duration which I feel passing within me and with me could not give me the idea of time in general: the first expresses only the rhythm of my individual life; the second should correspond to the rhythm of a life which is not that of any individual in particular, but in which all participate.[14] In the same way, finally, the regularities which I am able to conceive in the manner in which my sensations succeed one another may well have a value for me; they explain how it comes about that when I am given the first two phenomena whose concurrence I have observed, I tend to expect the other. But this personal state of expectation could not be confounded with the conception of a universal order of succession which imposes itself upon all minds and all events.

Since the world expressed by the entire system of concepts is the one that society regards, society alone can furnish the most general notions with which it should be represented. Such an object can be embraced only by a subject which contains all the individual subjects within it. Since the universe does not exist except in so far as it is thought of, and since it is not completely thought of except by society, it takes a place in this latter; it becomes a part of society's interior life, while this is the totality, outside of which nothing exists. The concept of totality is only the abstract form of the concept of society: it is the whole which includes all things, the supreme class which embraces all other classes. Such is the final principle upon which repose all these primitive classifications where beings from every realm are placed and classified in social forms, exactly like men.[15] But if the world is inside of society, the space which this latter occupies becomes confounded with space in general. In fact, we have seen how each thing has its assigned place in social space, and the degree to which this space in general differs from the concrete expanses which we perceive is well shown by the fact that this localization is wholly ideal and in no way resembles what it would have been if it had been dictated to us by sensuous experience alone.[16] For the same reason, the rhythm of collective life dominates and embraces the varied rhythms of all the elementary lives from which it results; consequently the time which it expresses dominates and embraces all particular durations. It is time in general. For a long time the history of the world has been only another aspect of the history of society. The one commences with the other; the periods of the first are determined by the periods of the second. This impersonal and total duration is measured, and the guide-lines in relation to which it is divided and organized are fixed by the movements of concentration or dispersion of society; or, more generally, the periodical necessities for a collective renewal. If these critical instants are generally attached to some material phenomenon, such as the regular recurrence of such or such a star or the alternation of the seasons, it is because objective signs are necessary to make this essentially social organization intelligible to all. In the same way, finally, the causal relation, from the moment when it is collectively stated by the group, becomes independent of every individual consciousness; it rises above all particular minds and events. It is a law whose value depends upon no person. We have already shown how it is clearly thus that it seems to have originated.

Another reason explains why the constituent elements of the categories should have been taken from social life: it is because the relations which they express could not have been learned except in and through society. If they are in a sense immanent in the life of an individual, he has neither a reason nor the means for learning them, reflecting upon them and forming them into distinct ideas. In order to orient himself personally in space and to know at what moments he should satisfy his various organic needs, he has no need of making, once and for all, a conceptual representation of time and space. Many animals are able to find the road which leads to places with which they are familiar; they come back at a proper moment without knowing any of the categories; sensations are enough to direct them automatically. They would also be enough for men, if their sensations had to satisfy only individual needs. To recognize the fact that one thing resembles another which we have already experienced, it is in no way necessary that we arrange them all in groups and species: the way in which similar images call up each other and unite is enough to give the feeling of resemblance. The impression that a certain thing has already

)een seen or experienced implies no classification. To recognize
he things which we should seek or from which we should flee, it
vould not be necessary to attach the effects of the two to their
:auses by a logical bond, if individual conveniences were the only
)nes in question. Purely empirical sequences and strong connec-
.ions between the concrete representations would be as sure guides
'or the will. Not only is it true that the animal has no others, but also
)ur own personal conduct frequently supposes nothing more. The
)rudent man is the one who has a very clear sensation of what must
)e done, but which he would ordinarily be quite incapable of
stating as a general law.

It is a different matter with society. This is possible only when
he individuals and things which compose it are divided into cer-
ain groups, that is to say, classified, and when these groups are
:lassified in relation to each other. Society supposes a self-con-
:cious organization which is nothing other than a classification.
This organization of society naturally extends itself to the place
vhich this occupies. To avoid all collisions, it is necessary that each
)articular group have a determined portion of space assigned to it:
n other terms, it is necessary that space in general be divided, dif-
erentiated, arranged, and that these divisions and arrangements
)e known to everybody. On the other hand, every summons to a
:elebration, a hunt or a military expedition implies fixed and es-
ablished dates, and consequently that a common time is agreed
ipon, which everybody conceives in the same fashion. Finally, the
:o-operation of many persons with the same end in view is possible
)nly when they are in agreement as to the relation which exists be-
ween this end and the means of attaining it, that is to say, when
he same causal relation is admitted by all the co-operators in the
:nterprise. It is not surprising, therefore, that social time, social
pace, social classes and causality should be the basis of the cor-
esponding categories, since it is under their social forms that these
lifferent relations were first grasped with a certain clarity by the
uuman intellect.

In summing up, then, we must say that society is not at all the
llogical or a-logical, incoherent and fantastic being which it has
oo often been considered. Quite on the contrary, the collective con-

sciousness is the highest form of the psychic life, since it is the consciousness of the consciousnesses. Being placed outside of and above individual and local contingencies, it sees things only in their permanent and essential aspects, which it crystallizes into communicable ideas. At the same time that it sees from above, it sees farther; at every moment of time, it embraces all known reality; that is why it alone can furnish the mind with the moulds which are applicable to the totality of things and which make it possible to think of them. It does not create these moulds artificially; it finds them within itself; it does nothing but become conscious of them. They translate the ways of being which are found in all the stages of reality but which appear in their full clarity only at the summit, because the extreme complexity of the psychic life which passes there necessitates a greater development of consciousness. Attributing social origins to logical thought is not debasing it or diminishing its value or reducing it to nothing more than a system of artificial combinations; on the contrary, it is relating it to a cause which implies it naturally. But this is not saying that the ideas elaborated in this way are at once adequate for their object. If society is something universal in relation to the individual, it is none the less an individuality itself, which has its own personal physiognomy and its idiosyncrasies; it is a particular subject and consequently particularizes whatever it thinks of. Therefore collective representations also contain subjective elements, and these must be progressively rooted out, if we are to approach reality more closely. But howsoever crude these may have been at the beginning, the fact remains that with them the germ of a new mentality was given, to which the individual could never have raised himself by his own efforts: by them the way was opened to a stable, impersonal and organized thought which then had nothing to do except to develop its nature.

Also, the causes which have determined this development do not seem to be specifically different from those which gave it its initial impulse. If logical thought tends to rid itself more and more of the subjective and personal elements which it still retains from its origin, it is not because extra-social factors have intervened; it is much rather because a social life of a new sort is developing. It is this international life which has already resulted in universalizing religious beliefs. As it extends, the collective horizon enlarges; the society ceases to appear as the only whole, to become a part of a much vaster one, with indetermined frontiers, which is susceptible of advancing indefinitely. Consequently things can no longer be contained in the social moulds according to which they were primitively classified; they must be organized according to principles which are their own, so logical organization differentiates itself from the social organization and becomes autonomous. Really and truly human thought is not a primitive fact; it is the product of history; it is the ideal limit towards which we are constantly approaching, but which in all probability we shall never succeed in reaching.

Thus it is not at all true that between science on the one hand, and morals and religion on the other, there exists that sort of antinomy which has so frequently been admitted, for the two forms of human activity really come from one and the same source. Kant understood this very well, and therefore he made the speculative reason and the practical reason two different aspects of the same faculty. According to him, what makes their unity is the fact that the two are directed towards the universal. Rational thinking is thinking according to the laws which are imposed upon all reasonable beings; acting morally is conducting one's self according to those maxims which can be extended without contradiction to all wills. In other words, science and morals imply that the individual is capable of raising himself above his own peculiar point of view and of living an impersonal life. In fact, it cannot be doubted that this is a trait common to all the higher forms of thought and action. What Kant's system does not explain, however, is the origin of this sort of contradiction which is realized in man. Why is he forced to do violence to himself by leaving his individuality, and, inversely, why is the impersonal law obliged to be dissipated by incarnating itself in individuals? Is it answered that there are two antagonistic worlds in which we participate equally, the world of matter and sense on the one hand, and the world of pure and impersonal reason on the other? That is merely repeating the question in slightly different terms, for what we are trying to find out is why we must lead these two existences at the same time. Why do these two worlds, which seem to contradict each other, not remain outside of each other, and why must they mutually penetrate one another in spite of their antagonism? The only explanation which has ever been given of this singular necessity is the hypothesis of the Fall, with all the difficulties which it implies, and which need not be repeated here. On the other hand, all mystery disappears the moment that it is recognized that impersonal reason is only another name given to collective thought. For this is possible only through a group of individuals; it supposes them, and in their turn, they suppose it, for they can continue to exist only by grouping themselves together. The kingdom of ends and impersonal truths can realize itself only by the co-operation of particular wills, and the reasons for which these participate in it are the same as those for which they co-operate. In a word, there is something impersonal in us because there is something social in all of us, and since social life embraces at once both representations and practices, this impersonality naturally extends to ideas as well as to acts.

Perhaps some will be surprised to see us connect the most elevated forms of thought with society: the cause appears quite humble, in consideration of the value which we attribute to the effect. Between the world of the senses and appetites on the one hand, and that of reason and morals on the other, the distance is so considerable that the second would seem to have been able to add itself to the first only by a creative act. But attributing to society this preponderating role in the genesis of our nature is not denying this creation; for society has a creative power which no other observable being can equal. In fact, all creation, if not a mystical operation which escapes science and knowledge, is the product of a synthesis. Now if the synthesis of particular conceptions which take place in each individual consciousness are already and of themselves productive of novelties, how much more efficacious these vast syntheses of complete consciousnesses which make society must be! A society is the most powerful combination of physical and moral forces of which nature offers us an example. Nowhere else is an equal richness of different materials, carried to such a degree of concentration, to be found. Then it is not surprising that a higher life disengages itself which, by reacting upon the elements of which it is the product, raises them to a higher plane of existence and transforms them.

Thus sociology appears destined to open a new way to the science of man. Up to the present, thinkers were placed before this double alternative: either explain the superior and specific faculties of men by connecting them to the inferior forms of his being, the reason to the senses, or the mind to matter, which is equivalent to denying their uniqueness; or else attach them to some super-experimental reality which was postulated, but whose existence could be established by no observation. What put them in this difficulty was the fact that the individual passed as being the *finis naturae*—the ultimate creation of nature; it seemed that there was nothing beyond him, or at least nothing that science could touch. But from the moment when it is recognized that above the individual there is society, and that this is not a nominal being created by reason, but a system of active forces, a new manner of explaining men becomes possible. To conserve his distinctive traits it is no longer necessary to put them outside experience. At least, before going to this last extremity, it would be well to see if that which surpasses the individual though it is within him, does not come from this super-individual reality which we experience in society. To be sure, it cannot be said at present to what point these explanations may be able to reach, and whether or not they are of a nature to resolve all the problems. But it is equally impossible to mark in advance a limit beyond which they cannot go. What must be done is to try the hypothesis and submit it as methodically as possible to the control of facts. This is what we have tried to do.

Notes

Introduction

1   *Moral Education*, p. 89. Full citations for Durkheim's major translated works can be found in the Bibliography.

2   *Sociology and Philosophy*, p. 59.

3   *Division of Labor*, pp. 398–99. See pp. 136–37 of this volume. The French word *conscience* can be translated "conscience" or "consciousness" depending on context. In this case I have substituted "consciousness" for the original translation's "conscience."

4   See my "Civil Religion in America" in *Beyond Belief* (New York: Harper and Row, 1970), pp. 168–89. The application to Durkheim will become clearer later in the Introduction.

5   Arthur Mitzman, *The Iron Cage* (New York: Alfred A. Knopf, 1970).

6   Georges Davy, "Emile Durkheim," *Revue de métaphysique et de morale* 6 (1920) : 194.

7   Edward Tiryakian, "Le Premier Message d'Emile Durkheim," *Cahiers internationaux de sociologie* 43 (1967) : 21.

8   Davy, "Emile Durkheim," p. 183.

9   Ibid.

10   Hannah Arendt discusses the German case in the introduction to Walter Benjamin, *Illuminations* (New York: Harcourt, Brace and World, 1968).

11   Davy, "Emile Durkheim," p. 184.

12   Ibid., p. 186; Marcel Mauss, introduction to Emile Durkheim, *Socialism and Saint-Simon*, p. 1.

13   Davy, "Emile Durkheim," p. 188. It is interesting how late the symbolism of the French Revolution was securely institutionalized. It was also in 1880 that the "Marseillaise" became the national anthem.

14   Emile Durkheim, "Discours aux lycéens de Sens," *Cahiers internationaux de sociologie* 43 (1967) : 25–32. See "Address to the *Lycéens*

of Sens," a translation especially prepared for this volume, below chapter 2. See also reference at footnote 7.

15   For a somewhat fuller treatment of this same material see a translation especially prepared for this volume: "Sociology in France in the Nineteenth Century," chapter 1 below. The original is "La sociologie en France au XIXe siècle," *Revue bleue*, 4e série, 13:609–13, 647–52.

16   Emile Durkheim, "Cours de science sociale: Leçon d'ouverture," *Revue internationale de l'enseignement* 15 (1888): 41.

17   Ibid., p. 42.

18   Ibid., p. 43.

19   Ibid., p. 45.

20   Ibid., p. 46.

21   Ibid., pp. 47–48.

22   This paragraph somewhat oversimplifies the political complexities of the Third Republic, though not, I think, Durkheim's place in them. A regime established on the blood of the Paris Commune was not without conservative elements. However, the monarchist majority of the early 1870s was replaced by a republican majority by 1880. From then until the First World War the French political scene was divided between a monarchist, aristocratic, and clerical right that several times sought to overthrow the republic; a middle-class republican center that was the chief support of the regime; and a working-class socialist left that was ambivalent about the regime but gave it crucial support in time of need. Durkheim's political position, as we will see later in the Introduction, was somewhere between the second and third groups. In view of Durkheim's later exaltation of the notion of "collective effervescence" and the several times he mentions the French Revolution as an example of it, it would be interesting to know his attitude toward the Commune. I have not, however, found any reference to it in his writings.

23   Harry Alpert, *Emile Durkheim and His Sociology* (New York: Columbia University Press, 1939), pp. 42, 61. Durkheim began teaching in Paris in 1902, but until 1906 he was a *chargé de cours*.

24   Ibid., pp. 38, 42.

25   Durkheim's remarks in "Pacifism et patriotisme," séance du 30 décembre 1907, *Bulletin de la Société française de philosophie* 8 (1908): 66–67.

26   Ibid.; *L'Allemagne au-dessus de tout: La mentalité allemande et la guerre* (Paris: Colin, 1915).

27   There is a helpful discussion of these issues in Ernest Wallwork, *Durkheim: Morality and Milieu* (Cambridge: Harvard University Press, 1972).

28   *Revue philosophique* 24 (1887): 33, 278.

29   Review of Ludwig Gumplowicz, *Grundrisse der Sociologie*, *Revue Philosophique* 20 (1885): 632.

30   p. 348.

31   *Sociology and Philosophy*, p. 29.

32   Ibid., p. 34.

33   Reprinted in this volume (chap. 10).

34   "La Science positive de la morale en Allemagne," *Revue philoso-phique* 24 (1887) : 45.

35   "Les études de science sociale," *Revue philosophique* 22 (1886) : 69.

36   *Division of Labor*, p. 173.

37   *Sociology and Philosophy*, p. 72.

38   *Division of Labor*, p. 227. See p. 111 of this volume.

39   Ibid. p. 402. See p. 139 of this volume.

40   For a discussion of the noncontractual elements in contract, that is, those elements that are assumed, that do not need to be negotiated into every contract, and that are enforceable at law even though not mentioned in the contract, see "Organic Solidarity and Contractual Solidarity," chapter 7 of this volume.

41   *Division of Labor*, p. 388.

42   Ibid., p. 172.

43   Ibid., pp. 407–8. See p. 144 of this volume.

44   Ibid., pp. 262–63, note 14.

45   Ibid., p. 171.

46   *Suicide*, p. 363.

47   Ibid., pp. 363–64.

48   Ibid., p. 369.

49   Ibid., p. 370.

50   Ibid., p. 386.

51   Ibid., pp. 386–87.

52   Ibid., p. 387.

53   *Socialism*, pp. 203–4.

54   Jean-Claude Filloux, Introduction to Emile Durkheim, *La science sociale et l'action* (Paris: Presses universitaires de France, 1970), pp. 36–45.

55   *Socialism*, pp. 19–20.

56   *Division of Labor*, p. 25.

57   Hannah Arendt, *On Revolution* (New York: Viking, 1965), pp. 251 ff.

58   *Division of Labor*, p. 28.

59   Published first in Turkey as *Leçons de sociologie* (new edition, Presses universitaires de France, 1969) and in English translation as *Professional Ethics and Civic Morals* (Glencoe, Ill.: Free Press, 1958).

60   *Professional Ethics and Civic Morals*, p. 63.

61   Ibid.

62   Ibid., p. 70.

63   Ibid., p. 69.

64   Ibid., p. 73.

65   Ibid., p. 74.

66   "L'individualisme et les intellectuels," *Revue bleue,* 4e série, 10 (1898) : 7–13. See "Individualism and the Intellectuals," especially translated for this volume, chapter 4 below. See also "Les principes de 1789 et la sociologie," *Revue internationale de l'enseignement* 19 (1890) : 450–56, especially translated for this volume as "The Principles of 1789 and Sociology," chapter 3 below. The latter article is helpful in understanding the two senses of individualism by indicating the importance of individualism as symbolism while questioning the particular theoretical understanding of the individual and society in enlightenment thought.

67   Summarized by Filloux, "Introduction," pp. 256–57.

68   Ibid., p. 257.

69   Terry N. Clark, "Emile Durkheim and the Institutionalization of Sociology in the French University System," *Archives européennes de sociologie,* 9 (1968) : 64.

70   Filloux, "Introduction," pp. 257–58.

71   Terry N. Clark, "The Structure and Functions of a Research Institute: The *Année sociologique,*" *Archives européennes de sociologie* 9 (1968) : 84.

72   "L'élite intellectuelle et la democratie," *Revue bleue,* 5e série, 1 (1904) : 705–6. See "The Intellectual Elite and Democracy," especially translated for this volume, chapter 5 below.

73   See p. 58 of this volume.

74   See p. 59 of this volume.

75   "Enseignement philosophique et l'agrégation de philosophie," *Revue philosophique* 39 (1895) : 121–47.

76   Alpert, *Emile Durkheim,* p. 61.

77   Clark, "Emile Durkheim," pp. 66–68.

78   See especially S. Deploige, *Le Conflit de la morale et de la sociologie* (Paris, 1912).

79   Clark, "Emile Durkheim," p. 65.

80   "Pédagogie et sociologie," *Revue de métaphysique et de morale* 11 (1903) : 37–54. An English translation appears as chapter 3 of Emile Durkheim, *Education and Sociology* (Glencoe, Ill.: Free Press, 1956).

81   The remaining lectures in the course did not appear in Durkheim's lifetime. They were published in France in 1925. I refer to the English translation, *Moral Education* (New York: Free Press, 1961).

82   Filloux, "Introduction," pp. 10, 67.

83   *Moral Education,* p. 12.

84   Ibid., p. 79.

85   Ibid., p. 11.

86   Ibid., p. 277.

87   Ibid., p. 123.

88   *Suicide,* p. 375.

89   *Moral Education*, p. 229.

90   Ibid., chap. 18.

91   Ibid., p. 235.

92   Filloux, "Introduction," p. 301.

93   *Elementary Forms*, p. 246. The first three parts of the chapter "Origin of the Idea of the Totemic Principle or Mana" are included below, chapter 11.

94   See p. 178 of this volume.

95   Ibid., pp. 178–79.

96   Lettres au directeur de la *Revue néo-scolastique* 14 (1907) : 606–7, 612–14.

97   *Division of Labor*, p. 402.

98   Translated in Emile Durkheim et al., *Essays on Sociology and Philosophy* (New York: Harper and Row, 1964), pp. 331–32. See p. 156 of this volume. The entire essay "The Dualism of Human Nature and Its Social Conditions" is reprinted below, chapter 10.

99   *Elementary Forms*, p. 475. See pp. 201–2 of this volume. The entire conclusion of *The Elementary Forms of the Religious Life* is reprinted below, chapter 12.

100   "La conception sociale de la religion," séance du 18 janvier 1914 de l' "Union de libres penseurs et de libres croyants pour la culture morale," in *Le sentiment religieux a l'heure actuelle*, Librairie philosophique J. Vrin, 1919, p. 104.

101   *The Elementary Forms of the Religious Life*, p. 262.

102   See pp. 200–201 of this volume. This quotation also bears on the "civil religion" idea.

103   *Sociology and Philosophy*, p. 92.

104   *Elementary Forms*, p. 262.

105   Ibid., p. 264.

106   See pp. 205–6 of this volume.

107   *Sociology and Philosophy*, p. 96.

108   See reference at note 4, p. 252. See also Talcott Parsons, "Durkheim on Religion Revisited: Another Look at the *Elementary Forms of the Religious Life*," in *Beyond the Classics*, ed. Charles Y. Glock and Phillip E. Hammond (Berkeley: University of California Press, 1972).

109   *Sociology and Philosophy*, p. 97.

110   See chapter 5 of this volume.

111   "The School of Tomorrow," in *French Educational Ideals of Today*, ed. Ferdinand Buisson and Frederic Farrington (New York: World Book Company, 1919), p. 189. The original appeared in *Manuel général de l'instruction primaire*, 15 December 1915.

112   Davy, "Emile Durkheim," p. 181.

113   Clark, "Structure and Functions of a Research Institute," pp. 89–91.

114   In America the only serious treatment of Durkheim's thought as a whole for many years was Talcott Parsons's *The Structure of Social Action* (New York: McGraw-Hill, 1937).

Chapter 1

1   *Social Physiology*, vol. 10 of *Complete Works*, p. 177.
2   Ibid.
3   *The Organiser*, vol. 4, p. 119.
4   *(The) Science of Man*, vol. 11, p. 187.
5   Ibid.
6   See our *Division of Labor in Society;* in our unpublished courses, we have studied crime, punishment, responsibility, and family from this same point of view. On this last question we have published a few isolated studies. In particular, see "The Prohibition of Incest," in *L'année sociologique*, vol. 1.
7   See our *Suicide* (Paris, 1897).
8   This point of view has been quite particularly developed in *L'année sociologique*, vols. 1, 2, and 3.
9   *Social Logic*, pp. 166–67.
10   As for Le Play and his system, we have said nothing about them because his preoccupations are much more practical than theoretical and because he takes as a fundamental postulate a religious prejudice. A doctrine which takes as an axiom the superiority of the Pentateuch has nothing to do with science. Let us nevertheless point out a recent tendency of this school toward more properly scientific research. It is this tendency which is represented by the *Social Science* of Demolins.

Chapter 2

1   Ernest Renan (1823–92), French writer and rationalist, in *Dialogues philosophiques*.

Chapter 3

1   (Paris: Hachette, 1889.)
2   See in particular *L'évolution politique* by Molinari.

Chapter 4

1   See the article by Ferdinand Brunetière, "Après le procès," *Revue des deux mondes*, 15 March 1898.

2   Let us note in passing that this very convenient word has in no way the impertinent sense that has so maliciously been attributed to it. The intellectual is not a man who has a monopoly on intelligence; there is no social function for which intelligence is not necessary. But there are those where it is, at one and the same time, both the means and the end, the agent and the goal. In them, intelligence is used to extend intelligence, that is to say, used to enrich it with new knowledge, ideas, or sensations. It thus constitutes the whole of these professions (the arts and sciences), and it is in order to express this peculiarity that the man who consecrates himself to them has quite naturally come to be called an intellectual.

3   See Rousseau, *The Social Contract*, book 1; book 2, chapter 3.

4   This is how it is possible, without contradiction, to be an individualist, all the while saying that the individual is more a product of society than its cause. It is because individualism itself is a social product just like all moralities and all religions. The individual receives from society even the moral beliefs which make him divine. This is what Kant and Rousseau failed to understand. They wanted to deduce their individualistic ethics not from society but from the notion of the isolated individual. This undertaking was impossible, and from it come the logical contradictions of their systems.

Chapter 6

1   Morgan, *Ancient Society* (London, 1870), pp. 62–122.

2   *Kamilaroi and Kurnai.* This state has, however, been passed through by the Indian societies of America. (See Morgan, *op. cit.*)

3   If, in its pure state, as we at least believe, the clan is made up of an undivided family which is confused, later particular families, distinct from one another, appear on the foundation of primitive homogeneity. But this appearance does not alter the essential traits of the social organization that we are describing; that is why this is no place to stop. The clan remains the political unity, and as families are similar and equal, society remains formed of similar and homogeneous segments, although, besides these primitive segments, new segmentations begin to appear, but of the same kind.

4   Morgan, *op. cit.*, p. 90.

5   *Afrikanische Jurisprudenz*, I.

6   See Hanoteau and Letourneux, *La Kabylie et les Coutumes kabyles*, II, and Masqueray, *Formation des cités chez les populations sédentaires de l' Algérie*, ch. v.

7   Waitz erroneously presents the clan as derivative from the family. The contrary is the case. Even if this description is important because of the competency of its author, it lacks some precision.

8   *Anthropologie*, I, p. 359.

9   Morgan, *op. cit.*, pp. 153 ff.

10   Thus, the tribe of Reuben, which comprised in all four *families*, consisted of according to *Numbers* (xxvi, 7), more than forty-three thousand adults above twenty years. (Cf. *Numbers*, ch. iii, 15 ff.; *Joshua*, vii, 14.—Munck, *Palestine*, pp. 116, 125, 191.)

11   "We have established the history of a belief. It is set up; human society is constituted. It modifies itself; society goes through a series of revolutions. It disappears; society undergoes a change" (*Cité antique*, end).

12   Spencer has already said that social evolution, just as universal evolution, begins in a stage of more or less perfect homogeneity. But this proposition does not in any wise resemble the one that we have just been developing. For Spencer, a society that was perfectly homogeneous would not truly be a society, for homogeneity is by nature unstable, and society is essentially a coherent whole. The social role of homogeneity is completely secondary; it may look towards an ulterior co-operation, but it is not a specific source of social life. At times, Spencer seems to see in societies such as we have just been describing only an ephemeral juxtaposition of independent individuals, the zero of social life. We have, on the contrary, just seen that they have a very strong collective life, although *sui generis*, which manifests itself not in exchanges and contracts, but in a great abundance of common beliefs and common practices. These aggregates are coherent, not in spite of their homogeneity, but because of their homogeneity. Not only is the community not too weak; but we may even say that it alone exists. Moreover, these societies have a definite type which comes from their homogeneity. We cannot treat them as negligible quantities.

13   See Tarde, *Lois de l'imitation*, pp. 402–412.

14   We shall see the reasons in Book II, ch. iv.

15   See Glasson, *Le droit de succession dans les lois barbares*, p. 19. It is true that the fact is contested by Fustel de Coulanges, despite the explicit statement of the text upon which Glasson relies.

16   See the heading *De Migrantibus* of the Salic Law.

17   *Deutsche Verfassungsgeschichte*, 2nd ed., II, p. 317.

18   In the comitia, the voting was done by curia, that is, by a group of *gentes*. There is a text which even seems to say that in the interior of each curia there was voting by *gentes*. (Gell., XV, 27, 4.)

19   Marquardt, *Privat Leben der Roemer*, II, p. 4.

20   Until Cleisthenes, and two centuries later, Athens lost her independence. Moreover, even after Cleisthenes, the Athenian clan, the γένος, while having totally lost its political character, retained a very strong organization. (Cf. Gilbert, *op. cit.*, I, pp. 142 and 200.)

21   We do not wish to imply that territorial districts are only a reproduction of old familial arrangements. This new mode of grouping results, on the contrary, at least in part, from new causes which disturb the old.

The principal of these causes is the growth of cities which become the centre of concentration of population (see Book II, ch. ii, 1). But whatever the origins of this arrangement may be, it is segmental.

22   Schmoller, *La division du travail étudiée au point de vue historique,* in *Révue d'écon. pol.* 1890, p. 145.

23   See Tarde, *Les Lois de l'imitation,* passim.

24   *Op. cit.,* p. 144.

25   See Levasseur, *Les classes ouvrières en France jusqu' à la Révolution,* I, p. 195.

26   Schmoller, *La division du travail étudiée au point de vue historique,* pp. 145–148.

27   See this book, ch. vii, § 2, and Book III, ch. i.

28   Perrier, *Le Transformisme,* p. 159.

29   Perrier, *Colonies animales,* p. 778.

30   *Ibid.,* Book IV, ch. v, vi, vii.

31   *Ibid.,* p. 779.

32   *Transformisme,* p. 167.

33   *Colonies animales,* p. 771.

34   See *Colonies animales,* pp. 763 ff.

35   *Principles of Sociology,* II, p. 153.

36   *Principles of Sociology,* pp. 154–155.

37   *Ibid.,* III, pp. 426–427.

38   We find here confirmation of a previously enunciated proposition which makes governmental power an emanation of the inherent life of the collective conscience.

Chapter 7

1   *Principles of Sociology,* III, pp. 332 ff.

2   *Ibid.,* III, p. 808.

3   *Principles of Sociology,* II, p. 160.

4   *Ibid.,* III, p. 813.

5   *Ibid.,* III, pp. 332 ff.—See also *Man versus the State.*

6   This is what Fouillée does in opposing contract to pressure. (*Science sociale,* p. 8.)

7   *Moral Essays,* p. 194 note.

8   Of course, the case is the same for the dissolution of the conjugal bond.

9   Smith, *Marriage and Kinship in Early Arabia,* p. 135. Cambridge, 1885.

10   Krauss, *Sitte und Brauch der Südslaven,* ch. xxxi.

11   Viollet, *Précis de l'histoire du droit français,* p. 402.

12   Accarias, *Précis de droit romain,* I, pp. 240 ff.

13   Viollet, *op. cit.,* p. 406.

14   *Ancient Society*, p. 81.

15   Krauss, *op. cit.*, pp. 113 ff.

16   *Salic Law*, LX.

17   For example, in cases of guardianship, of interdiction, where public authority sometimes intervenes officially. The progress of this regulatory action does not deny the regression, mentioned above, of collective sentiments which concern the family. On the contrary, the first phenomenon supposes the other, for, in order for the sentiments to diminish or become enfeebled, the family must have had to cease to confound itself with society and constitute itself as a sphere of personal action, distinct from the common conscience. But this transformation was necessary in its becoming an organ of society, since, as an organ, it is an individualized part of society.

18   In his work on ethics.

19   *Moral Essays*, p. 187.

20   See Book III, ch. i.—See particularly the preface [to the second edition—G. S.] where we have expressed ourselves more explicitly on this point.

21   *Principles of Sociology*, III, pp. 822–834.

22   *Moral Essays*, p. 179.

23   This censure, moreover, just as all moral punishment, is translated into external movements (discipline, dismissal of employees, loss of relations, etc.).

Chapter 8

1   *Laws of Manou*, I, 87–91.

2   *Cours de Philosophic positive*, VI, p. 505.

3   *Principles of Sociology*, II, p. 57.

4   Wundt, *Physiological Psychology* (tr. Fr.), I, p. 234.

5   Notice the experiment of Kühne and Paul Bert reported by Wundt, *ibid.*, p. 233.

6   *Ibid.*, I, p. 239.

7   *Principles of Sociology*, III, p. 406.

8   We do not here have to look to see if the fact which determines the progress of the division of labor and civilization, growth in social mass and density, explains itself automatically; if it is a necessary product of efficient causes, or else an imagined means in view of a desired end or of a very great foreseen good. We content ourselves with stating this law of gravitation in the social world without going any farther. It does not seem, however, that there is a greater demand here than elsewhere for a teleological explanation. The walls which separate different parts of society are torn down by the force of things, through a sort of natural usury, whose effect can be further enforced by the action of violent causes. The

movements of population thus become more numerous and rapid and the passage-lines through which these movements are effected—the means of communication—deepen. They are more particularly active at points where several of these lines cross; these are cities. Thus social density grows. As for the growth in volume, it is due to causes of the same kind. The barriers which separate peoples are analogous to those which separate the different cells of the same society and they disappear in the same way.

9   *First Principles*, pp. 454 ff.

10   See his work on ethics.

11   The definition of de Quatrefages which makes man a religious animal is a particular instance of the preceding, for man's religiosity is a consequence of his eminent sociability.

12   Transformations of the soil, of streams, through the art of husbandry, engineers, etc.

13   This is the case in societies where the matriarchal family rules.

14   To cite only one example of this, religion has been explained by the movements of individual feeling, whereas these movements are only the prolongation in the individual of social states which give birth to religion. We have developed this point further in an article in the *Révue Philosophique, Etudes de science sociale*, June, 1886. Cf. *Année Sociologique*, Vol. II, pp. 1–28.

15   *Study of Sociology*, ch. i.

16   This is a sufficient reply, we believe, to those who think they prove that everything in social life is individual because society is made up only of individuals. Of course, society has no other substratum, but because individuals form society, new phenomena which are formed by association are produced, and react upon individual consciences and in large part form them. That is why, although society may be nothing without individuals, each of them is much more a product of society than he is its maker.

Chapter 9

1   See Book I, ch. iii, § 2.

2   There is, however, probably another limit which we do not have to speak of since it concerns individual hygiene. It may be held that, in the light of our organico-psychic constitution, the division of labor cannot go beyond a certain limit without disorders resulting. Without entering upon the question, let us straightaway say that the extreme specialization at which biological functions have arrived does not seem favorable to this hypothesis. Moreover, in the very order of psychic and social functions, has not the division of labor, in its historical development, been carried to the last stage in the relations of men and women? Have not

there been faculties completely lost by both? Why cannot the same phenomenon occur between individuals of the same sex? Of course, it takes
time for the organism to adapt itself to these changes, but we do not see
why a day should come when this adaptation would become impossible.

3   Among the practical consequences that mght be deduced from the
proposition that we have just established there is one of interest to education. We always reason, in educational affairs, as if the moral basis of
man was made up of generalities. We have just seen that such is not the
case at all. Man is destined to fill a special function in the social organism,
and, consequently, he must learn, in advance, how to play this role. For
that an education is necessary, quite as much as that he should learn his
role as a man. We do not, however, wish to imply, that it is necessary to
rear a child prematurely for some certain profession, but that it is necessary to get him to like the idea of circumscribed tasks and limited horizons. But this taste is quite different from that for general things, and
cannot be aroused by the same means.

4   There is nothing that forces the intellectual and moral diversity of
societies to be maintained. The ever greater expansion of higher societies,
from which there results the absorption or elimination of less advanced
societies, tends, in any case, to diminish such diversity.

5   Thus, the duties that we have toward it do not oppress those which
link us to our country. For the latter is the only actually realized society
of which we are members; the other is only a desideratum whose realization is not even assured.

6   The word is de Molinari's, *La morale économique*, p. 248.

7   Beaussire, *Les principes de la morale*, Introduction.

Chapter 10

1   *Les formes élémentaires de la vie religieuse* (Paris: Félix Alcan,
1912). [Translated as *The Elementary Forms of Religious Life* by Joseph
Ward Swain ([1915] Glencoe, Ill.: Free Press of Glencoe, Illinois, 1947).]

2   To sensations, one should add images, but since images are only
sensations that survive themselves, it is useless to mention them separately.
The same is true for those conglomerations of images and sensations which
are called perceptions.

3   No doubt there are egoistic desires that do not have material
things as their objects, but the sensory appetites are the type par excellence of egoistic tendencies. We believe that desires for objects of a different kind imply—although the egoistic motive may play a role in them—
a movement out of ourselves which surpasses pure egoism. This is the
case, for example, with love of glory, power, and so on.

4   Cf. our communication to the French Philosophical Society, "La
détermination du fait moral," *Bulletin de la Société française de philoso-*

phie, VI, (1906), 113–39. [Translated as "The Determination of Moral Facts," in Durkheim, *Sociology and Philosophy*, trans. D. F. Pocock, with an Introduction by J. G. Peristiany (Glencoe, Ill.: Free Press of Glencoe, Illinois, 1953), pp. 35–62.]

5   We do not mean to deny the individual the capacity to form concepts. He learns to form representations of this kind from the collectivity, but even the concepts he forms in this way have the same character as the others: they are constructed in such a way that they can be universalized. Even when they are the product of a personality, they are in part impersonal.

6   We say our individuality and not *our personality*. Although the two words are often used synonymously, they must be distinguished with the greatest possible care, for the personality is made up essentially of supra-individual elements. Cf., on this point, *Les formes élémentaires de la vie religieuse*, pp. 386–90.

7   Cf. *ibid.*, pp. 320–21, 580.

8   Cf. "La détermination du fait moral," p. 125.

9   Cf. *Les formes élémentaires de la vie religieuse*, pp. 268–342.

10   *Ibid.*, pp. 329 ff.

11   *Ibid.*, pp. 53 ff.

12   Cf. *De la division du travail social* ([1893] 3rd ed.; Paris: Félix Alcan, 1907), *passim* and esp. pp. 391 ff. [Translated as *The Division of Labor in Society*, by George Simpson ([1933] Glencoe, Ill.: Free Press of Glencoe, Illinois, 1947).]

13   *Les formes élémentaires de la vie religieuse*, pp. 616 ff.

14   *Ibid.*, pp. 12–28 ff., 205 ff., 336, 386, 508, 627.

Chapter 11

1   Pickler, in the little work above mentioned, had already expressed, in a slightly dialectical manner, the sentiment that this is what the totem essentially is.

2   See our *Division du travail social*, 3rd ed., pp. 64 ff.

3   Ibid., p. 76.

4   This is the case at least with all moral authority recognized as such by the group as a whole.

5   We hope that this analysis and those which follow will put an end to an inexact interpretation of our thought, from which more than one misunderstanding has resulted. Since we have made constraint the *outward sign* by which social facts can be the most easily recognized and distinguished from the facts of individual psychology, it has been assumed that according to our opinion, physical constraint is the essential thing for social life. As a matter of fact, we have never considered it more than the material and apparent expression of an interior and profound

fact which is wholly ideal: this is *moral authority*. The problem of sociology—if we can speak of *a* sociological problem—consists in seeking, among the different forms of external constraint, the different sorts of moral authority corresponding to them and in discovering the causes which have determined these latter. The particular question which we are treating in this present work has as its principal object the discovery of the form under which that particular variety of moral authority which is inherent in all that is religious has been born, and out of what elements it is made. It will be seen presently that even if we do make social pressure one of the distinctive characteristics of sociological phenomena, we do not mean to say that it is the only one. We shall show another aspect of the collective life, nearly opposite to the preceding one, but none the less real.

6   Of course this does not mean to say that the collective consciousness does not have distinctive characteristics of its own (on this point, see *Représentations individuelles et représentations collectives*, in *Revue de Métaphysique et de Morale*, 1898, pp. 273 ff.).

7   This is proved by the length and passionate character of the debates where a legal form was given to the resolutions made in a moment of collective enthusiasm. In the clergy as in the nobility, more than one person called this celebrated night the dupe's night, or, with Rivarol, the St. Bartholomew of the estates (see Stoll, *Suggestion und Hypnotismus in der Völkerpsychologie*, 2nd ed., p. 618, n. 2).

8   See Stoll, *op. cit.*, pp. 353 ff.

9   *Ibid.*, pp. 619, 635.

10   *Ibid.*, pp. 622 ff.

11   The emotions of fear and sorrow are able to develop similarly and to become intensified under these same conditions. As we shall see, they correspond to quite another aspect of the religious life (Bk. III, ch. v).

12   This is the other aspect of society which, while being imperative, appears at the same time to be good and gracious. It dominates us and assists us. If we have defined the social fact by the first of these characteristics rather than the second, it is because it is more readily observable, for it is translated into outward and visible signs; but we have never thought of denying the second (see our *Règles de la Méthode Sociologique*, preface to the second edition, p. xx, n.1).

13   Codrington, *The Melanesians*, pp. 50, 103, 120. It is also generally thought that in the Polynesian languages, the word *mana* primitively had the sense of authority (see Tregear, *Maori Comparative Dictionary*, s.v.).

14   See Albert Mathiez, *Les origines des cultes rèvolutionnaires* (1789–1792).

15   *Ibid.*, p. 24.

16   *Ibid.*, pp. 29, 32.

17   *Ibid.*, p. 30.

18   *Ibid.*, p. 46.

19   See Mathiez, *La Théophilanthropie et la Culte décadaire*, p. 36.

20   See Spencer and Gillen, *Nor. Tr.*, p. 33.

21   There are even ceremonies, for example, those which take place in connection with the initiation, to which members of foreign tribes are invited. A whole system of messages and messengers is organized for these convocations, without which the great solemnities could not take place (see Howitt, *Notes on Australian Message-Sticks and Messengers*, in *J.A.I.*, 1889; *Nat. Tr.*, pp. 83, 678–691; Spencer and Gillen, *Nat Tr.*, p. 159; *Nor. Tr.*, p. 551).

22   The corrobbori is distinguished from the real religious ceremonies by the fact that it is open to women and uninitiated persons. But if these two sorts of collective manifestations are to be distinguished, they are, none the less, closely related. We shall have occasion elsewhere to come back to this relationship and to explain it.

23   Except, of course, in the case of the great bush-beating hunts.

24   "The peaceful monotony of this part of his life," say Spencer and Gillen (*Nor. Tr.*, p. 33).

25   Howitt, *Nat. Tr.*, p. 683. He is speaking of the demonstrations which take place when an ambassador sent to a group of foreigners returns to camp with news of a favourable result. Cf. Brough Smyth, I, p. 138; Schulze, *loc. cit.*, p. 222.

26   See Spencer and Gillen, *Nat. Tr.*, pp. 96 f.; *Nor. Tr.*, p. 137; Brough Smyth, II, p. 319.—This ritual promiscuity is found especially in the initiation ceremonies (Spencer and Gillen, *Nat. Tr.*, pp. 267, 381; Howitt, *Nat. Tr.*, p. 657), and in the totemic ceremonies (*Nor. Tr.*, pp. 214, 298, 237). In these latter, the ordinary exogamic rules are violated. Sometimes among the Arunta, unions between father and daughter, mother and son, and brothers and sisters (that is in every case, relationship by blood) remain forbidden (*Nat. Tr.*, pp. 96 f.).

27   Howitt, *Nat. Tr.*, pp. 535, 545. This is extremely common.

28   These women were Kingilli themselves, so these unions violated the exogamic rules.

29   *Nor. Tr.*, p. 237.

30   *Nor. Tr.*, p. 391. Other examples of this collective effervescence during the religious ceremonies will be found in *Nat. Tr.*, pp. 244–246, 365–366, 374, 509–510 (this latter in connection with a funeral rite). Cf. *Nor. Tr.*, pp. 213, 351.

31   Thus we see that this fraternity is the logical consequence of totemism, rather than its basis. Men have not imagined their duties towards the animals of the totemic species because they regarded them as kindred, but have imagined the kinship to explain the nature of the beliefs and rites of which they were the object. The animal was considered a relative of the man because it was a sacred being like the man; but it was not treated as a sacred being because it was regarded as a relative.

32   At the bottom of this conception there is a well-founded and persistent sentiment. Modern science also tends more and more to admit that

the duality of man and nature does not exclude their unity, and that physical and moral forces, though distinct, are closely related. We undoubtedly have a different conception of this unity and relationship than the primitive, but beneath these different symbols, the truth affirmed by the two is the same.

33 We say that this derivation is sometimes indirect on account of the industrial methods which, in a large number of cases, seem to be derived from religion through the intermediacy of magic (see Hubert and Mauss, *Théorie générale de la Magie, Année Sociol.*, VII, pp. 144 ff.) ; for, as we believe, magic forces are only a special form of religious forces. We shall have occasion to return to this point several times.

Chapter 12

1 William James, *The Varieties of Religious Experience.*

2 Quoted by James, *op. cit.*, p. 20.

3 Only one form of social activity has not yet been expressly attached to religion: that is economic activity. Sometimes processes that are derived from magic have, by that fact alone, an origin that is indirectly religious. Also, economic value is a sort of power or efficacy, and we know the religious origins of the idea of power. Also, richness can confer *mana*; therefore it has it. Hence it is seen that the ideas of economic value and of religious value are not without connection. But the question of the nature of these connections has not yet been studied.

4 It is for this reason that Frazer and even Preuss set impersonal religious forces outside of, or at least on the threshold of religion, to attach them to magic.

5 Boutroux, *Science et Religion*, pp. 206–207.

6 On this same question, see also our article, "Représentations individuelles et représentations collectives," in the *Revue de Métaphysique*, May, 1898.

7 William James, *Principles of Psychology*, I, p. 464.

8 This universality of the concept should not be confused with its generality: they are very different things. What we mean by universality is the property which the concept has of being communicable to a number of minds, and in principle, to all minds; but this communicability is wholly independent of the degree of its extension. A concept which is applied to only one object, and whose extension is consequently at the minimum, can be the same for everybody: such is the case with the concept of a deity.

9 It may be objected that frequently, as the mere effect of repetition, ways of thinking and acting become fixed and crystallized in the individual, in the form of habits which resist change. But a habit is only a tendency to repeat an act or idea automatically every time that the same circum-

stances appear; it does not at all imply that the idea or act is in the form of an exemplary type, proposed to or imposed upon the mind or will. It is only when a type of this sort is set up, that is to say, when a rule or standard is established, that social action can and should be presumed.

10   Thus we see how far it is from being true that a conception lacks objective value merely because it has a social origin.

11   Lévy-Bruhl, *Les fonctions mentales dans les sociétés inférieures,* pp. 131–138.

12   *Ibid.,* p. 446.

13   William James, *Principles of Psychology,* I, p. 134.

14   Men frequently speak of space and time as if they were only concrete extent and duration, such as the individual consciousness can feel, but enfeebled by abstraction. In reality, they are representations of a wholly different sort, made out of other elements, according to a different plan, and with equally different ends in view.

15   At bottom, the concept of totality, that of society and that of divinity are very probably only different aspects of the same notion.

16   See our *Classifications primitives, loc. cit.,* pp. 40 ff.

Bibliography

ALTHOUGH DURKHEIM published only five or six books in his life-time, his output of articles, reviews, and occasional pieces was prodigious and is not always easy to track down. The most accessible, though far from complete, bibliography is that contained in Harry Alpert's *Emile Durkheim and His Sociology* (New York: Columbia University Press, 1939). The following list includes those books which Durkheim himself wrote, collections of essays published during his lifetime but not gathered in book form until after his death, and volumes based on manuscripts of lectures left among his papers at the time of his death.

The Division of Labor in Society. Glencoe, Ill.: Free Press, 1947. (First French edition, 1893.)

The Rules of Sociological Method. Glencoe, Ill.: Free Press, 1958. (First French edition, 1895.)

Suicide. Glencoe, Ill.: Free Press, 1951. (First French edition, 1897.)

The Elementary Forms of the Religious Life. New York: Free Press Paper-back, 1965. (First French edition, 1912.)

"Germany above All": German Mentality and the War. Paris: Colin, 1915. (First French edition, 1915.)

Education and Sociology. Glencoe, Ill.: Free Press, 1956. (First French edition, 1924.)

Sociology and Philosophy. Glencoe, Ill.: Free Press, 1953. (First French edition, 1924.)

Moral Education. New York: Free Press, 1961. (First French edition, 1925.)

Socialism and Saint-Simon. Yellow Springs, Ohio: Antioch Press, 1958. (First French edition, 1928.)

L'évolution pédagogique en France. 2 vols. Paris: Félix Alcan, 1938.

Professional Ethics and Civic Morals. Glencoe, Ill.: Free Press, 1958. (First French edition, 1950.)

Montesquieu and Rousseau. Ann Arbor: University of Michigan Press, 1960. (First French edition, 1953.)

Pragmatisme et Sociologie. Paris: Vrin 1955. (Partially translated in Emile Durkheim et al., *Essays on Sociology and Philosophy.* New York: Harper and Row, 1964, pp. 386–436.)

Journal sociologique. Paris: Presses universitaires de France, 1969. (Contains all of Durkheim's articles and most of his reviews from *L'année sociologique.*)

Books and Articles on Emile Durkheim

Aron, Raymond. *Main Currents in Sociological Thought.* Vol. 2. *Durkheim/Pareto/Weber.* New York: Basic Books, 1967.

Bellah, Robert N. "Durkheim and History." *American Sociological Review,* 24 (1959) : 477–61. (Reprinted in Robert A. Nisbet, *Emile Durkheim.*)

Filloux, Jean-Claude. Introduction to Emile Durkheim, *La science sociale et l'action,* pp. 5–68. Paris: Presses universitaires de France, 1970.

Neyer, Joseph. "Individualism and Socialism in Durkheim." In *Essays on Sociology and Philosophy,* by Emile Durkheim et al., pp. 32–76. New York: Harper and Row, 1964.

Nisbet, Robert A. *Emile Durkheim.* Englewood Cliffs, N.J.: Prentice-Hall, 1965.

Parsons, Talcott. *The Structure of Social Action.* New York: McGraw-Hill, 1937.

Pizzorno, Alessandro. "Lecture actuelle de Durkheim." *Archives de sociologie européennes,* 4 (1963) : 1–36.

Tiryakian, Edward A. *Sociologism and Existentialism.* Englewood Cliffs, N.J.: Prentice-Hall, 1962.